# Metropolitan Migrants

# Metropolitan Migrants

*The Migration of Urban Mexicans
to the United States*

Rubén Hernández-León

UNIVERSITY OF CALIFORNIA PRESS
*Berkeley     Los Angeles     London*

University of California Press, one of the most
distinguished university presses in the United States,
enriches lives around the world by advancing scholarship in the humanities, social sciences, and natural
sciences. Its activities are supported by the UC Press
Foundation and by philanthropic contributions from
individuals and institutions. For more information,
visit www.ucpress.edu.

University of California Press
Berkeley and Los Angeles, California

University of California Press, Ltd.
London, England

Library of Congress Cataloging-in-Publication Data

Hernández-León, Rubén.
    Metropolitan migrants : the migration of
urban Mexicans to the United States / Rubén
Hernández-León.
        p.    cm.
    Includes bibliographical references and index.
    ISBN: 978-0-520-25673-6 (cloth : alk. paper)
    ISBN: 978-0-520-25674-3 (pbk. : alk. paper)
    1. Mexicans—United States—Case studies.
2. United States—Emigration and immigration—
Economic aspects—Case studies.   3. Structural
adjustment (Economic policy)—Mexico—Monterrey.
4. Monterrey (Mexico)—Economic conditions.
5. Monterrey (Mexico)—Emigration and
immigration.   6. Mexicans— Texas—Houston.
7. Houston (Tex.)—Emigration and immigration.
I. Title.
E184.M5H437   2008
973.00468'72—dc22                    2007044596

Manufactured in the United States of America

17  16  15  14  13  12  11  10  09  08
10  9  8  7  6  5  4  3  2  1

This book is printed on Cascades Enviro 100, a
100% post consumer waste, recycled, de-inked fiber.
FSC recycled certified and processed chlorine free.
It is acid free, Ecologo certified, and manufactured
by BioGas energy.

# Contents

# Illustrations

# Acknowledgments

The journey that led to this book started nearly fifteen years ago when I began to learn and research about Mexico-U.S. migration. What caught my attention at that time is, that with a handful of notable exceptions, study after study on the sending side focused on rural settings—hamlets, ranches, and small towns. Clearly, this seeming paradox is easily explained through the history of Mexican migration to the United States. Still, in a mostly urban country, the puzzle remained as to how Mexican cities participated in the phenomenon. In the years since I began to conceptualize this study, conduct fieldwork and analysis and to write this book, scholars have devoted considerably more attention to Mexican urban areas as sending sources of U.S.-bound migration.

In its long and circuitous career this book received the support of many advisors, colleagues, friends and institutions. In its earliest incarnation, as a dissertation, the project benefited from the steadfast and careful supervision of Martin Murray and the close reading and friendly commentary and critique of Anthony D. King, both at Binghamton University. Bryan Roberts of the University of Texas at Austin provided advice, enthusiastic insights and important financial assistance to make field research in Houston possible. I'm most grateful to my *compadre* Néstor Rodríguez and my colleague and friend Jacquie Hagan, at one point co-directors of the Center for Immigration Research at the University of Houston, who welcomed me at the center and in their homes countless times as I made repeated visits to the Bayou City, tracking and re-interviewing Houston-based *regiomontanos*. My association with their projects—in what Néstor used to dub the center's "secret weapon" at the border—provided additional opportunities to continue my research and keep one foot in Monterrey and another in Houston.

My fieldwork in Monterrey was supported with a grant from the Inter-American Foundation and the hard work of several field assistants, notably Efrén Sandoval, Renée Tarango, Fátima Soto, Eleocadio Martínez and Gustavo Rojas. Also in the *Sultana del Norte* I benefited from the advice of my *hermano mayor* Víctor Zúñiga, who commented on the survey I implemented in La Fama and always warned me about vulgar economic explanations of migration. The following pages illustrate that I have not always heeded his wise words.

As I made my own second migration *al norte,* I benefited from a two year postdoctoral fellowship with Douglas Massey's and Jorge Durand's Mexican Migration Project (MMP) then at the University of Pennsylvania. Although the survey data collection I undertook in Monterrey preceded my affiliation with the MMP, there is no question that it was inspired by its methods and understanding of international migration. I am deeply grateful to Douglas Massey who provided generous financial support to return to Monterrey, Houston and to conduct fieldwork in a rural sending area in Nuevo León, and its daughter community in Atlanta, Georgia. The qualitative data generated through field research in rural Nuevo León is referenced in chapter 4 of this book and served as helpful contrast with the findings obtained earlier in Monterrey. My gratitude to Doug Massey goes beyond the academic nexus, extending to an area of his persona that others know well: his compassion and solidarity when dark clouds hovered over my family and little Paloma in Philadelphia. This book has also gained from the conversations and joint work I undertook with MMP affiliates, such as my *comadre* Nadia Flores and my friend Beth Fussell, on the issue of urban migration from Mexico to the United States. I would like to think, perhaps immodestly, that our conversations helped spark a metropolitan origin migration revival within the MMP.

I would like to thank Jorge Durand, with whom I spent many hours, lunches and dinners exchanging about the topic of Mexico-U.S. migration. My arrival to Los Angeles coincided with his stint as visiting professor at UCLA. Interestingly, Jorge read and stimulated more than ten years ago some of the very early products of this study, always providing direct and helpful suggestions and insights. I also recognize the support provided by the Institute of American Cultures, the University of California Committee on Latino Research, and the UCLA Chicano Studies Research Center through a Latino Policy Studies research grant.

I owe much gratitude to many colleagues in the Department of Sociology at UCLA, who read multiple versions of the chapters that now make up this book. Roger Waldinger read the manuscript several times throughout its various stages of development. His observations helped me sharpen ideas and push timidly stated arguments to their ultimate sociological conclusions. I also benefited from the critical yet sympathetic eye of Ivan Light with whom I have sustained a constant and fruitful exchange on issues of ethnic and immigrant entrepreneurship since my arrival at UCLA. Jack Katz read the entire manuscript more than once and always provided enthusiastic encouragement along with his keen eye for important ethnographic themes I had ignored. César Ayala reviewed early drafts of the manuscript, offering many useful suggestions and his unabashed endorsement of its arguments and findings. Above all, I thank him for his friendship and collegial support. I also thank Stefan Timmermans (my academic productivity whip of the past two years), Rogers Brubaker, Ruth Milkman and Greta Krippner, all of whom read and gave useful feedback on various parts of the manuscript. All of these colleagues promptly and generously provided feedback, making the Department of Sociology at UCLA a welcoming and supportive institution to bring the project to fruition.

I would like to express my gratitude to the two reviewers and the member of the faculty board commissioned by the University of California Press to evaluate the book manuscript. Their comments and suggestions helped me improve the flow of the multiple arguments I make throughout the book, correct methodological mistakes and avoid mischaracterizations and omissions. Special thanks go to Naomi Schneider, executive editor at UC Press, who from the beginning demonstrated her commitment to the manuscript and efficiently and effectively moved it through the publication process.

Finally, I thank *mi familia:* my parents, Emilia and Aurelio, whose love and support have been a constant in my life. Their lifelong commitment to education and social justice as profoundly moral beings is the greatest gift a son can be given. This book is dedicated to *mis tres mujeres:* Janna, Olín, and Paloma, who shine and cast their bright light upon me every wonderful day we are together.

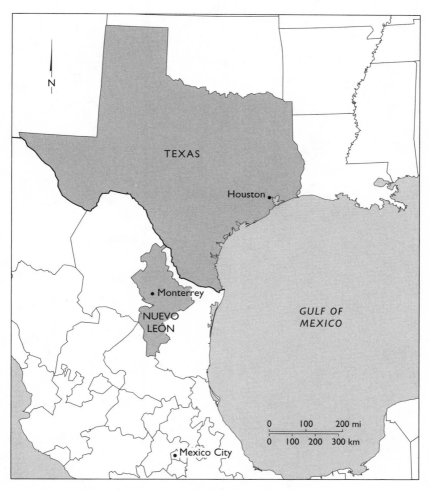

Locations of Monterrey and Houston. Map by Verónica Terríquez.

# CHAPTER I

# The Migration of Urban Mexicans to the United States

*This is the neighborhood of La Fama, an industrial working-class district in the metropolitan area of Monterrey, Mexico's version of Pittsburgh, Detroit, or Chicago (depending on your preference) because of its history of heavy manufacturing. It is the Sunday after New Year's Day, and several families are getting ready to return to the United States after spending the holidays in Monterrey. These families are also celebrating the birthday of a boy in the driveway of one of the homes. As such celebrations often are in Mexico, the party is open to everybody in the neighborhood. After a clown's performance, the children break the piñata and get ready to sit down and eat their tamales. At the same time, on the sidewalk, the adults are exchanging information about* la pasada, *the crossing into the United States, specifically about conditions on the highway leading to the border and the traffic congestion on the bridges in the Laredo area. The children are being served dinner and are now eating their tamales. As I listen to their conversation, I am able to grasp this snapshot of immigrant life: Just like their parents, some children are also discussing their trip back to the United States. The crux of their exchange is the question of how many tamales they need to take in order to make it to Houston and Chicago without going hungry. It is clear to them that those traveling to Chicago should bring more tamales because of the additional distance to be covered after Houston. Thus, these kids are already aware of the geographical distance separating three different points of the migratory circuit they inhabit. By measuring distance in terms of a culinary and cultural item (the tamale) so familiar to them, they are also establishing links between these distant cities.*

*It is Friday afternoon at a small strip mall in a busy intersection of Houston's Summerland area. One of the businesses at this intersection is a courier service that shuttles between Houston and Monterrey, carrying remittances in cash, parcels with mostly used goods, correspondence, and a handful of passengers. Customers begin to crowd in the small storefront, turning in their remittances. Two women receive the money and count it, placing each customer's cash in a white envelope, writing the Monterrey delivery address on the envelope, and registering all this information in a log book. At the end of each transaction, the women ask the customer to sign the flap of the envelope after it has been sealed. The owner of the courier service supervises the operation, chatting with patrons and quoting them the cost for shipping parcels to Monterrey. A man approaches the owner to inquire about a pickup truck wheel that had not yet been delivered in Mexico, two weeks after he took them to the courier's office. The owner argues that he hasn't had space in his van. The customer reacts angrily, leaving the store at once. The owner responds by saying that he doesn't know why people ship such "crazy stuff" to Mexico. But it is getting late, and he and his employees have to load the van and the trailer with boxes and bags containing an assortment of used goods, foodstuffs, small and large appliances, and electronics. They will drive all night, arriving in Monterrey in the morning to immediately begin deliveries throughout the westernmost neighborhoods of the city.*

*It is a grey and rainy fall day in La Fama. Two new developments are worth noting since my last field visit: the demolition of the textile mill and the celebration of the first La Fama Antigua (Old La Fama) festival. Paradoxically, the festival celebrates the 150 years of the textile mill that gives its name to the neighborhood. It is Sunday and the bulldozers that are razing the mill's buildings have the day off, offering a spectacle of silent destruction. At this point, only the walls of the mill remain standing, surrounded by overgrown bushes and trees. Later in the day, the festival organizers get ready to honor the former mill workers in a union hall located in the heart of the neighborhood. The ceremony begins with an array of Mexican folk dances performed by middle and high school troupes from the surrounding public schools, followed by a few speeches by the organizers and the mayor. The main part of the event is a medal award ceremony for retired mill workers and for those who lost their jobs when the factory closed in 2003. Their names are read from a long list, and, one by one, they go to the podium to receive their medals. The master of ceremonies makes reference to the community contributions of these former workers and states that although the mill is closed now, "we should not be sad," reminding the participants that the motto of the festival is "la alegría que nos une" (the joy that brings us together). As they continue to receive their medals, I talk to a few former workers. Those who lost their jobs when the factory closed are basically unemployable. They tell me that no company in Monterrey will hire a fifty-plus-year-old worker. If it happens, it will be to sweep floors. One of the workers gives me a long lecture about his skills in industrial welding, providing multiple examples of his technical problem-solving abilities. Another one, an electrician and union leader, mentions that the union hall is up for sale. I ask him if any of his acquaintances from the mill have headed north to work in the United States. He answers, "No. We don't do that stuff here." A few moments later he tells me that he just spent three months in the United States painting houses and doing yard work.*

This book is about the migration of urban and, more specifically, metropolitan Mexicans to the United States. Using the Monterrey-Houston migratory circuit to observe the causes and social organization of metropolitan emigration, I argue that the restructuring of the Mexican economy—prompted by the transition from a development model of import substitution industrialization (ISI) to a policy of export-oriented industrialization (EOI)—has driven urban households in Monterrey to increasingly deploy the labor of their members internationally. Through the lens of a case study, I show how the migration of skilled working-class *regiomontanos* (the people of Monterrey) to the United States is being sustained not only by strong kinship networks, but also by weak friendship ties established in the context of the urban neighborhood. In Monterrey's blue-collar districts, the employment and residential stability characteristic of ISI have allowed for these weak ties to be conduits of migratory social capital. Still, migrant networks are not the sole social infrastructure easing international human mobility. Here, I contend that migration is also facilitated by a matrix of migration entrepreneurs—recruiters, smugglers, couriers—who connect "here" and "there" at a profit. Combined, migrant networks and migration entrepreneurs have successfully channeled *regiomontanos* to Houston, a global city for the oil industry with an increasingly diversified economy, where these Mexican urbanites have formed settlements and occupational niches.

Known as the Chicago (Snodgrass 2003) and the Pittsburgh (Langley 1994) of Mexico, Monterrey boasts a history of early industrialization stimulated by the geopolitical proximity to the American Industrial Revolution. Such history began at the dusk of the nineteenth century, when local merchants and financiers started to invest their fortunes in manufacturing, a move uncommon in Latin America. This experience shaped the city's capitalist future, its labor markets, and its social demographic patterns. Fifty years later, Monterrey had become the country's third-largest metropolitan area, its most important heavy manufacturing industrial center, and a prime destination of internal migratory flows.[1]

During the last two decades of the twentieth century, prompted by Mexico's transition from ISI to EOI, the economic specialization of the Monterrey metropolitan area shifted from production for largely protected internal markets to manufacturing and services in a free-trade environment—developments that forced local firms to engage in various forms of industrial restructuring. Unfolding in a macroeconomic context of recurrent financial crises, restructuring has produced a variety of outcomes, many of which have particular relevance for this book. One notable development was the substantial weakening of a regime of industry-labor relations that afforded male workers in local manufacturing many of the contractual arrangements enjoyed by their peers in developed countries: a family wage, lifelong employment, the passing-down of jobs from fathers to sons, and perquisite packages that included housing and health benefits. The erosion of these labor relations during the past two decades has occurred not only because of the downsizing, closure, merger, and takeover of firms, which in the 1980s translated into massive layoffs, but also because of legal changes in the labor code that together have restricted the access of new generations to stable, formal employment in the large corporations dominating the local labor market (Pozas 2002).

During the 1990s, in the context of the opening of the economy and the implementation of the North American Free Trade Agreement (NAFTA), Monterrey reindustrialized: Local manufacturing conglomerates restructured and internationalized their holdings, establishing joint ventures and subcontracting arrangements with foreign companies while foreign direct investment flocked to export-oriented production, including light, assembly-type manufacturing, or *maquiladoras*.[2] Unsurprisingly, employment in light manufacturing and services does not provide the wages, security, and benefits typical of traditional heavy industry jobs. It is in this context of transformation that Monterrey has emerged as a source of migratory flows to the United States and to Texas in particular.

## EXPLAINING URBAN MEXICANS' MIGRATION TO THE UNITED STATES

In contrast with their rural counterparts, Mexican urbanites have only recently begun migrating across the border in sizable numbers. In the 1980s and early 1990s, researchers started to document, analyze, and debate the causes, consequences, social organization, and actual numbers of urban dwellers in Mexico who were joining the migratory stream across the international border. Still, until the 1990s, scholars of the prolific Mexico-U.S. migration literature were primarily concerned with rural settings, that is, with the villages and towns that, for most of the twentieth century, had been the predominant sites of out-migration. By 1990, only a handful of studies had analyzed the role of cities in connection with the population flows to *el norte* (Massey et al 1987; Verduzco Igartúa 1990; Cornelius 1992). In the past fifteen years, critical knowledge about the specificity, social dynamics, and outcomes of urban-origin migration has begun to emerge (Arias and Woo Morales 2004; Flores, Hernández-León, and Massey 2004; Fussell and Massey 2004; Hernández-León 1999; Lozano Ascencio 2000; Zúñiga 1993). Still, the sizable literature reporting the findings and methods of research conducted in rural areas in central and western Mexico continues to be a necessary reference for the emerging studies of cities as sending areas of international migration.

Why is the study of cities as source areas of sojourning important for the overall investigation of Mexico-U.S. migration? There are two reasons. First, the participation of Mexican cities is part of a series of new developments changing the face of population flows between the two countries in the last twenty-five years. There is a scholarly consensus that in this period Mexican migration to the United States has undergone a great transformation (Durand, Massey, and Parrado 1999; Roberts, Frank, and Lozano Ascencio 1999), an argument echoed by Martin, who suggests, "Mexico today is on the verge of its *Great Migration*" (1997: 79). Thus, fundamental changes in the characteristics and dynamics of this migration have occurred both at the origin and at the destination. The Mexican population in the United States more than doubled in the 1990s, growing from 4.3 million in 1990 to 9.2 million in 2000 (Grieco 2003). Mexican migrants have gradually become concentrated in metropolitan labor markets, reflecting the occupational shift from agriculture to services and manufacturing (Waldinger 1989). Urban employment has contributed to the growing pattern of long-term settlement and family migration. The passage and implementation of the Immigration Reform and Control Act of 1986, which included a comprehensive amnesty program, reinforced these trends. Moreover, the legalization of 2.3 million undocumented Mexicans in the United States allowed for larger numbers of documented migration under family reunification provisions and created conditions for the diversification of areas of destination (Baker 1997; Durand, Massey, and Charvet 2000; Hernández-León and Zúñiga 2000).

In Mexico, the maturation of social networks, the consolidation of immigrant communities abroad, and successive economic crises produced changes in the social and geographical selectivity of U.S.-bound migrants (Cornelius 1992; Roberts and Hamilton 2005). More single and married women and elderly people have joined the international flow (Donato 1993). Furthermore, the economic crises of the 1980s and 1990s triggered the migration of middle-class Mexicans. Also, new sending regions have emerged in central and southern Mexico, allowing the participation of indigenous groups and the rise of new migration systems linking internal and international flows (Durand and Massey 2003; Fox and Rivera-Salgado 2004; Kearney 1998). Another new development of the past twenty years has been the Mexican government's growing involvement in the affairs of expatriate political and civic associations in the United States in an attempt to control such organizations (Smith 1998). In sum, Mexican cities are part of the profound transformation of Mexico-U.S. migration, participating in the phenomenon in ways they had not in the past.

The second reason why the study of cities as source areas of U.S.-bound sojourning is of significance to the field is that urban environments offer the opportunity to put to the test old and new hypotheses on the causes and social organization of international migration and to verify whether existing explanations are context specific or can cut across different social settings of origin. Leading researchers have long cast doubts about the ready applicability of theories, concepts, and analytical tools developed in rural contexts to urban settings, often characterized by social differentiation, anonymity, and an advanced division of labor. As Massey and his associates argue, "The dynamics of international migration from large metropolitan areas have not been well studied," suggesting that "the social dynamics of migration from major cities are sufficiently different from those of smaller towns and cities to warrant separate study" (Massey, Goldring, and Durand 1994: 1503, 1506).

This task has been undertaken by scholars of Mexico-U.S. migration since the mid-1990s, and they have posed and reframed questions in ways that point to the distinctive nature of metropolitan settings. What is the relation between the structural transformation of the Mexican economy in the past twenty years and international out-migration from the country's urban areas? What is the social organization of migration in urban environments? Does migration have a similar capacity to transform urban sending communities the way it changes rural localities? What are the distinct impacts that migration can have on urban contexts (in contrast with rural settings)? An emerging strand of scholarship has sought to respond to these and other questions. Thus, a series of qualitative and quantitative studies have uncovered social networks and a migration industry structuring flows between Mexican cities and the United States yet have also found that the cumulative causation and the motivations associated with rural sending areas and traditional labor migration do not unfold in urban settings exactly as predicted by existing theories. These same studies have identified fundamental differences in the types of social groupings and relations that support migration in cities and in rural contexts (Flores 2001; Flores, Hernández-León, and Massey 2004; Fussell and Massey 2004; Hernández-León 1997, 1999). Other scholars analyzing urban-origin migration have discovered streams that are not necessarily structured by social networks in which people who migrate are relatively isolated and have weak connections to their own places of origin (Roberts, Frank, and Lozano Ascencio 1999; Lozano Ascencio 2000).

The scholarship on Mexican cities as source areas of U.S.-bound migration has also produced explanations about the causes of the phenomenon. Seeking to explain a changing profile of Mexican immigration, Cornelius argues that "rather than simply absorbing internal migrants from the countryside and provincial cities . . . Mexico's large urban centers today are serving increasingly as platforms for migration to the United States" (1991: 162). He and others attributed this "urbanization of the flow" to the severe crises that affected the Mexican economy during the 1980s, which provoked a sharp decline in real wages and a saturation of urban labor markets (Cornelius 1992; Roberts and Escobar Latapí 1997). Disputing this interpretation and the factual evidence behind it, Durand, Massey, and Zenteno (2001) countered that rather than a changing profile and urbanization of the social origins of migrants, the broader flow displayed an increasing bifurcation, with towns of fewer than 15,000 people contributing 57 percent of the migration and cities of more than 100,000 making up more than 30 percent of the stream by the late 1980s. In their view, international out-migration from cities was due not to the social impact of the crises as much as to the secular urbanization of Mexican society in general. Echoing an argument made earlier in *Return to Aztlan* (Massey et al. 1987), Durand, Massey, Alarcón, and Gonzáles contend that "as Mexico has urbanized, families have brought their migratory experiences and network contacts from the countryside to the city, so that the flow now embraces urban as well as rural workers" (2001: 124).

Lozano (2001) offered yet another explanation of the causes and profile of urban migration from Mexico to the United States. Using data from a national demographic survey on return migrants collected in the late 1990s, Lozano demonstrated that even though migration from places with fewer than 2,500 inhabitants increased in the 1970–97 period, U.S.-bound population movements from cities with more than 100,000 people amplified—reaching a peak in the 1985–89 period when they became more than 40 percent of the total outflow—but then declined in the 1995–97 period to slightly over 28 percent. However, by differentiating between traditional and nontraditional regions of migration in Mexico in his analysis,[3] Lozano also showed that in the nontraditional states, migration from cities remained higher than the outflow from rural localities, with nearly 40 percent and 32 percent, respectively, in 1995–97. Lozano interpreted these fluctuations in the social composition of the stream as the result of patterns of foreign investment in Mexico during the 1990s and as evidence of the intersection between macroeconomic transformation and its uneven impact in the national territory *and* the regional origins of migrants.[4] In their analysis of the Mexican Census, Roberts and Hamilton (2005) determined that about 29 percent of U.S. migrants in the 1995–2000 period came from cities of more than 100,000 inhabitants. The authors also analyzed the fourth quarter wave of the 2002 Encuesta Nacional de Empleo (National Employment Survey), which collected data on U.S. migration between 1997 and 2002. According to this survey, large- and medium-sized cities accounted for nearly 40 percent of all U.S.-bound trips during the period of reference (Roberts and Hamilton 2005).

In sum, these studies show that there is not linear growth of Mexican urbanites in the broader flow to the United States and that the relation between crises and other sources of structural change and out-migration is not obvious. At the same time, however, these studies prove that Mexico's urban residents are resorting in significant numbers to U.S. migration and that large cities are already an important and sizable source of population flows between the two countries—one that still has garnered relatively little attention.

Utilizing Monterrey and the Monterrey-Houston migratory circuit as what Merton (1987) called strategic research materials, this book raises questions related to the *urban* specificity of urban-origin migration from Mexico to the United States. What are the distinctive causes, dynamics, and outcomes of the international migratory flows that originate in Mexican cities and metropolitan areas? In what respects are the root causes of migration, the social networks, and their social ecology typically urban? How are the types of networks and social capital, household arrangements, experiences of labor market incorporation at the destination, and the overall social process of migration associated with the city origin of migrants? In urban contexts, is international migration an individual or a household strategy? Why and under what circumstances do urban households deploy their labor internationally? Do urban social relations allow for the development of support networks that sustain migration over time? If so, what are the characteristics of the networks that support city-origin migration? How are these networks established, and how are they mapped out on urban space? What forms of social capital arise as such urban networks unfold? Does transnationalism and transnational forms of social organization develop in cities and metropolitan source areas of international migration? What are the settlement experiences of urban-origin migrants? How do the networks these migrants use influence their patterns of incorporation at the destination?

## IS THE MONTERREY-HOUSTON CONNECTION A 'TRANSNATIONAL' MIGRATORY CIRCUIT?

The chief destination of migrants from Monterrey to the United States is Houston, Texas, a global city for the oil industry and its multiple branches (i.e., management, extraction, tools, and technology).[5] Together, Monterrey and Houston constitute an international migratory circuit. Durand (1988) uses the term *migratory circuit* to refer to a social system of intertwined international and internal population flows, which generate a "complex ensemble of social and economic relations. . . . including the mobility of information, goods, capital, services. . . . This continuous traffic resembles an integrated circuit of alternate current, through which flows move in multiple directions and with different intensity" (1988: 26, 43). Focusing on the migratory streams from western Mexico to the United States, Durand's conceptualization provides a comprehensive and systemic view of migration, incorporating historic, geographic, economic, and social dimensions of this border-spanning phenomenon. In so doing, Durand in fact pioneered a perspective applied later on to transnational studies of Mexico-U.S. migration (see Rouse 1989).

However, this early conceptualization of a migratory circuit remained incomplete in one vital way: its political dimension. An *international* migratory circuit—and international migration in general—is fundamentally a sociopolitical phenomenon, ultimately defined by the crossing of borders, the involvement of two or more nation-states, and migrants' entry into and exit out of distinct and separate polities. This is what in essence differentiates international migratory circuits from domestic ones—regardless of whether they are interconnected. Such a distinction is not just a nominal one. State policies and practices toward emigration and immigration and the relations *between* the states in which a given flow is nested shape much of what is at stake in a migratory circuit. As this book shows, the sending state has played a vital role in the formation of the Monterrey-Houston circuit, because the mix of macroeconomic policies that Mexico has pursued since the mid-1980s have eroded the safety net that its skilled working-class urban residents enjoyed for decades and that turned cities—specially Monterrey—into virtual barriers against cross-border migration. As early as the 1940s, the Mexican government prevented the formation of networks and a culture of migration in cities by excluding Mexico's urbanites from the recruitment schemes of the Bracero program—the 1942–64 bilateral agreement that funneled millions of guest workers to U.S. agriculture—a move designed to retain its growing, skilled urban-industrial population while channeling rural dwellers to the international labor market, albeit temporarily (Durand 1998; Fitzgerald 2006a).

The United States government, in turn, has been at the center of a scheme to import migrant labor to the Southwest for more than a century, allowing this region to become a source of agricultural products and raw materials for the American Industrial Revolution (Galarza 1964). The relations between the two states have also shaped cross-border population movements. Clearly, the territorial and economic expansion of the United States during the nineteenth century created the political and geographic conditions that transformed Mexico into a vast labor pool for states like California and Texas. Although less powerful than its U.S. counterpart, the Mexican government has by no means been a passive actor, using legal and undocumented migration to get rid of critics, export excess labor resulting from economic modernization, and finance the direct and indirect costs of development through remittances.

The emphasis placed here on the primacy of states does not dismiss the social and cultural dimensions of international migratory circuits, including the flows of services, information, goods, and capital that follow the trails opened by migrants that are referenced in Durand's (1988) definition. Such dimensions are important in their own right: as part of the lived experience of individuals and families; as dependent and independent variables of migration-induced social change in sending and receiving communities; as part of the types of sociability that infuse network dynamics and motivations for migration; and as social institutions that state actors confront when designing and implementing emigration and immigration policy. But their meaning would ultimately be different if migration were to occur *within* the confines of a single nation-state. Consequently, to talk about the Monterrey-Houston migratory circuit is, first and foremost, to talk about a border-spanning process, not a border-blurring phenomenon.

With this revised notion of an international migratory circuit in hand, it is worth asking: Is the Monterrey-Houston connection a transnational migratory circuit? For the last ten years, the transnational perspective has swept international migration research. Thus, scholars have flocked to study and define what has alternatively been called transnational communities (Rodríguez 1996), transnational social spaces (Faist 2000; Pries 2001), transnational life (Smith 2001, 2006), transnational social formations (Guarnizo and Smith 1998) and transnationalism (Basch, Glick Schiller, and Szanton-Blanc 1994; Portes, Guarnizo, and Landolt 1999). Proponents of transnationalism argue that immigrants keep a continued political and social belonging in their country of origin while asserting rights and making membership claims at their destination (Guarnizo 1998; Levitt 2000). According to this view, immigrants use this dual membership as a strategic resource to confront discrimination and marginalization and to negotiate their incorporation into the host society (Portes 1999). Still other scholars have argued that immigrant transnationalism sheds light on the limitations of the methodological nationalism that has dominated the study of international migration (Wimmer and Glick Schiller 2003).

As with other trendy developments in the social sciences, the word *transnational* has been faddishly pegged to almost anything remotely connected with migration, prompting academics to warn, "Transnationalism thus runs the risk of becoming an empty conceptual vessel" (Guarnizo and Smith 1998: 3). To date, most of the debate between proponents and critics of this approach revolves around the distinctiveness and specificity of transnationalism (Waldinger and Fitzgerald 2004), the durability of transnational practices beyond the immigrant generation (Smith 2006), the extent of migrants' participation in transnational activities (Portes, Haller, and Guarnizo 2002), and the newness and contingency of the phenomenon in question (Foner 2000; Guarnizo and Smith 1998; Kivisto 2001; Portes, Guarnizo, and Landolt 1999). There is no consensus among students of transnationalism about who or what exactly is included in the phenomenon. Scholars researching immigrant transnational entrepreneurship have contended that the proper unit of analysis is the individual and her networks, hence defining transnationalism as the "exchanges, the new modes of transacting, and the multiplication of activities that require cross-border travel and contacts on a sustained basis" (Portes, Guarnizo, and Landolt 1999: 219). Others have argued that it is in fact the immigrant's community or social group of reference that should be considered the fundamental unit of analysis, stating, "Individual actors cannot be viewed in isolation from the transnational social field in which they are embedded" (Levitt 2001: 7; see also Kivisto 2001). These competing definitions illustrate what is one of the most salient shortcomings of the transnational perspective: the lack of a coherent theory of transnational migration, namely, a body of concepts and propositions that describes the phenomenon and differentiates it from other types of migration, establishing the conditions for the emergence, scope, duration, and demise of transnational practices.[6]

As recent critiques have shown (Waldinger and Fitzgerald 2004), very often studies of immigrant transnationalism are in fact studies of migratory circuits (see Rouse 1989; Levitt 2001; Smith 2006), defined by the orientation to and circulation of migrants between two localities situated in two countries—a brand of research that could be characterized as the bilocal-binational strand of transnationalism. Yet another type of research observes the emergence of transnational migration between postcolonial, quasi-national societies (the island nations of the Caribbean, for example) and core countries that economically and politically continue to play the role of the old metropolis (see the collections of Glick Schiller, Basch, and Szanton Blanc 1992 and Basch, Glick Schiller, and Szanton Blanc 1994). In both strands of research, the intensity of the social, economic, and political life of the transnational sphere, the presence of weak and failed states in the sending countries, and the constant and often successful efforts of newcomers to surmount the barriers that receiving states continue to build around their borders have provided clues for scholars to see migrants operating in a social field that lies beyond the national.

Still, scholars of transnationalism should be credited with bringing sending states "back in." Indeed, a more recent wave of studies inspired by the transnationalist framework have shown how the less powerful and economically dependent states of sending countries have promoted the incorporation of expatriate populations into the body politic through diasporic notions of nationhood. Responding to the changing dynamics of national politics, to new regional and international geopolitical realities, and to the growing economic significance of remittance flows, said states often create new institutions, policies, and legal frameworks to incorporate, control, and mobilize migrants on behalf of government interests. As this literature has shown, this is by no means a one-way street: Diasporic or transnational fields, increasingly legitimized in the form of dual nationality, expatriate political rights, and other types of legislation, created opportunities for social movements, organizations, and entrepreneurial migrants to conduct local and cross-border politics (Goldring 2002; Guarnizo 1998; Smith 2003; Smith and Bakker 2005).

Clearly, the social, economic, and political realities of the Monterrey-Houston circuit are firmly embedded in the context of two nation-states. Migrants from Monterrey, and from Mexico in general, come from a fully *nationalized* society (Waldinger and Fitzgerald 2004) in which individuals' and households' social experiences and identities are (and have been over the course of generations) profoundly shaped by multiple and effective state institutions, from public schools to political parties. These institutions' historical backgrounds and day-to-day operations are fundamentally different from those of the United States. To Houston-bound migrants from Monterrey, the beginning of their migration to the United States is not an entry into a *trans*national realm. On the contrary, their sojourning is the start of a series of constant encounters with the institutions of sending and receiving nation-states, which begin well before the journey commences. Thus, would-be legal entrants need to obtain a passport and apply for a U.S. visa in the local consulate and then travel to the border, where they will face more paperwork, along with the queries of customs and immigration inspectors. Illegal migrants will most likely require the services of the migration entrepreneurs—smugglers and guides—to circumvent the entrance restrictions established by the state and its border enforcement agencies, such as the Border Patrol (Hernández-León 2005). The ability to evade these restrictions—effectively becoming a clandestine immigrant—is by no means a sign of transnationalism but rather a symptom of how much the state matters in setting the terms of entry and presence of foreigners in the receiving polity.

As a migratory circuit, Monterrey and Houston form a binational social field where border-spanning networks channel migrants from specific urban neighborhoods back home to distinct areas of settlement in Houston and labor market niches in this city's economy. The Monterrey-Houston connection stems from Mexico's process of urban-industrial restructuring of the last twenty years and an even earlier round of recruitment of Monterrey's skilled industrial workers to aerospace and oil industries in the United States. Throughout this period, state policy, informal immigration practices, and the unintended consequences of both have had a profound effect on the circuit, creating not a transnational community, but a highly differentiated population composed of legal residents, U.S. citizens, a resident undocumented population of families and single men and women, and documented and illegal males whose spouses and children remain in Monterrey and who therefore shuttle back and forth between the two cities. A thriving and profitable migration industry (Castles and Miller 1998) facilitates movement and communication of people on both sides of the circuit, bridging the border, time, and distance in multiple ways.

Still, other things take place within the confines of the Monterrey-Houston connection besides labor migration, including the interactions and intense exchanges of individuals and families aimed at social and cultural reproduction, namely binational and bilocal child-rearing strategies and the emergence of a second generation, reciprocity, and solidarity, but also opportunism and breaking of trust in social relations, redefinition of gender and family roles, cultural production and consumption, formation of small-business ventures, and movement of material and cultural remittances. This book explains (1) the structural origins of the Monterrey-Houston connection and the types of migratory patterns that have evolved in this binational intermetropolitan circuit, (2) the nature of networks and social life of households and extended families inhabiting this social field, and (3) the migration industry that provides an often-overlooked infrastructure for population mobility, communication, and remittance transactions.

## THE STRUCTURAL ORIGINS OF MIGRATION IN THE MONTERREY-HOUSTON CIRCUIT

The emphasis of current theories of international migration on social networks has at times obscured the continued significance of historical-structural forces in the initiation of migratory flows. Still, the sea change of Mexico's political economy over the past twenty years has kept the scholarly eye on the relations between structural conditions and international migration, although not necessarily with a focus on urban settings. During the 1990s, the connection between structural economic transformations and out-migration from rural areas attracted new scholarly interest. Researchers suggested an imminent mass rural exodus due to the effects of agricultural reforms—including the privatization of the *ejido* (the system of communal farms enshrined in the Mexican Constitution), the elimination of subsidies and guaranteed prices for foodstuffs, and the liberalization of agricultural imports—coupled with the implementation of the NAFTA.[7] Because of these reforms, redundant labor in the Mexican countryside would be displaced, and many of the 24 to 27 million people making a living from agricultural activities would have to find nonfarm employment, either by commuting to urban jobs in nearby cities or by participating in long-distance internal and cross-border migration (Cornelius and Martin 1993; Harvey 1996; Martin 1993, 1997). As a result of this "agricultural revolution,"[8] it was estimated that as much as 30 percent of the agricultural workforce in Mexico would be displaced (Yúnez-Naude 1991, quoted in Martin and Taylor 1992) and that as many as 3 to 4 million rural households engaged in farming jobs would have to look for nonagricultural occupations (Martin 1997).[9]

Researchers have identified at least two ways in which NAFTA is connected with increasing out-migration from Mexico's countryside. The deregulation of agricultural imports from the United States, a policy that began in the late 1980s, has affected agricultural producers by heightening competition, which lowers the profits that can be obtained from local commodities, thus threatening the viability of Mexican farms and allied industries (Cornelius 1998; Gereffi and Martínez 2005). Another way in which NAFTA may be contributing to cross-border migration is through the expansion of agro-export production. According to Zabin and Hughes (1995), the NAFTA-induced growth of export agriculture activity fosters international migration by recruiting mostly indigenous laborers in southern states, such as Oaxaca and Guerrero, with little prior tradition of working in the United States. As people migrate to the agro-export zones of northwest Mexico, they are able to accumulate the contacts and knowledge that allows them to move across the border following a two-stage migration strategy. Thus, export-oriented agriculture, boosted under NAFTA, appears to be fostering linkages between internal and external migratory streams, which historically had been differentiated by networks, selectivity, and geographical origins of migrants (Lozano Ascencio, Roberts, and Bean 1997).

In contrast with the plethora of studies focusing on rural economic change and international migration, the linkages between economic transformation and urban U.S.-bound migration have received little attention.[10] The issue is most important because Mexican cities and metropolitan areas have been the setting of fundamental changes in the country's pattern of capitalist development. Forced by the exhaustion of the prior strategy of ISI, the economic and debt crisis of the 1980s, and a changing international context, the Mexican government and the country's economic elites embarked on a new path of EOI. This profound reorientation of the Mexican economy required the restructuring of the country's urban-industrial base, a process that in turn entailed the opening and liberalization of national markets and the modernization of the manufacturing and service sectors. During the 1980s and 1990s, the government took a number of active steps in this direction, including joining the General Agreement on Trade and Tariffs (GATT), closing and selling many state-owned companies, deregulating import and export activities, promoting the growth of export manufacturing, reprivatizing the banking system, liberalizing financial services, and deepening the country's economic integration with the United States through NAFTA (Crandall 2005; Dussel Peters 2000; Pastor and Wise 1998).

In this book I argue that Mexico's twenty-year-long experience of economic restructuring has provoked the incorporation of members of the country's urban-industrial working class into the U.S.-bound migratory stream. Because it forced many public and private companies to shut down, downsize, and modernize by adopting new technologies and methods of production, increasing unemployment in the short run and degrading the overall occupational structure of Mexico's urban-industrial centers in the long run, restructuring has entailed the uprooting of thousands of members of the formerly protected skilled and semiskilled working class, prompting them to participate in the international labor market.

## NETWORKS, SOCIABILITY, AND CUMULATIVE CAUSATION IN URBAN SETTINGS

Studies of Mexican migration to the United States have generated substantial evidence about the significance of networks in the social organization of international migration. Through migrant networks, individuals and families obtain information about and access to work opportunities, lodging, and services that are necessary for either permanent settlement or temporary presence in the country of destination. These social networks are also used to minimize the costs and risks of migration by making available information and material resources, which in turn contribute to the success of the migratory experience (Massey 1987). Network members exchange information, favors, and support following the logic of reciprocity. Reciprocal exchanges maintain and enrich networks because the favors that have been received become obligations and debts, which will be repaid later on with other favors (Mair 1965; Gouldner 1973; Lomnitz 1976).[11]

Because the scholarship on international networks follows studies on the social ties of domestic migrants moving between countryside and cities (Balán, Browning, and Jelin 1973; Lomnitz 1976), researchers have rarely made a concerted effort to distinguish one set of connections from the other, overlooking the question of what happens to the structure, dynamics, and life span of a social network when it crosses a border (see Durand 1988). This old problem took on a new dimension during the 1990s as proponents of transnationalism built an entire research perspective on the border-spanning capacity of social networks. As Waldinger and Fitzgerald (2004) have noted, the development of a social infrastructure linking "here" and "there" is not exclusive of international networks but an attribute of long-distance migration in general. However, in an era of increasingly stiff restrictions to international migration, cross-border networks may put their members in direct confrontation with the state while domestic migratory networks generally do not (Rodríguez 1996; Waldinger and Fitzgerald 2004).

Not surprisingly, in the Mexico-U.S. case, most studies on networks and the social context of origin have been conducted in the rural localities of central and western Mexico (Massey et al. 1987; Durand and Massey 1992). In contrast, significantly less has been written about social migratory networks in urban and metropolitan contexts. The existing knowledge on Mexico-U.S. migration suggests that the flows originating in the cities and metropolitan areas of Mexico are also organized through social networks. Still, it is less clear whether urban-origin migrants develop strong ties similar to those of the international sojourners from the towns and villages of the Mexican countryside. But what is the role of social networks in urban-origin migration? Do urbanites establish the same kind of social infrastructure that their rural counterparts do to support their migration? If not, what types of social ties sustain the sojourning of urban residents? What are the characteristics, dynamics, and social underpinnings of such ties? Do these networks have a distinctively urban contour, or are they interlocked with those stemming from Mexico's rural world?

Prior research provides important clues to these questions. Analyzing the case of a working-class neighborhood in Guadalajara, Mexico's second-largest metropolitan area, Massey et al. (1987) showed that the networks utilized by urban dwellers for U.S. migration did not originate in the city. Rather, urbanites resorted to networks that stemmed from rural areas that were home to a long-standing migratory tradition. Rural networks composed of *paisanos* (natives of the same hometown) cut across the city, connecting it with communities and workplaces in the United States. According to Massey and his colleagues, the relationships of *vecinazgo* (ties between neighbors) developed in the city were weaker than those of *paisanaje* (ties between natives of the same town or village), explaining why specifically urban networks in support of international migration could not emerge (Massey et al. 1987).

Thus, Massey and his associates contend, "The city in general, and the barrio of San Marcos [Guadalajara] in particular, do not generate their own social networks. Rather, migrants from the city use the long-established networks of their home communities, which have demonstrated efficacy. People from San Marcos migrate through contacts based in the town of their family's origin" (Massey et al. 1987: 168).

Offering an alternative hypothesis, Roberts (1995) has argued that migrants from urban origins often pursue individualized migratory strategies. According to him, this type of strategy unfolds when "conditions in home communities are heterogeneous, community ties are weak, and people are affected diversely by economic change. This is often the case in urban communities. In towns and cities, size, residential mobility, and a highly differentiated occupational structure are likely to weaken social cohesion" (Roberts 1995: 47).

This contention suggests that the conditions of urban sociability influence the nature of networks. In developing this hypothesis, Roberts and his associates have suggested, for example, that transnational communities formed by migrants of urban origin tend to be weaker than those set up by migrants of rural background because, in contrast with those in rural areas, people living in urban settings rely less on economic cooperation and are more mobile due to work and residential dynamics, making their social relations and networks less stable (Roberts, Frank, and Lozano Ascencio 1999).

The arguments of Massey and Roberts are based not only on empirical observations but also on classical sociological statements about the consequences of urbanization, the nature of urbanism, and the contrasting social relations and forms of solidarity prevailing in rural and urban contexts. Building on Durkheim's work on mechanic and organic solidarity as well as on the studies of the Chicago school (Wirth 1938), sociologists and social anthropologists have long differentiated between the social networks of rural settings and those of urban areas. Thus the former display "*close-knit* social networks in which everybody knows and interacts with everyone else," whereas urban contexts are characterized by "social networks [that] are loose-knit and allow greater anonymity and independence of action" (Scott 1988: 117, in reference to Frankenberg 1966). Gaetz (1992), in turn, has argued that urban spaces (i.e., neighborhoods, districts, boroughs) are heterogeneous and, given that their boundaries are usually arbitrary, might lack social solidarity. Hence, these spaces do not favor the development of social networks, casting doubts on the validity and usefulness of the concept of community in urban settings. Gaetz thus contends that the notion of community, as applied to urban contexts, may serve ideological purposes, such as containing conflict and encouraging cooperation "within geographically-bounded entities rather than within more socially significant collectivities" (1992: 94).

A series of studies using data from the Mexican Migration Project (http://mmp.opr.princeton.edu) confirm the significance of context of origin in the formation of migratory social networks and migration-relevant social capital and on the overall dynamics of the social process of international migration (Hernández-León 1999; Flores 2001; Flores, Hernández-León, and Massey 2004; Fussell and Massey 2004). Taken together, these studies question the applicability of existing theories of migration to urban settings. Largely developed in the Mexico-U.S. context, the theory of cumulative causation is one such conceptual construct.

This theory posits that, as a social process, migration unfolds in a form that is self-feeding. That is, once it begins, migration creates the conditions for subsequent flows to arise. This occurs because at the core of this process of cumulative causation rests the fact that migration functions and spreads through social networks. It is the first wave of migrants, then, that lays the foundation for an unfolding support network that, in turn, provides the social infrastructure for the continuation of migratory flows (Massey 1990; Massey, Goldring, and Durand 1994).

As networks broaden, so does their social base. In the beginning, a migratory flow is usually composed of single men who are members of a community's middle strata and who are able to confront the risks and costs of migration. Over time, as the network unfolds and matures, individuals of lower socioeconomic class join the flow, taking advantage of the infrastructure of contacts and opportunities set in place by fellow migrants. So do women, children, and the elderly, who are also incorporated into the stream as changes in selectivity continue to happen. In communities with long-established flows, mature networks, and an advanced process of cumulative causation, migration tends to be a more prevalent phenomenon. That is, people participate in crossborder movement to a level at which, given a locality's total population, migration becomes a mass social process (Durand and Massey 1992; Massey, Goldring, and Durand 1994; Massey et al. 1987; Massey 1990). It is at this point that cumulative causation has the greatest impact on the sending community, producing a culture of migration (Alarcón 1992; Durand 1994; López Castro 1989).[12]

Although proponents of the cumulative causation model were always cautious about the applicability of this theory to urban-origin migration—contending that it is most relevant for "migrant circuits arising in nonmetropolitan locations" (Massey, Goldring, and Durand 1994: 1503)—the aforementioned studies have demonstrated empirically that economic and social conditions in cities do not allow for the kind of migratory dynamics long observed in the *ranchos* and small towns of rural Mexico. In large cities, prospective migrants rely on kinship contacts to support U.S.-bound sojourning yet do not resort to friendship and (nonkin) hometown networks, something that their rural counterparts commonly do. Urbanites' choice of social network stems from the anonymity, feeble solidarity, and heterogeneity that prevail in cities (Flores 2001).

Without the strong ties that bind urban residents to each other, migration cannot gain the momentum it normally attains in rural settings, when U.S. labor market and border-crossing experiences have become a readily available community resource. In other words, urban sociability does not provide the conditions for the accumulation of social capital, therefore preventing the development of the expansive, self-feeding mechanism leading to mass migration (Fussell and Massey 2004). In addition, labor markets and general economic conditions in cities provide low-skill and impoverished urban dwellers with alternatives to migration, which for the most part are absent in rural areas. These alternatives include informal income, credit- and capital-generating opportunities, and more-developed housing markets. Moreover, formal urban employment offers access to Mexico's retirement and pension system, which, despite its underdevelopment, provides workers with some disability and health insurance protection and the elderly with some financial security (Flores, Hernández-León, and Massey 2004; Fussell and Massey 2004).

Contrary to these findings, I argue that for the purpose of U.S.-bound migration, under certain conditions, urbanites may be able to substitute the weak ties that link them to (nonkin) neighbors, coworkers, and schoolmates in the city for the strong (rural-type) ties they lack. For some time now, network theorists have maintained that weak ties play a significant role in the diffusion of information and social behavior (Granovetter 1973). Whereas strong ties often provide redundant information to small numbers of closely interconnected individuals, weak ties function as bridges between groups, extending beyond the reach of people's immediate contacts and therefore diversifying the resources a person is able to access. According to Granovetter, weak ties and the indirect contacts they facilitate "are then of importance in that they are the channels through which ideas, influences, or information socially distant from ego may reach him. The fewer indirect contacts one has the more encapsulated he will be in terms of knowledge of the world beyond his own friendship circle." (1973: 1370–1371).

Conversely, Granovetter continues, "those to whom we are weakly tied are more likely to move in circles different from our own and will thus have access to information different from that which we receive" (1973: 1371). Weak ties effectively extend opportunities generally unavailable to those to whom one is closely connected. From the point of view of their strength, weak ties are an intermediate category between strong ties and the absence of substantive relations. Weak ties are indeed less dense than strong ties but not entirely void of emotion, trust, and reciprocal interactions.

I use these theoretical insights in combination with the findings of a rich, ethnographic, urban sociological and anthropological literature, which cautions about viewing the city as a wasteland for the formation of social ties that can support international migration. These studies, conducted in Mexico and the United States, have shown that working-class and low-income populations use the urban neighborhood as an effective space to establish social ties and to develop support networks and social capital. This tradition of urban ethnography has demonstrated that city residents do not live an anonymous social life in the metropolis. On the contrary, economically disadvantaged urbanites develop connections with fellow neighbors and deploy these links to support social movements, undertake informal economic activities, and form solidarity networks between households (Fernández-Kelly 1994; Gutmann 2002; Lomnitz 1975; Miraftab 1997; Suttles 1968; Vélez-Ibáñez 1988). In this book, I utilize the contributions of these strands of sociological network theory and urban ethnography to inquire: Do urban settings give rise to a social infrastructure supporting migration? Under what conditions does urban sociability engender migratory social capital? What kinds of networks emerge in urban contexts and how do they operate? How do urban contexts limit and shape the ability of networks to be the conduits of such migratory social capital?

The chapters of this book provide answers to these questions and, at the same time, contain a critique of current perspectives on networks, social capital, transnationalism, and international migration. In the Mexico-U.S. case, studies have often focused on the capacity of family and hometown ties to sustain migration and provide the necessary resources for immigrant settlement (i.e., shelter, information, job contacts, and other migration-relevant knowledge; Durand 1994; Durand and Massey 1992; Massey et al. 1987). This emphasis on the positive traits and outcomes of networks has prompted critics to question whether "a network [should] be viewed as a big and happy family" (Escobar Latapí et al. 1998: 229). Thus, Escobar Latapí and his associates have argued that "more refined analyses are needed to determine when and how networks break up; when and how individuals decide to migrate in spite of weak or no links to networks; and when and how a 'binational community' reconstitutes itself in the U.S., as when most women and children join men abroad" (Escobar Latapí et al. 1998: 229).

Indeed, scholars have paid little attention to issues of conflict, power, and long-term sustainability of kinship and friendship ties. Specifically, researchers have overlooked intranetwork conflict arising from the uneven control and distribution of resources among men and women, youths and adults, and legal and illegal immigrants within the same network. Similarly, little is known about the impact that social and economic conditions at origin and destination have on the stability of networks. Even though contributions to the economic sociology of immigration have referred to the issue of freeloaders who use but do not contribute to a group's social capital (Portes and Sensenbrenner 1993), little empirical research has been conducted to assess the consequences of opportunism for the social networks established by immigrants.

A new generation of scholarship has begun to present a more nuanced view of immigrant social networks. Such networks are gendered in ways that express the different roles of men and women in key migration-related decisions (i.e., how one, when one, and who gets to migrate), in their ability to tap into social capital and employment opportunities, and in their capacity to control the tangible and symbolic benefits of sojourning (Hagan 1998; Hondagneu-Sotelo 1992). These studies show that as migration brings about social change affecting the original roles, motivations, and resources available to migrants, tension and conflict arise within networks, families, and households, not only between genders but also between members of different generations (Espinosa 1998; Hirsch 2003). Other studies have demonstrated that networks are neither infallible nor immune to the changing political and socioeconomic contexts they inhabit and that such contexts greatly affect their capacity to deliver valuable resources and useful assistance to members. Thus protracted poverty, violence, and social fragmentation may severely limit the ability of networks to dispense social capital and effectively keep participants connected to each other (Guarnizo and Diaz 1999; Guarnizo, Sánchez, and Roach 1999; Mahler 1995; Menjivar 1997, 2000).

This study shows that despite the predictions of scholars regarding the effect of urbanism on the formation and resilience of social ties, migrants in the Monterrey-Houston circuit make use of their contacts with neighbors, friends, and fellow urbanites to establish networks that are effective conduits of migratory support. However, these networks are not smoothly functioning devices. On the contrary, they are fraught with inequality, conflict, and differing motives for migration among members. Because networks have a structuring capacity—channeling immigrants to alternative destinations, jobs, and housing markets—such dynamics are not anecdotal details but important characteristics that are likely to affect the fate of sojourners and their international migratory circuits.

## THE MIGRATION INDUSTRY

Despite being the focus of much scholarly attention, migrant networks are not the sole social infrastructure connecting home and destination. I contend that the migration industry constitutes an infrastructure distinct from networks that facilitates mobility between Monterrey and Houston.[13] Not an industry in the traditional sense of the term, the migration industry consists of a matrix of private and specialized services that facilitate and sustain international human mobility and its related behaviors, including settlement, mobility, communication, and resource transfers. Migration entrepreneurs render these services for a fee, and the main objective is turning a profit. Still, because migration industry services are often embedded in immigrant networks and ethnic economies, the behavior of these entrepreneurs is also mediated by relations of kinship and fictive kinship, bounded trust, patron-client relationships, and coethnicity (Harney 1977; Krissman 2000; Spener 2004).

Migration industry actors make functionally distinct contributions to the process of migration depending on the stage and nature of the migratory regime, "greasing" the system's engines (Harney 1977). These contributions include (but are not limited to) stimulating, initiating, facilitating, and sustaining human mobility, opening and institutionalizing new destinations for migration, mediating newcomers' incorporation into host societies, and, in the current regime of heightened restrictions to international migration, bypassing border controls and internal inspections aimed at detecting clandestine entrants and residents. Finally, the migration industry also eases contacts between migrants and stay-at-home individuals in the country of origin by providing communication, transportation, and in-kind and monetary resource transfer services. Migration industry activities and services include trafficking and labor recruitment, lending funds to finance migration, providing passenger transportation and travel agency services, sending monetary and in-kind remittances, applying for and producing authentic and counterfeit documents, legal counseling, and supplying telecommunications services for emigrants and their home communities. Still, the actors and activities integrating the migration industry have varied historically according to emigration and immigration policies, labor demand, social and economic conditions in sending and receiving countries, and the size of the immigrant population at the destination.

Following Froud et al. (1998) and their study of motoring, I contend that the migration industry can be best understood as a sector matrix of services and activities organized around international mobility and associated behaviors. The case of motoring is useful to the study of the migration industry because, just as buying a car leads the customer to consume bundles of services, such as financing and repair (Froud et al. 1998), the immigrant needs an array of services before, during, and after international mobility takes place. Such services are not organized in a chainlike form, where the consumption of one leads to another, but instead represent a matrix of interrelated services and activities in which providers simultaneously compete, cooperate, and articulate their activities with other actors. Yet another advantage of this matrix perspective is that formal and informal services as well as legal and illegal activities are considered integral components of the overall sector, providing insight into how services evolve or straddle the line of official recognition, how legal and illegal services are used throughout the migratory journey, and how entrepreneurs and services adapt to shifting economic circumstances and larger legal and political realities.

As a matrix of mobility services, the migration industry and its assortment of entrepreneurs do not cease to operate once migratory flows begin and social networks kick-in. On the contrary, I argue that migration industry entrepreneurs are ever present in the social process of international migration, interacting in complex and still largely unexplored ways with sojourners and their support ties, employers of immigrant labor, state institutions, and advocates of migrant workers. In addition to the entrepreneurs facilitating the initiation of migration, such as recruiters and smugglers, a panoply of transportation, communication, and remittance transfer providers work to secure the continuation and long-term reproduction of cross-border mobility in the Monterrey-Houston circuit.

## ORGANIZATION OF THE STUDY

This book is the result of a ten-year study of the causes, social organization, and consequences of international migration in Monterrey—a city long known for anchoring its residents to local industries through lifetime, stable employment instead of channeling them into international labor markets—and Houston, the chief destination of this flow. The chapters, conclusions, and methodological appendix that follow present the findings of three interrelated case studies analyzing the structural causes that gave rise to international migration in the industrial working-class neighborhoods of metropolitan Monterrey; the social networks and

economic incorporation of blue-collar *regiomontanos* in Houston; and
the migration service industry that efficiently and effectively connects the
two cities.

I begin, in chapter 2, by reviewing Mexico's urban-industrial development from the 1940s to the present. Part 1 of the chapter deals with
dominant patterns of economic growth, urbanization, labor market
dynamics, and social policy during the period of ISI. Part 2 takes notice
of recent changes in urban-industrial development in Mexico, including
the transition to a model of EOI, the economic crises, and the structural economic transformations that have fostered the rise of U.S-bound
urban migration. In section 3, I outline Monterrey's processes of urbanization and industrialization and discuss in great detail the political,
geographic, and social circumstances that led to this city's accumulation
of capital and economic development from the nineteenth century to the
present.

The empirical core of this book are chapters 3 through 5, each presenting the settings, participants, and findings of the three strategic
research sites. Chapter 3 introduces La Fama, an industrial working-class
neighborhood located in the Monterrey metropolitan area and proud
cradle of this city's industry. In La Fama, I found a fertile environment
of blue-collar households making increasing use of migration across the
border to confront the effects of industrial restructuring and changing
urban labor markets. In this neighborhood, I implemented a survey to a
final sample of 168 randomly selected households. The instrument was
modeled after the Mexican Migration Project's ethnosurvey (Massey
1987) but included open-ended questions and equally detailed sections
on the migratory networks of men and women heads of household. The
purpose of the survey was to obtain systematic data on migratory patterns and long-term trends rather than to formally test hypotheses about
the phenomenon. I triangulated the results of the survey with Mexican
census data, ethnographic (participant and nonparticipant) observations, structured and unstructured interviews, and life histories of the
migration pioneers from La Fama. Some U.S. migrants identified in this
neighborhood were interviewed multiple times throughout the years in
Houston and again in Monterrey.

Chapter 4 deals with two interrelated issues: the role of networks in
the social organization of migration and the incorporation of La Fama
and *regiomontano* immigrants into Houston's labor market. I begin
by showing how in addition to kinship ties, city-origin migrants utilize
friendship networks stemming from the social space of the urban neigh-

borhood to support their international mobility. I argue that residential and employment stability and the presence of institutions that provide social cohesion to working-class neighborhoods, such as La Fama, have allowed residents to develop migratory social capital out of the normally weak ties that link them to their neighbors.

This chapter also shows how skilled blue-collar immigrants from La Fama and surrounding neighborhoods have been able to transfer the technical abilities acquired in Monterrey's heavy manufacturing workplaces to the industrial labor markets of Houston, particularly to the petrochemical and oil-technology plants of the Bayou City. However, not all *regiomontano* newcomers have been able to benefit from such skill transfer, as many have become incorporated into low-skill (though not necessarily low wage), high-risk jobs, such as asbestos removal. Finally, engaging the literature on immigrant transnationalism, I ask whether the Monterrey-Houston connection represents a transnational community. By showing how the receiving state and state borders affect mobility and immobility, I demonstrate that despite the relative proximity of Monterrey, Houston-based *regiomontanos'* ability to participate in cross-border activities is largely determined by their legal status in the United States. Needless to say, my aim is not to disprove the main claims of the transnational approach but to argue that immigrant transnationalism is contingent on the policies and practices of states—an argument that resonates with recent scholarship on this topic (see Smith 2003, 2006).

The chapter draws from a snowball sample of forty immigrant households originally from Monterrey settled in new and historic Mexican neighborhoods in the eastern and western sections of Houston and from a small subsample of *regiomontano* cultural activists and small-business entrepreneurs. It is precisely in one of these newer immigrant neighborhoods of the Bayou City where immigrants from La Fama have established a daughter community. As I describe in detail in the methodological appendix, I discovered this daughter community early in my fieldwork in Houston as I searched for contacts with *regiomontano* families. Indeed, in the Summerland district and adjoining neighborhoods of western Houston, I encountered a surprising density of families and single men who were from La Fama and who knew and supported each other, forming a series of interconnected social networks. Although years later some of the single men told me jokingly that they initially thought that I was working for *la migra* (the Border Patrol and, more generally, U.S. immigration enforcement agencies), I managed to gain their trust by deploying my own linguistic, geographic, and cultural skills as a fellow Mexican and, just as important, as a fellow *regiomontano*. I kept in touch with many of these individuals and families from La Fama throughout the entire study period of ten years and re-interviewed, called, and spent time with them as they moved back and forth between Monterrey and Houston. This was the case with the Gonzalez family I depict in the last section of the chapter.

Chapter 5 analyzes the migration industry that facilitates international human mobility between Monterrey and Houston. Through the lens of a case study, I offer an in-depth ethnographic look into the workings of courier services operating in this circuit. Often seen as either an extension of social networks or as a subsector of the ethnic economy, the migration industry has received little systematic attention in most theorizing about international migration. Here, I claim that the matrix of entrepreneurs and services that make up the migration industry—smugglers, recruiters, transportation operations, remittance companies, lawyers, and others—is at the heart of the social organization of international migration. This ensemble of migration entrepreneurs has a multidimensional and fluid relationship with states, advocacy organizations, employers of immigrants, and the immigrants themselves, articulated by their profit-seeking motivation and their interest in the continuation and expansion of cross-border flows.

I explain the place Monterrey and Houston occupy as hubs for migration industry services in the Mexico-U.S. migratory system, a fact that is relatively evident in the case of the Bayou City but remains unknown in the case of La Sultana del Norte (The Sultan of the North, as Monterrey is dubbed in Mexico). The chapter then focuses on the case of a small business established by a *regiomontano* migrant to transport cash and in-kind remittances, correspondence, and people between the two cities. Deeply embedded in the immigrant social networks and operating on both sides of the border, the case of this informal business showcases in great detail the workings and significance of the migration industry in the social organization of this international migratory circuit, easing the movement of resources aimed at household reproduction and facilitating contact between members of *casas divididas* (divided households).

This is the most ethnographic chapter of the larger qualitative study of the Monterrey-Houston circuit. I closely followed the ups and downs of the family-run operation for several years, also tracking the businesses that replaced it after its demise. I established a close relationship with the owner, visiting his "offices" and riding his vans in Monterrey and Houston numerous times to conduct participant interviews and make unobtrusive observations along delivery routes. Thus, I was able to gain in-depth knowledge not only of the inner workings of the service but also of the cleavages and disputes that existed between the owner and his extended family, his employees, and even his customers. A long-term and intimate connection to the courier service also allowed me to witness the effects that border and customs enforcement (by both U.S. and Mexican authorities) had on the success and survival of this informal migration industry business. Finally, the case study and the chapter as a whole also benefited from my interviews with other courier operators, my observations and informal conversations at bus depots in Monterrey and Houston, and my own experiences as passenger and border-crosser traveling the highways that connect the two cities.

In addition to summarizing the major findings of the book, chapter 6 elaborates on the specificity of metropolitan migration by explicitly comparing rural- and urban-origin migrations in the Mexico-U.S. context. Clearly useful, such comparisons need to be drawn carefully so as not to dwell on stagnant and stereotypical images of one kind of migration in an attempt to shed light on the other. Indeed, just as urban flows have started to attract attention, rural flows have undergone substantial changes of their own. For example, immigration and border enforcement policies of the last twenty years coupled with transformations in Mexican and U.S. agriculture have turned yesterday's "birds of passage" into settled immigrants today (Durand and Massey 2003). Still, it is safe to argue that there are significant differences between urban and rural flows. For instance, urbanites are unlikely to use migration as a risk-management strategy. Instead, work abroad is likely to be utilized as a coping strategy to fully substitute for employment lost at home. Moreover, as I illustrate throughout the book, to the extent that they rely on nonfamilial networks to support their journeys, metropolitan migrants may have to build and resort to the weak ties that connect them to neighbors, friends, and coworkers to support their stints in the United States.

Finally, in the methodological appendix I provide a detailed account of the methods of data collection and analysis and the criteria used to identify and select research sites and subjects. As a multifocal and multisite study of an international migratory circuit, the fieldwork experience entailed my own back-and-forth movement between Monterrey and Houston and between multiple locales in each of those two cities: homes, bus stations, cantinas, street corners, soccer fields, parties and festivals, community centers, churches and plazas, outdoor markets, commercial strips, and workplaces. The research experience also involved understanding migration from the point of view of numerous diverse actors: skilled industrial male workers at both ends of the migratory stream and their stay-at-home wives in Monterrey; female migrants employed in services and light manufacturing in Houston; and migration entrepreneurs, such as smugglers and courier van operators, and their associates, employees, and clients. Making sense of their experiences, social position, and relations in the process of international migration has required the use of an array of methods, ranging from surveys and focus groups to life histories and ethnographies. For similar reasons, this book actively utilizes and critically engages a diverse group of theories and concepts, including the new economics of migration; structural-historical models; transnationalist, network, and social capital perspectives; and urban and economic sociology approaches. This is less the embracing of eclecticism than the open recognition that migration is a multidimensional social process that precludes either methodological phobias or theoretical dogmatism.

# CHAPTER 2

# Urban-Industrial Development in Mexico, 1940-2005

The migration of urban Mexicans to the United States has taken place in the aftermath of the model of import substitution industrialization (ISI), which set the path for urban-industrial development in Mexico for nearly half a century. Since the 1980s, the country has been enmeshed in a process of economic restructuring and modernization, moving Mexico away from ISI toward a pattern of export-oriented industrialization (EOI). In Monterrey, this transition and its ensuing effects on industrial-labor relations and the reproduction of working-class households have unleashed uncharted migratory streams to the United States.

From the late 1930s until 1982, Mexico adopted an economic model of ISI, which accelerated urbanization and rapidly transformed this rural society into a predominantly urban one. Throughout this period, the Mexican government sought to directly and indirectly develop the country's industrial base, creating and financing infrastructural projects, instituting protections and subsidies to manufacturing production, and improving the work and living conditions of the country's urban population. A byproduct of the ISI model was the growth of a large skilled and semiskilled urban working class, which benefited from low inflation, price controls on food staples, and expanding public and private employment. A beneficiary of the sustained economic growth of the 1950s and 1960s, the urban-industrial working class not only had few incentives to migrate to the United States but also had been purposefully excluded from the Bracero program (1942–64) and the emerging binational labor market (Durand 1998).

The year 1982 signaled the beginning of Mexico's most severe economic crisis of the last fifty years and the starting point of a profound process of restructuring, which entailed the demise of ISI and the shift to a new model of EOI and international competitiveness. Restructuring has also meant the unevenly paced dismantling of the social and political institutions that were the pillars of industrial-labor relations during the ISI era and their replacement by new institutional arrangements reflecting the realities of EOI. The common denominator of these new arrangements is the introduction of flexibility in the workplace, in the labor market, and in industrial-labor relations in general. In other words, the modernization of Mexico's industrial firms and infrastructure required a modernization of labor relations in the workplace and in the broader legal and societal arenas (Pozas 2002). It is in this context of transformation that labor from Mexico's primary urban-industrial centers has begun to migrate to the United States.

Monterrey represents a strategic research site to study the relationship between economic restructuring and U.S.-bound migration as well as the incorporation of industrial workers into migratory circuits linking Mexico and the United States. As pioneers of Mexico's heavy manufacturing production, the Monterrey economic elite led early efforts to implement ISI, an endeavor that prompted it to develop its own supply of skilled industrial manpower. Being close to the border, local industrialists faced one important threat to their steady supply of skilled and semiskilled workers: the constant pull of higher wages from the binational labor market (Mora-Torres 2001). In the early twentieth century, the Monterrey bourgeoisie developed a series of corporate paternalist labor relations policies and practices aimed at attracting, retaining, and controlling industrial workers. Later on, the social welfare provisions of Mexico's postrevolutionary state challenged but also reproduced and extended similar policies to broader segments of the urban-industrial working class (Rojas and Garza 1985).

This combination resulted in an institutional regime of industrial-labor relations that has been called "peripheral Fordism" (Gutiérrez Garza, 1988, 1990) because it mimicked, in the context of a peripheral country, elements of Fordist regimes in the industrialized world. The set of institutionalized practices that made up this regime allowed for the formation and reproduction of a skilled industrial working class with firm roots in the city, one that for decades would not be enticed by the higher wages to be found on the other side of the border. In the early 1980s, as the economic model of ISI that Mexico had embraced during the postwar years collapsed, so did the institutions of peripheral Fordism. The ensuing process of economic restructuring has transformed the nature of industrial-labor relations, eroding job stability and downgrading the overall quality of employment in the labor market. As a result, international migration has now emerged as a salient option for the urban-industrial working class.

I begin this chapter by outlining the ISI model and its impact on urban-industrial development in Mexico, including the formation of a metropolitan skilled and semiskilled working class. I close this section by explaining the demise of ISI. In part 2 of this chapter, I describe and analyze the most important characteristics of EOI and its effect on the country's urban-industrial centers and working-class households from 1982 to the present. In part 3, I introduce the case of Monterrey and the historical, geopolitical, and economic processes that led to its emergence as a heavy manufacturing powerhouse in the twentieth century. I conclude by describing the context of crisis and forces of restructuring responsible for unleashing new urban migratory flows to the United States and to Houston, Texas, in particular.

## ISI AND POSTWAR URBANIZATION (1940–82)

### Import Substitution and the Mexican Miracle

Mexico is today a predominantly urban-industrial country. Whereas only 22 percent of the country's inhabitants lived in urban areas in 1940, more than 70 percent of the national population lived in cities in 1990, and 75 percent in 2000 (INEGI 2005; Jones and Ward 1998; Ward 1991).[1] The economic, demographic, and policy changes that most forcefully accelerated Mexico's urban-industrial development began to occur in the late 1930s and early 1940s (Garza 1992) as a result of ISI, the economic model adopted in Mexico on the heels of postrevolutionary reconstruction (Garza and Rivera 1993). Even though such a model exhibited signs of exhaustion during the latter part of the 1960s and throughout the 1970s, it was the 1982 crisis that forced Mexico to move away from ISI and turn toward an EOI program.

The early phase of ISI began in Mexico during the 1930s, less as the result of purposeful economic policy than as the outcome of structural circumstances in the world economy that affected the links between metropolitan and peripheral countries. The fall in price of agricultural and extractive export products, the high cost of imports, and the decline in investment and lending capital flows from core nations, provoked by the 1929 crisis, forced Mexico to begin its own process of industrialization. This process started with the local production of nondurable consumer goods such as food and clothing, that is, commodities that were labor rather than capital intensive and for which a vast market existed (Guillén Romo 1985).

During the 1940s and 1950s, as the process of import substitution moved forward and additional types of manufactures were produced nationally, industrialization started to require more active participation by the state. It is at this point that ISI became an actual economic policy. State intervention responded to the costs, problems, and constraints that entrepreneurs faced when producing intermediate, durable, and capital goods. The Mexican state financed the establishment of businesses, subsidized industrial production through the low cost of public utilities, invested heavily in the development of the country's infrastructure, and protected national industries from international competition, restricting the kinds and volume of goods that could be imported. The state also intervened through the direct ownership of enterprises in key economic sectors (i.e., oil, electricity, and steel), taking over inefficient private companies and effectively creating and presiding over a mixed economy in which the government played a crucial role in setting up the basis for modern industrial development (Guillén Romo 1985; Story 1990). Such forms of government economic intervention would not have been possible without the corporatist system established during the postrevolutionary period (1920–40), which allowed for the direct and indirect political control of civil society. In this system of corporate political control, the state functioned as mediator between labor and capital, setting up arbitration councils between unions and employers and co-opting those unions, and as the designer and executor of a revolutionary program centered on economic justice and social policy issues (Aguilar Camín and Meyer 1993; Escobar Latapí 1992).

With the deepening of import-substitution during the 1950s, the growth of new industries and the production of more sophisticated goods demanded the importation of expensive equipment and technology. To produce such manufactures, Mexico had to import the capital goods that were not available in the domestic market, including advanced technologies brought in by the subsidiaries of transnational corporations (Story 1990). To pay for these costly imports and the subsidies and tax exemptions to the private sector and to handle the ensuing trade deficit, the Mexican government (and businesses) resorted to international loans and foreign investment (Guillén Romo 1985). Although the issue of indebtedness did not become a major problem until the 1982 crisis, by 1970 Mexico was using the equivalent of nearly 24 percent of the value of its exports to service its foreign debt (Guillén Romo 1985; Ward 1991).

Despite these imbalances and intrinsic limitations, the import-substitution model was successful in transforming the country's economic structure. This transformation is clearly reflected in manufacture's growing share of both the gross national product (GNP) and the economically active population (EAP) and the declining participation of agriculture in both GNP and EAP. Thus, the proportion of manufacturing activities in the GNP increased from 15.40 percent in 1940 to 22.55 in 1970, while the sector's share of the EAP rose from 12.3 percent in 1950 to 18.5 in 1970. In contrast, agriculture's participation in the GNP declined from 19.41 percent in 1940 to 11.51 in 1970, while the sector's share of the EAP decreased from 58.7 percent in 1950 to 39.4 percent in 1970 (Garza and Rivera 1993). Moreover, manufacturing production increased by 7.5 percent annually between 1960 and 1976, with subsectors such as auto assembly, machines, and household appliances (i.e., refrigerators, washing machines, television sets) growing by 12 to 16.3 percent yearly during the same period (Guillén Romo 1985). At the same time, the national economy registered annual average growth rates of 5.73 percent from 1940 to 1955 and 6.74 percent from 1956 to 1970. During this latter period, known as "the stable development" (*el desarrollo estabilizador*) and "the Mexican miracle" (*el milagro mexicano*) epoch, such growth rates were attained while also sustaining low inflation and a stable peso to U.S. dollar exchange rate.[2]

## The Social Consequences of ISI

ISI policies had significant social and demographic consequences. The most notable impact was the rapid urbanization of the country, which followed a pattern of high population concentration in a few metropolitan areas, particularly Mexico City. This pattern had its most visible effect during the 1940–70 period and resulted from the concentration of industrial production, manufacturing jobs, services, and most public and private investment in the capital city. Thus, the metropolitan area of Mexico City grew from nearly 2 million people in 1940 to slightly more than 9 million in 1970. In 1960, 48 percent of the nation's urban inhabitants were concentrated in Mexico City. Guadalajara and Monterrey, the country's second- and third-largest cities, increased their populations from 290 thousand and 220 thousand in 1940 to 1.51 million and 1.27 million, respectively, in 1970. By the end of the 1960–70 decade, nearly 51 percent of all urban dwellers were concentrated in these three metropolitan areas. This pattern of urban growth and population redistribution came at the expense of Mexico's intermediate and small cities and of the towns and villages of the countryside and resulted in the primacy of Mexico City over the rest of the urban system (Garza and Rivera 1993; Ruiz Chiapetto 1994; Ward 1991).

The model of economic development adopted between 1940 and 1982 provoked not only a rapid urbanization of the country but also a dramatic abandonment of the rural and agricultural life that had characterized Mexico. The above-mentioned declining share of agriculture in the GNP and the EAP during this period attests to this claim. However, such decline barely reveals the impact of ISI and its pattern of high urban concentration on rural Mexico. Although the government had aggressively implemented its agrarian reform laws under the Cárdenas administration during the 1930s, the process of land distribution did not provide small farmers with the necessary capital and technology to make their economic units fully productive.

Aside from the irrigation projects that were concentrated in the large agribusiness districts of northern Mexico, this period was defined by disinvestment in agricultural production and the use of export agriculture surpluses to finance industrialization, providing the foreign currency to pay for the import of capital goods and raw materials. At the same time, the government controlled the prices of food staples, such as corn and beans, which small farmers produced for the internal market. This strategy of price control was aimed at subsidizing the cost of living of the urban labor force and at eliminating inflationary pressures on industrial wages. A consequence of this policy was the impoverishment and near bankruptcy of small agricultural producers. In addition, the agricultural sector underwent its own transformation during this period as more land and financial resources were allotted for the production of export commodities (i.e., tobacco, coffee, and cotton) and animal feed goods (i.e., sorghum, soybean, and alfalfa). Produced in large estates, using more efficient green revolution technologies, these commodities contributed to the displacement of the rural labor force (Barkin 1991; Guillén Romo 1985; Valenzuela Feijoo 1986).

These effects unleashed internal and international migratory flows stemming from the countryside and directed toward Mexico's metropolitan areas and the United States. These flows were connected to the dislocations fostered by the process of development under ISI (Martin 1991; Massey 1988). Between 1940 and 1970, besides natural population growth, it was internal migration that contributed to the rapid urbanization of the country.[3] Even though rural to urban migrations occurred following different patterns, the dominant trend was one of permanent migration to the country's metropolitan areas. In that sense, internal and international flows had different effects on their places of origin and on the country as a whole: Permanent internal migrations reinforced the process of urbanization and metropolitanization, whereas U.S.-bound migration, due to its circularity, contributed to the survival of towns and institutions in Mexico's rural world (Durand 1994).[4]

The expanding economy was able to absorb many of these immigrants. But as import-substitution moved toward a more capital-intensive phase and as the model began to reach its limits, this pattern of industrialization revealed its growing incapacity to provide employment for the new entrants to the urban labor market. To be sure, such new entrants provided an abundant supply of labor to modern industry, but in the absence of unemployment insurance, they had to invent "employment around the fringes of the urban economy" (Portes 1989: 8). The resulting informal employment developed as a byproduct of capital-intensive industrialization and as a survival strategy for those who could not find jobs in formal labor markets. This so-called marginal sector was not peripheral to the performance of the mainstream economy. On the contrary, informal work became articulated with formal employment in private and public enterprises. Such articulation stemmed from the hidden subsidies transferred to the formal sector in the form of cheap goods and services produced under informal work conditions. Much like government subsidies, these transfers of value helped keep the cost of the social reproduction of urban labor low (Escobar Latapí 1992).

ISI had other important social consequences. Chief among them was the making of an urban working class and a salaried urban middle class. Following the principles of the regulation school, students of Mexican industrialization have applied the notion of peripheral Fordism (Lipietz 1987; Gutiérrez Garza 1988) to analyze the social, economic, and legal institutions that allowed for the making and reproduction of the industrial working-class and that regulated industrial-labor relations under the ISI model.[5] According to this explanation, peripheral

Fordism begins to unfold in Mexico during the late 1950s through the use of technologies both imported from abroad and transferred by the subsidiaries of transnational corporations and large local enterprises— technologies conceived following Fordist principles of the production process (Gutiérrez Garza 1988). As was the case in core countries, Fordism entailed more than just a type of organization of the work process (Coriat 1991; Harvey 1990). As Harvey puts it, Fordism involved the "recognition that mass production meant mass consumption, a new system of the reproduction of labour power, a new politics of labour control and management" (1990: 126).

In Mexico, the expansion of the internal market on the basis of more expensive, capital-intensive goods that national firms had begun to produce during the 1950s necessitated mass consumption. Large-scale consumption required, in turn, establishing a link between the wages paid to industrial workers, their productivity, and the cost of living. A series of institutional arrangements made this possible. In 1962, new legislation instituted the professional minimum wage, homogenizing the salaries for skilled and trade workers, and divided the country into a series of economic zones to determine the respective minimum wage. The same legislation established a national management, union, and government commission that would resolve disputes regarding wage increases, centralizing the salary arbitration process. Different from metropolitan Fordism, the institutional arrangements enshrined in the law in Mexico presupposed a corporatist system in which the state exercised great control of union federations in exchange for political positions for the union leadership, rhetorical support for workers' demands in the bargaining process, and social policies that benefited the urban working class. Yet the impact of these policies and institutions on the salaries and living standards of workers was no rhetorical matter: The daily real minimum wage grew from 1.24 pesos in 1955 to 3.37 pesos in 1976 while inflation remained low throughout the period (Gutiérrez Garza 1988, 1990).

In the manufacturing centers where peripheral Fordism institutional arrangements dominated, industrial working-class households exhibited a rigid division of labor by gender, with domestic groups predominantly composed of nuclear families and headed by a male breadwinner earning a family wage. Typically, women did not participate in the labor market. Their contribution to household reproduction was centered on child rearing and domestic labor. Still, these forms of unpaid labor were crucial to peripheral Fordism as they helped keep the cost of household sustenance low and, consequently, salary levels down (Cravey 1997).

The social programs of the Mexican state supplemented the family wage of the industrial worker, in a way similar to the welfare state social provision that arose in developed countries after World War II. Moreover, employers provided a series of benefits that, as part of the indirect wage, became a sizable portion of the worker's overall income.[6] Thus, the state established the Instituto Mexicano del Seguro Social (IMSS) in 1943 to provide medical attention, child care, and retirement benefits to workers and their families. A similar system for public servants, the Instituto de Seguridad y Servicios Sociales de los Trabajadores del Estado, was created in 1961. In 1972, the federal government created several funds to provide affordable (owner-occupied) housing to salaried workers, notably the Instituto del Fondo Nacional de la Vivienda para los Trabajadores (INFONAVIT). Between 1965 and 1974, the state also implemented a variety of programs to subsidize or finance the consumption of durable and nondurable goods. In turn, private and state-owned corporations assisted employees directly by supplying or subsidizing food, work clothes, transportation to workplaces, educational and recreational activities, and end-of-year bonuses. By 1980, this indirect, or social, wage represented 44 percent of the income of a manufacturing worker (Cravey 1997; Gutiérrez Garza 1988; Rojas and Garza 1985).

However, the benefits of peripheral Fordism and the welfare state included only those workers employed in the formal sector of the economy, particularly industrial operatives and the salaried middle class. Hence, vast segments of the population were excluded from the expanding social rights that the Mexican miracle brought about as a precondition of economic growth. Almost the entire rural population was among those excluded, together with the urban poor, those who were underemployed and engaged in informal economic activities, and the unemployed.[7] According to estimates developed by Gutiérrez Garza (1988), in 1970 only 50 percent of the economically active population had been incorporated into the institutional arrangements that came to define peripheral Fordism.[8]

In sum, by the end of the 1970s, ISI, peripheral Fordism, and the social provision of the welfare state had demonstrated a profound urban bias. The combined effect of these processes and institutions had transformed Mexico into an urban country: By 1980, the majority of the population was living in cities (56.26 percent). The beneficiaries of economic growth, consumption, and expanding social rights were also part of the urban population: the industrial and commercial bourgeoisie, the salaried middle class, and the skilled industrial working class. The redistribution of wealth that higher salaries and a social wage entailed favored middle-class groups at the expense of both the high- *and* low-income strata. Middle-class families, making up 55 percent of the total number of families in the country, had increased their share of the income distribution, from 45.50 percent in 1950 to 63.60 percent in 1977. However, during the same period, low-earning households, constituting 40 percent of all households in Mexico, had experienced a decreasing participation in the income distribution, from 14.30 percent to 10.94 percent. Thus, ISI and the institutional arrangements that accompanied it did little to redress income inequality, suggesting that the country's most impoverished families were excluded from the benefits of peripheral Fordism and the employment-related social wage (Guillén Romo 1985; Gutiérrez Garza 1988, 1990; Ward 1991).

## The Exhaustion of ISI

The crisis of the ISI model in Mexico can be attributed, in part, to the exclusion of such a large portion of the population from the benefits of economic growth. Because import substitution was sustained on a type of development where industrial production was geared for local and national consumers rather than for world markets (Ward 1991), continued growth depended on the protracted expansion of the internal market. But the capacity of the national market to absorb durable and capital goods manufactured by local industries began to reach its limits during the 1970s. Created and protected by the state's restrictions on imports, these industries lacked the ability to compete in international markets. Even though the federal government implemented policies aimed at diversifying exports, Mexico continued to rely heavily on agricultural, mining, and oil industries to obtain foreign currency. A weak capacity to export, in the context of a global economic recession, led to an escalating deficit in the balance of payments. This deficit went from 726.4 million dollars in 1971 to more than 3 billion dollars in 1976 (Guillén Romo 1985; Gutiérrez Garza 1988).

Other causes also contributed to the exhaustion of the import-substitution model. By the late 1960s, the agricultural sector showed signs of its inability to continue subsidizing industrialization. In the early 1970s, Mexico turned from being an exporter of agricultural products to being a net importer of basic grains, hence signaling the end of the country's self-sufficiency in the production of food staples. These transformations resulted in part from new patterns of land use in which agricultural commodities that yielded higher returns in national and world markets displaced the cultivation of basic grains. However, these changes also resulted from the transfer of resources from agriculture to industrial production, particularly in the form of low-cost staples that subsidized the price of the urban labor force. Given that the government had kept the prices of corn and beans stagnant since 1963, small farmers had no incentive to produce for the market. Still, in 1969, these small farmers contributed 38 percent to the total agricultural production in Mexico. With limited access to credit and modern technology, small producers withdrew from the market, abandoning their lands and seeking employment in Mexican cities and the United States. The decline in Mexico's output of agricultural staples forced the importation of these products. Consequently, the reproduction cost of the urban-industrial labor force escalated, undermining a pillar of ISI and peripheral Fordism (Barkin 1991; Guillén Romo 1985; Gutiérrez Garza 1988).

Mexico's increasing dependency on foreign borrowing also signaled the exhaustion of ISI policies. Thus, by 1970, foreign debt was 4.2 billion dollars, representing 10.6 percent of the GNP. During the 1970–76 administration, as the deficit grew and the Mexican state revealed its inability to implement a fiscal reform that would raise internal sources of revenue, foreign debt increased at an annual rate of almost 30 percent, reaching 19.6 billion dollars by the end of the term. It is worth noting that parastate enterprises contracted 85.4 percent of said debt during the period in question. These were precisely the industries that subsidized the growth of the private sector through the low cost of utilities and public services such as fuel, gas, and electricity (Guillén Romo 1985; Wyman 1983). But the rapid growth of foreign debt also resulted from the surplus availability of petrodollars in the international banking system, produced in turn by the rise in oil prices during the oil shock of 1973 (Harvey 1990). During this period, the Mexican government was able to borrow substantial amounts of money at low interest rates but soon began to require new loans to service its foreign debt (Guillén Romo 1985).

In 1976, in the context of rising inflation, deficits in the balance of payments, and growing foreign debt, the government devalued the peso for the first time since 1954. Despite the circumstances and the massive flight of private capital, the government averted the implementation of a stabilization program negotiated with the International Monetary Fund

(IMF) as the discovery of new oil reserves allowed Mexico to continue borrowing from international banks and to resume economic growth.[9] The federal government, which controls oil production and processing through the parastate corporation Petróleos Mexicanos, acquired new loans to exploit these newly found resources. Three major consequences resulted from this economic juncture: First, Mexico became increasingly dependent on oil revenues, which by 1981 came to represent 61 percent of the country's total exports; second, the deficit in the balance of payments surpassed 6.5 billion dollars, almost tripling in three years and reflecting Mexico's dependency on imports for continued economic growth; and third, the foreign debt nearly doubled between 1978 and 1981, reaching the unprecedented figure of 71 billion dollars (Guillén Romo 1985; Wyman 1983).

Two developments that unfolded in the world economy during 1981 forced Mexico into a debt-induced financial crisis: the decline in oil prices and the rise of interest rates. The collapse in oil prices signified the loss of six billion dollars in expected earnings in 1981. The government responded to the shortfall of resources through heavy borrowing, taking out variable-interest short-term loans. As rates increased, the country saw its foreign reserves shrink to minimum levels and was basically unable to service its maturing international debt. By 1982, the crisis was in full force as the government attempted a series of desperate measures to stabilize the economy and contain capital flight: devaluation of the Mexican peso, implementation of exchange controls, a two-tiered exchange rate system, and, most important, the nationalization of the banking system (Guillén Romo 1985; Wyman 1983).

Concerned about the impact of the Mexican debt crisis on world financial markets, U.S. and other international banking institutions came to the rescue. This rescue effort was anchored on an agreement, reached at the end of 1982, between the Mexican government and the IMF. Mexico agreed to implement a severe austerity program in exchange for access to 3.9 billion dollars in loans. The centerpiece of this program was the reduction of the deficit, viewed as the driving cause of inflation and indebtedness. Thus, the government slashed expenditures on public works, health, and education, raised the price of utilities, and eliminated price controls and subsidies for consumer goods and basic staples (Grindle 1991; Lustig 1992; Rivera Ríos 1992; Wyman 1983). In a country where public spending had played a key developmental role for more than forty years, this austerity program entailed severe social and economic costs.

CRISIS, EOI, AND URBAN-INDUSTRIAL RESTRUCTURING
(1983–2005)

*The Effects of the 1980s Crisis*

I now turn to the social and economic consequences of the 1980s crisis, the significance of the crisis as a transition period in the move toward EOI, and the impact of both the crisis and EOI on urban-industrial restructuring in Mexico from 1983 to the present. The period in question actually encompasses two distinct crises with arguably different origins: the 1980s debt-induced crisis, which began in 1982 and included the 1986 recession, and the 1994–95 crisis linked to the overvaluation of the peso and to the Mexican economy's dependence on highly movable speculative capital (Pastor 1998). Still, it was the 1980s crisis—the worst of the postwar era—which had the most profound socioeconomic consequences: the decline in real wages and in the standard of living of working- and middle-class Mexicans; the growth of informal labor, underemployment, and unemployment; the saturation of urban labor markets due to the contraction of available jobs; and the decline in the rate of urbanization and in the rate of growth of the three largest metropolitan areas. The crisis also signaled the transition from ISI to EOI (Escobar Latapí and Roberts 1991). This transition comprised not only the demise of old economic policies but also the establishment of new models of industrial organization, a new regime of industrial-labor relations, changes in urban economic specialization, and a tighter connection between Mexico and the world economy. In short, the shift from ISI to EOI entailed complete economic restructuring.

One of the most significant consequences of the 1980s crisis was the abrupt decline in real wages (Bortz 1992). During the 1982–89 period, the real minimum wage dropped 50 percent as inflation reached 159 percent in 1987 and the cost of basic food staples increased as a proportion of the minimum wage, from 30 percent in 1982 to over 50 percent in 1986. Real urban wages fell 27 percent between 1982 and 1986, and the average real manufacturing wage declined by 35 percent. Households responded to the fall of real wages with a variety of strategies, which included incorporating more family members into the labor market and raising income from nonwage sources. Thus, nonwage income increased its share of total income, from 60 percent in 1981 to 71.5 percent in 1988. Among the urban labor force, the proportion of wage earners declined from 83.4 percent in 1982 to 76.2 percent in 1985 while the propor-

tion of self-employed workers increased from 12.1 percent to 15 percent
and the number of unpaid family workers rose from 2.1 percent to 4.6
percent. This emerging pattern of employment was coupled with a surge
in urban unemployment. The unemployment rate in Mexico generally
underestimates the extent of this phenomenon because the government's
definition of employment includes all individuals who have worked
at least one hour during the week of reference. Thus, the unemployment rate does not take into account those who are underemployed and
engaged in precarious employment. The "implicit" unemployment rate
does take into account these other forms of employment, hence showing that the proportion of those who were unemployed grew from 11.4
percent in 1980 to 20.3 percent in 1985. In sum, households reacted to
the decline of real wages by having more members join the workforce, by
resorting to self-employment, and by using unpaid family labor for the
production of goods and services (Cortés and Rubalcava 1993; Escobar
Latapí and Martínez Catellanos 1991; Friedmann, Lustig, and Legovini
1995; Grindle 1991; Lustig 1992; Pastor 1998; Trejo Reyes 1992).

Women's labor market participation played a central role in the way
urban households responded to the aftermath of the crisis and to the program of austerity and adjustment implemented by the Mexican government. Thus, single and married women entered the labor force in growing numbers, conducting both formal and informal work in exchange for
salaried and nonwage income.[10] For instance, married women increased
their labor market participation by 32 percent between 1982 and 1987,
and women with more than three children by more than 60 percent during the same period. The growing feminization of the labor force was
particularly important in manual self-employment and manufacturing,
where women gained ground as operatives in *maquiladora* (assembly)
plants (García Guzmán 1993). Children and the elderly were also incorporated (or reincorporated) into the labor force as part of the household strategies to maximize potential sources of income. Families also
responded by reducing consumption, allocating previous health and education expenditures to the satisfaction of basic needs, and increasing
household size to share living expenses (Cortés and Rubalcava 1993; De
Oliveira and Roberts 1993; Gabayet and Lailson 1991; García Guzmán
1993; González de la Rocha 1994; González de la Rocha and Escobar
Latapí 1991; Miraftab 1997).

These transformations in employment patterns and household strategies suggest that the 1980s crisis fostered the growth of informal work
in the labor market (Escobar Latapí 1992; Escobar Latapí and Martínez

Castellanos 1991). Roberts (1994) contends that the informal economy provided families with work and income to weather the effect of the crisis, becoming a central component of the strategies for household survival (see also De Oliveira and Roberts 1993). During the 1980s, new labor market entrants found employment in the urban informal sector. This sector's share of total nonagricultural employment increased from about 24 percent in 1980 to 33 percent in 1987. But despite the fact that informal work grew, unregulated businesses and the informal sector as a whole became less dynamic, partly as a result of the lack of demand from the formal sector. By the end of the decade, informality also arose from the flexibility and deregulation of industrial-labor relations, the shift toward services in many urban economies, the growing use of subcontracting, and the privatization of state-owned companies. Thus, the rise of informal economic activities was linked not only with the aftermath of the crisis but also with the transition to a new model of industrial development, an issue to which I come back below. For many workers, however, incorporation into the informal labor force during the 1980s meant the loss of benefits that were part of the social wage, including social security, health care, and other formal sector job-related perks. When compounded with the low earnings associated with informal employment, such experiences came to signify entry into the ranks of the urban poor (Alba Vega and Roberts 1991; De Oliveira and Roberts 1993; Escobar Latapí 1992; García Guzmán 1993).[11]

What was the effect of the crisis on the patterns of urbanization and industrialization that had unfolded in Mexico during the 1940–82 period? The 1980s crisis unleashed substantial transformations in the style of urban and industrial development, countering previous trends. Cities, urban labor markets, and manufacturing activities bore the brunt of the crisis, particularly during the first four to five years of the economic downturn (1982–86).[12] This comes as no surprise considering the pattern of high urban-industrial concentration that Mexico had pursued under ISI. As domestic demand declined, so did growth in manufacturing. This sector grew at a low 1.3 percentage rate between 1981 and 1985 and actually experienced negative growth rates in 1982 and 1983, -3 percent and -8.1 percent, respectively. Moreover, manufacturing accounted for only a 4 percent increase in the number of firms between 1980 and 1989 and for only 25 percent of the jobs created during this period (compared to commerce, which accounted for a 50 percent increase in the number of firms and a 39 percent raise in the number of jobs). Given that manufacturing was highly concentrated in cities, the decline and slow growth of this sector had a major impact on urban labor markets, rural-urban migration, and on the entire Mexican urban hierarchy (Aguilar 1997; Cornelius 1991; Garza and Rivera 1993).

The labor markets of the major metropolitan areas of the country lost jobs as a result of the manufacturing crisis. The Mexico City metropolitan area lost 2,466 industrial firms and nearly 38,000 jobs between 1980 and 1985. The Monterrey metropolitan area, in turn, lost almost 56,000 posts and reduced its contribution to the national manufacturing product from 10.3 percent in 1980 to 6.7 percent in 1985. In contrast to Mexico City and Monterrey—cities with industries that specialized in the production of capital and durable goods—the metropolitan areas of Guadalajara and Puebla, with industrial sectors that concentrated on processing food and other nondurable consumer goods, actually held ground and experienced modest growth in the number of firms, jobs, and output. Despite this mixed picture of stagnation and modest growth, these two large cities combined only contributed a small proportion to the industrial activity nationwide: 8.2 percent of the total number of establishments in the country, 8.6 percent of the employed labor force, and 9.7 percent of the national industrial product. In sum, the largest urban labor markets in Mexico contracted and underwent saturation, expelling workers and losing the capacity to absorb new entrants to the workforce, particularly in the industrial sector (Cortés and Rubalcava 1993; Garza and Rivera 1993; Roberts and Escobar Latapí 1997).

The patterns of urbanization and internal migration that unfolded in Mexico during the 1980s reflected the contraction of job opportunities in the country's largest cities. Even though city growth continued during the 1980–90 decade, the index of urbanization increased at a slow annual rate of 0.8 percent, the lowest growth rate in the twentieth century. Furthermore, the annual rate of expansion of the urban population declined from 5.2 percent during the 1970s to 2.8 percent during the 1980s.[13] As expected, metropolitan areas of more than 1 million inhabitants (with the exception of Puebla) bore the brunt of this decline: Whereas Mexico City, Guadalajara, Monterrey, and Puebla made up 51.3 percent of the country's urban population in 1980, by 1990 these cities only contributed 45.1 percent of the total. The population of Mexico City grew at a slow 0.7 percentage rate throughout the 1980s (compared with 4.4 percent during the previous decade), resulting in the decline of this city's primacy over the national urban system. Thus, Mexico City not only ceased to attract internal migrants but also began to lose population during the 1980–90 decade (Browning and Corona 1995; Garza and Rivera 1993; Lozano Ascencio, Roberts, and Bean 1997; Ruiz Chiapetto 1994). Browning and Corona (1995) have estimated that during the 1987–92 period nearly 661,000 people emigrated from the Mexico City metropolitan area to other states in the country.[14]

The border cities and the northern region of the country experienced the most significant gains in this reorientation of internal migrations. Lozano Ascencio, Roberts, and Bean (1997) have shown that on average border cities received more internal migrants from other states as a proportion of their total populations (9.75 percent) during 1985–90 than did other categories of cities, namely, the capital cities of Mexico's northern states (4.28 percent) and the metropolitan areas of the country (3.66 percent). Tijuana alone received 19.4 percent of immigrants from other states in 1985–90, thus contributing to the 5.3 percent growth rate the city experienced during the 1980–90 decade. Ciudad Juárez, in turn, accommodated 10 percent of interstate immigrants in 1985–90, reaching a rate of increase of 3.8 percent between 1980 and 1990. This pattern of northern border city growth can also be observed from the perspective of the inter-regional migrations taking place during the 1985–90 period (a national total of 1.5 million people). When these inter-regional flows are compared, the northern region of the country appears as the only one with a favorable net-migration balance (355,610 persons) (Garza and Rivera 1993; Lozano Ascencio, Roberts, and Bean 1997).[15]

The changes in urban labor markets, internal migratory flows, and patterns of city growth outlined above have prompted researchers to refer to the 1980s as a period of crisis for the urban system in Mexico and, most importantly, to contend that international migration during the decade stemmed from this crisis "as the capacity of the urban system to absorb labor was substantially diminished" (Roberts and Escobar Latapí 1997: 70; see also Cornelius 1991). International migration arguably became an alternative for both internal migrants and native city dwellers who encountered urban labor markets dominated by diminishing opportunities for salaried work, especially in manufacturing, and growing informal labor and self-employment, particularly in commerce and services (Roberts and Escobar Latapí 1997). Indeed, the 1980s became a landmark decade in the record number of Mexicans who migrated to the United States either directly or via step internal migration; they surpassed the 2 million mark (Corona 1993; Lozano Ascencio, Roberts, and Bean 1997).[16]

## The Transition to EOI

The crisis of the 1980s signaled the exhaustion of the model of ISI and the launching of a new pattern of development based on EOI. In a country that had long protected its industrial manufacturing sector, what Gereffi and Martínez (2005: 119) have called an "extreme example of . . . development model shift" from ISI to EOI entailed a profound process of economic restructuring, affecting Mexico's urban-industrial patterns, urban labor markets, industrial-labor relations, and international migration dynamics. Students of restructuring have primarily focused their attention on the transformations that industrialized countries underwent after the 1973 world crisis, signaling the advent of postindustrial, post-Fordist economies and a new positioning of cities in the world economy (Bluestone and Harrison 1982; Coriat 1992; Harvey 1990; Sassen 1990, 1991; Smith and Feagin 1987; Soja 1989). Social scientists have paid less attention to restructuring processes taking place in peripheral and middle-income nations, where experiences of industrialization were also affected by the changing world economy of the 1970s and 1980s. A more recent wave of studies has addressed the politics, economics, and social consequences of restructuring in Mexico (Pastor and Wise 2005; Cook, Middlebrook, and Horcasitas 1994; Cravey 1997; Dussel Peters 1998; Gutiérrez Garza 1990; Otero 1996; Pozas 2002, 1993a; Pozos Ponce 1996).

At the heart of the Mexican experience of restructuring is the transformation of an overprotected and inward-looking manufacturing sector into an export-oriented, internationally competitive one. The state institutions and national and transnational corporations leading the restructuring process have followed a twofold strategy. First, these economic actors have modernized the manufacturing sector through the incorporation of new technologies and flexible systems of production and the establishment of strategic alliances between local and foreign capital. Second, the Mexican government rapidly completed the liberalization of trade, the opening of the economy, and its integration with the United States by lowering duties and eliminating import restrictions, joining GATT in 1986 and later establishing NAFTA with the United States and Canada (Gereffi and Martínez 2005; Pozas 1992; Story 1990; Wise 1998). The outcome of this two-prong strategy of restructuring has been the dismantling of the institutions of peripheral Fordism erected during the ISI period and the emergence of a new model of industrial-labor relations, which Cravey (1997) has called "a new factory regime." This emerging regime presupposes "changing relations among state, market, and households" (Cravey 1997: 171). The rest of this section deals with the features and impact of restructuring by analyzing the combined effect of industrial manufacturing modernization and the liberalization of the economy. Together, these processes signify the restructuring process that has driven urban working-class Mexicans to seek jobs in the international labor market to face the dislocations effected by the transition to EOI.

The technological and organizational modernization of the manufacturing sector began in the 1980s in the midst of the state's implementation of the austerity program to manage the crisis. The purpose of the modernization program was clear: to create a manufacturing sector capable of exporting and competing in the world market. The obstacles to achieving this goal were not only the sector's inward-looking orientation and dependency on imports of technology and capital but also the industrial-labor relations constructed under ISI and enshrined in the labor code (Gutiérrez Garza 1992, 1988; Pozas 1992).[17]

To raise productivity, the sector's leading firms have adopted new flexible technologies and systems of organizing production which have had major effects on the labor process and the ways wages, skills, job categories, and employment tenure are negotiated in the workplace. The quest for flexibility, within and beyond the workplace, has been at the center of a variety of restructuring paths (Pozas 1992). Researchers have associated flexibility with the development of technologies and new forms of industrial organization that have allowed firms to overcome the obstacles to accumulation posed by the systems of production, industrial labor-relations, and institutions of the Fordist era, such as the inability to adapt to rapidly changing markets, which frequently left corporations with unsold inventories. Thus, implementing flexible systems of industrial organization presupposed dismantling the Fordist definition of the labor process in which operatives conducted clearly specified repetitive tasks, institutionalized in the workplace as part of a seniority-based occupational structure negotiated between management and unions through collective bargaining. This type of operative was replaced by a multiskilled and multifunctional worker. However, moving toward flexibility has also entailed the attempt by management to do away with the institutional arrangements that had emerged from the Fordist labor process: contracts, a high-profile role for unions in the workplace and the labor market, highly regulatory labor legislation, and comprehensive welfare protection (Gutiérrez Garza 1992, 1990, 1985).[18]

Social scientists have produced a number of case studies that illustrate the impact of flexibility and other strategies of restructuring in specific industries, regions, and cities of Mexico. In analyzing the experience of firms which are part of Grupo Monterrey, an industrial conglomerate that has been at the forefront of restructuring, Pozas (1992) found that the introduction of flexible automated technologies allowed specific plants to reduce the number of workers by as many as two-thirds in some cases.[19] The new equipment required fewer operatives, allowing the companies to lay off temporary and unskilled auxiliary workers, keep the skilled ones, and reduce the number of occupational categories on the shop floor. According to Pozas, workers have perceived these transformations as an additional burden that is not compensated by wage increases (Pozas 1992). Similar experiences have taken place in the cement industry in which the automation of the labor process has eliminated jobs and affected the structure of occupational categories within firms (Girón 1985).

In the automobile industry, dominated by transnational corporations and highly integrated to the U.S. market, restructuring actually began in the late 1970s and early 1980s with the construction of new factories in northern Mexico. In the new plants, workers were paid less than in the older facilities of central Mexico at the same time that the introduction of advanced technologies required a worker capable of monitoring computerized processes instead of executing skilled manual tasks. In these new factories, automation also contributed to flattening the occupational structure of the plant (Arteaga 1985; see also Rothstein 2004).[20] In a study of a parastate mining company in northern Mexico, Contreras and Ramírez Sánchez (1992) found that restructuring and privatization produced a dramatic transformation of the type of workplace that existed under ISI: introduction of modern flexible technologies, dismissals, reduction in the number of occupational and wage categories (from 143 to 4), internal mobility and promotion on the basis of skill rather than seniority, management's flexible rotation of workers to different tasks, and diminishing control of the union of the labor process as well as in the hiring of new operatives (Pozas 1993a; see also Zapata 1992).

Still, restructuring through flexibility has not been restricted to the workplace. The associations representing the largest industrial firms in Mexico have lobbied for changes in the federal labor code that reflect what has been occurring at the level of the shop floor. Calling for a *nueva cultura laboral* (new labor culture), these associations have developed and advocated for proposals that include greater flexibility in hiring and dismissal practices, longer work shifts, introduction of hourly payment instead of the current workday wage, and elimination of the occupation-specific minimum salary to be replaced by wages reflecting skill and productivity. In short, these measures seek to deregulate the labor market, which would weaken employment security and other worker protection regulations enshrined in Mexico's constitution (Pozas 2002, 1992; Palacios 2003). Pozas (2002) provides an example of how these reforms have contributed to the erosion of the peripheral Fordism regime of industrial-labor relations. In the mid-1990s, following modification of the law regulating Mexico's workers' health and pension system, the federal government drastically reduced its contributions to the system's central agency, the Instituto Mexicano del Seguro Social (IMSS, or Mexican Institute for Social Security). As a result, employers had to boost their own contributions to the IMSS. To accommodate this increase and its effect on profits, companies cut back on workers' benefits, including retirement and savings account programs as well as recreational centers and activities for employees and their families (Pozas 2002: 232).

The liberalization and opening of the economy complements the modernization of manufacturing. The purpose of this second strategy has been to open the national economy to foreign investment and products, to foster the international competitiveness and export capacity of Mexican industry, and to redefine Mexico's position in the world economy by deepening economic integration with the United States. The Mexican state has played a rather crucial role in this process, developing, negotiating (internally as well as internationally), and implementing the regulatory framework to reach these objectives.[21]

What has been the impact of this restructuring strategy on workers, labor markets, and migration? The opening of the economy had severe consequences for the small- and medium-sized companies that were once dependent on a captive internal market. When less expensive imports from Asia saturated the Mexican market in the late 1980s, particularly in the shoe and clothing industries, these firms faced serious economic problems. Between 1988 and 1993, the number of registered small- and medium-sized firms declined by 54 percent, representing a loss of 43,000 jobs. During this period, these companies and traditional industrial sectors like textiles, garment and leather, wood products, and structural metal goods lost jobs, contributing to the decline of manufacturing employment. This decline began in 1991 and hit the lowest point during 1996 as a result of the crisis, when manufacturing became only

9.42 percent of total employment (excluding *maquiladoras*) (Alba Vega and Roberts 1991; Dussel Peters 1998; Pastor and Wise 1998).

The opening of the economy also led to a rapid increase in imports during the late 1980s and early 1990s, which produced a deficit in the balance of trade that reached nearly 18.5 billion dollars in 1994.[22] According to the government program, the growth in imports would be compensated for by an increase in exports, and even though such exports had been growing since 1987, foreign-made goods simply outpaced them. Much of the steady expansion of exports was due to the tremendous growth of the *maquiladora* industry (see below). When *maquiladora* activities were excluded from the calculation, exports were not only erratic but were also completely dwarfed by imports. In 1992, the proportion of imports to exports reached a dramatic twelve to one ratio. This trade imbalance forced the government to finance the deficit with foreign portfolio investment directed to the Mexican stock exchange. This highly mobile and speculative investment began to leave Mexico in 1994 in response to local political instability and rising interest rates in the United States. The government converted its short-term peso-issued debt into dollars to keep foreign investors from withdrawing their funds. As the strategy failed and foreign reserves were depleted, the federal government devalued the peso, sparking the crisis of 1994–95. While some researchers have interpreted the 1990s economic crash as a crisis that resulted from the opening and liberalizing of the economy and the deregulation of financial flows, others have emphasized the inability of the manufacturing sector to export in the new economic context, hence contributing indirectly to the growth of the trade deficit (Dussel Peters 1998; Heath 1998; Pastor 1998; Pozas 1993a; Ros and Lustig 2001).

Regardless of the interpretation, the impact on workers and employment patterns was evident: Real wages fell to 1991 levels and the open unemployment rate reached 7.6 percent, a level not even seen during the 1982 economic downturn. Workers who lost their jobs in formal labor markets due to the impact of restructuring found employment in services and in the informal sector. By the mid-1990s, between 25 percent and 40 percent of Mexico's economically active population was employed in informal sector enterprises, which absorbed job losses experienced in manufacturing. The growth of informal sector activities can be gauged, albeit indirectly, from the proliferation of small businesses, the rise in service and commerce employment, and the job increases in economic sectors such as construction and communal services. These sectors were actually the most important in employment generation between 1988 and 1996 (excluding *maquiladora* activities), prompting observers to argue that the jobs being created during this period were of lower quality, further signaling the deterioration of the urban labor market and the polarization in the urban occupational structure between skilled and unskilled workers (Aguilar 1997; Dussel Peters 1998; Heath 1998; Pastor and Wise 1998).

The Mexican economy survived the peso crisis thanks to the financial bailout put together by the Clinton administration in 1995. The boom of the U.S. economy in the late 1990s stimulated Mexico's recovery and growth, spearheaded by the significant rise in foreign direct investment and exports. However, the country's expansion stalled in 2001 as a result of the recession in the United States. Despite negative gross domestic product (GDP) growth, Mexico weathered the effects of the recession with the help of remittances, which more than doubled between 2002 and 2005, becoming a top source of foreign earnings. With more than 85 percent of its exports going north—a phenomenon facilitated by NAFTA—Mexico's economic cycle is now intimately tied to the ups and downs of the U.S. economy. The upsurge in the U.S. economy once again fostered the resumption of growth south of the border: In 2006, Mexico registered an estimated 4.5 percent increase of its GDP (Crandall 2005; Pastor and Wise 2005; Gereffi and Martínez 2005). Despite that "Mexico's export-oriented strategy indeed has ushered in an extraordinary economic transformation in the past decade" (Gereffi and Martínez 2005: 124), some analysts have contended that the gains in productivity and the volume of manufactured exports have not been matched by a significant growth in manufacturing jobs. At the same time, real wages remain depressed and have not come up to their pre–peso crisis levels (Polaski 2004, 2006).

## The Maquiladora Question

It is important to briefly address the question of *maquila* growth because this sector has been at the heart of the strategy of opening and economically liberalizing the Mexican economy and because in cities like Monterrey employment in *maquiladoras* has become a more prevalent alternative for new generations of blue-collar workers and for those displaced from traditional sectors of industrial work.[23] Even though the Border Industrialization Program that established *maquiladora* plants with the purpose of alleviating unemployment along Mexico's northern border had been in place since 1965, *maquilas* did not experience significant growth until the 1980s and 1990s. The number of export assembly plants increased from 620 in 1980 to more than 2,000 in 1992. Similarly, the number of persons employed in these industries during this period grew from 100,000 to 518,000. By the mid-1990s, *maquiladoras* accounted for 11 percent of total manufacturing jobs. In 1998, *maquiladora* employment represented 25 percent of all manufacturing jobs.[24] By 2000, nearly 1.3 million people worked in the *maquila* sector, basically doubling the estimated labor market expansion of the industry. However, *maquiladora* employment has declined recently due to the U.S. economic recession and the relocation of companies to China. Despite such decline, by early 2004 the sector accounted for 45 percent of all manufacturing jobs (Polaski 2004; Bustamante 1983; Gereffi 1996; INEGI 2005).

*Maquiladoras* have undergone substantial transformations that indicate the maturation of this industry. These transformations include the emergence of a new generation of technologically sophisticated assembly plants, concentrated in the automobile and electronics subsectors, holding significant linkages to the domestic economy via supplier networks; the growing recruitment of men as operatives;[25] and the geographic dispersion of investments beyond the border to cities of the northern states and other localities of the Mexican interior, contributing to a shift in manufacturing from the traditional industrial core (Mexico City, Guadalajara, Monterrey, Puebla) to the northern region. The *maquiladora* industry has also changed in terms of location, plant size, internal labor markets, salary and work conditions, rate of unionization, and level and use of technological innovations and flexible forms of industrial organization (Aguilar 1997; Carrillo and Hualde 1992; Cravey 1997; Gereffi 1996; Gereffi and Martínez 2005; Pastor and Wise 1998).

Despite these changes, *maquiladoras* still operate on the basis of a simple premise: the attraction of foreign direct investment from core and, more recently, middle-income countries to a nation that offers a plentiful pool of cheap unskilled labor. *Maquiladoras* have become an integral part of Mexico's new internationally competitive manufacturing sector and a clear path, if not the only one, for Mexico's integration with the United States and the rest of the world in an era of open and restructured economies (Carrillo and Hualde 1992; Gereffi 1996; Gutiérrez Garza 1988; Pastor and Wise 1998).[26] *Maquiladoras* represent the prototype of the new factory regime that has gradually displaced the old, inward-looking type of manufacturing (Cravey 1997). The assembly plant regime is characterized by the low average wages and benefits paid to workers, which represent only half of the average earnings in non-*maquila* manufacturing. Furthermore, the high turnover rates and low levels of average seniority that *maquiladora* jobs exhibit show that these posts are also less stable than employment in the industries of the old factory regime. Thus, urban working-class households cannot achieve day-to-day and long-term reproduction on the basis of a family wage earned by a single male breadwinner. This has had multiple consequences for such households, including new gender and family dynamics, new strategies to access extra-salary benefits that used to be covered by state and corporate social provision, and the use of nonwage sources of income to supplement the salary (Carrillo and Hualde 1992; Cravey 1997; Pastor and Wise 1998).

It is in this context of crisis, restructuring, and transition to a new model of industrialization and a new factory regime that urban working-class households have begun to incorporate international migration into their ensemble of reproduction strategies, a development clearly taking place in Monterrey—Mexico's most important concentration of heavy industry for more than one hundred years.

## THE CASE OF MONTERREY: HEAVY INDUSTRY, FORMAL LABOR MARKETS, AND RESTRUCTURING

### The Origins

Monterrey, located in northeastern Mexico, had its geopolitical and economic circumstance change dramatically in the middle of the nineteenth century when the U.S.-Mexico War of 1846–48 pushed the border southward, bringing the city within one hundred and twenty-five miles of the United States.[27] Merchants and politico-military leaders based in Monterrey and the surrounding area were able to use this geopolitical development to their advantage, constructing a regional economic space that spanned the states of northeast and north-central Mexico and southeast Texas.

Several circumstances coincided to make Monterrey the de facto capital of this regional economic space. First, the liberal governor of Nuevo León since 1855, Santiago Vidaurri, consolidated politico-military power—at a time when a true nation-state with a centralized power had yet to emerge in Mexico. Vidaurri led an economy of war regime, creating an army of about five thousand men to fight centralist and conservative forces and battle belligerent, seminomadic Indians, annexing neighboring Coahuila and exercising significant control over the coastal state of Tamaulipas. This regime fostered a strong demand for credit and supplies that was largely satisfied by local merchants. Vidaurri took control of international trade in the region by establishing export and import posts along the border (all coordinated from Monterrey), taxing foreign goods, allowing the export of Mexican silver, and retaining customs revenue. Vidaurri's mercantile allies greatly benefited from these decisions (Cerutti 1992a, 1992b, 1995).

Second, a group of merchants based in and around Monterrey consistently took advantage of the opportunities provided by the border's proximity and Mexico's civil wars. For instance, local businessmen became the purveyors of war supplies, transportation equipment, agricultural staples, and other commodities to the Confederate army during the U.S. Civil War. These entrepreneurs (and Vidaurri's government) provided the means and the geographic outlet for the Confederacy to export its cotton to industrial markets when Union forces besieged the South's ports. Thus, Monterrey bourgeois groups successfully engaged in all sorts of commercial, credit, and agricultural activities in a vast regional and binational economic space that encompassed northeast Mexico and sections of Texas as part of the accumulation of capital (Cerutti 1992a, 1992b, 1995).

Third, the economic and demographic growth of Texas and the southwestern United States brought prosperity to the Monterrey region. American merchants based in the lower Rio Grande, controlling trade and contraband, established business partnerships with their Mexican counterparts, benefiting not only from war-driven demand but also from the reconstruction of both national economies during the 1870s and 1880s. The development of the railroad infrastructure south of the border strengthened the integration of northeast Mexico with the United States as northbound train lines crisscrossed the region. Monterrey got its own railroad connection with the United States in 1882 (before being connected with Mexico City), and by the turn of the century, the city became the hub of a modern communications network with four railroad connections to Texas. Such connections signified profitable linkages with the U.S. economy and the world market that allowed the regional bourgeoisie to import equipment and capital goods and to export iron and steel to Texas. These linkages and the railroad network that tied Monterrey with the rest of Mexico also gave this city a prominent role in the country's nascent national market (Cerutti 1992a, 1992b, 1995; González Quiroga 1993; Hibino 1992).

Beginning in 1890, the local bourgeois families that had accumulated their fortunes through commercial and lending activities started to shift their investments to industry. In so doing, they exploited opportunities made available to them by the demand for raw and processed minerals during the boom of the U.S. economy at the end of the nineteenth century and by the formation of Mexico's own national market, which also called for manufacturing products. The federal and state governments encouraged and facilitated investment in mining and industrial pursuits, guaranteeing private property rights on the subsoil and declaring, in Monterrey, a twenty-year tax exemption for all new enterprises whose capital exceeded a thousand pesos. Thus, the shift to industry that occurred between 1890 and 1910 implied a profound reorganization of the city and its regional economy.

Surprisingly, heavy industrial manufacturing was the driving force behind this economic transformation, particularly large-scale metallurgical production, a development unforeseen in the rest of Latin America. In Mexico's northeast, mining produced dynamic effects, connecting the region with the national and world economies and fostering backward and forward linkages. Between 1890 and 1900, three smelting plants were established in Monterrey to process the ores extracted from north-central and northeastern states (including Nuevo León) destined for the U.S. market.[28] Once again, local entrepreneurs extended their economic reach, continuing with their regional strategy by investing in mining and the processing and production of metals, frequently in association with foreign businessmen, a few of whom had actually immigrated to Monterrey. The process of industrial expansion reached a milestone in 1903 with the establishment of Fundidora de Fierro y Acero de Monterrey, S.A., the first iron and steel plant of its type in Latin America, which was set up with an initial investment of five million dollars. From its inception until 1986, the year it was shut down, Fundidora came to represent Monterrey's industrial calling in the urban landscape (Cerutti 1992a; Flores 2000; Hibino 1992).

Companies producing consumer and intermediate goods—some strongly identified with the industrialization of this city—were also established during the 1890–1910 period. The brewery Cervecería Cuauhtémoc was founded in 1890, with the majority of its capital coming from local investors. It was wholly owned by Mexican entrepreneurs and could initially produce five thousand barrels of beer per year. At the turn of the century, Cervecería employed one thousand workers. Monterrey's brick and glass industries were also created during this period. By 1906, the Compañía Manufacturera de Ladrillos de Monterrey produced twenty-five million bricks annually, exporting some of this output to places like Texas and Havana, Cuba. In turn, the Vidriera de Monterrey, after a failing start as Fábrica de Vidrios y Cristales de Monterrey, was financially and technologically restructured and, by the mid-1910s, produced up to one hundred thousand glass bottles per day, becoming the main supplier for the national market.

Still, what built Monterrey's reputation as a leader in early industrialization in Latin America was the making of commodities destined for use as capital goods and inputs in the production process: mining equipment, agricultural machinery, steel, and nonferrous industrial metals. This sector was the driving force behind Monterrey's industrialization because of the large investments it required, the technology it utilized, and the number of people it employed, fostering demand for raw materials, services, and transportation infrastructure and creating linkages with regional, national, and international markets (Cerutti 1992a; Hibino 1992). In explaining the structural conditions that fostered the development of the Monterrey regional economy and of this city as a center for heavy manufacturing, Cerutti argues that

> the fact of being located next door to the industrial revolution produced in this Latin American space a particularly dynamic economy, all the more notable if one takes into account capitalism's overall level of development in turn-of-the-century Mexico. This area of the country, and especially Monterrey, benefited from the opportunity to operate simultaneously in two markets: the domestic market, slow-paced and slow to take shape; and the neighboring market (with which an ancient web of commercial ties existed), the most rapidly accelerating market of the time. To some degree, the industrial revolution seeped into border areas, and that seepage clearly affected the spatial organization and the complexity of economic activities there. (1992b: 155)

This industrial expansion required the making of a manufacturing labor force. At first, the Monterrey bourgeoisie recruited skilled German and American workers, whose efforts, according to historian Mora-Torres (2001), were supplemented by numerous unskilled laborers coming from a hinterland that included rural Nuevo León, neighboring northern states, and even central Mexican states, such as Guanajuato and Aguascalientes (see also Cerutti 1995). Monterrey's proximity to the border and the pull of the U.S. labor market and its high wages forced industrialists to adopt a proactive strategy to create and retain a native, skilled industrial labor force. Thus, to "recruit workers [Monterrey's industrialists] raised wages and engaged in a variety of labor practices . . . including offering wage bonuses, housing, and schooling and promoting Mexican unskilled labor to higher skills" (Mora-Torres 2001: 127). By 1910, the city boasted a 10,000-strong working class. Reflecting the effect of these labor practices and its overall economic dynamism, Monterrey's population increased from about 45,000 in 1885 to nearly 79,000 in 1910 (Cerutti 1995; Mora-Torres 2001).

## Revolutionary Upheaval and Postrevolutionary Reconstruction

The Mexican Revolution (1910–17) disrupted economic activities in the entire country, and Monterrey was no exception. The local bourgeoisie, now transformed into an industrial capitalist class, experienced tremendous losses at the hands of revolutionary factions and endured exile in the United States.[29] Despite these experiences, the Monterrey elite remained united and, in the absence of a legitimate political power during the critical revolutionary years, became the de facto government of the city and the state. The Monterrey business class survived the revolutionary upheaval yet was faced with a new, socially progressive constitution and a national context that drastically differed from the ancien régime under which it had thrived. A steel workers' strike at Fundidora in 1918 showed industrialists the need to exercise direct control of labor in their plants and to seek an organized representation for their economic and political interests vis-à-vis the new revolutionary regime. In response to the challenges posed by labor, Cervecería's owners created an employee cooperative in 1918, the Cooperativa Cuauhtémoc y Famosa, a company union that served as a model for the business elite to implement paternalistic practices and to eliminate any independent organizing drive on the part of workers. Clearly, the industrial bourgeoisie confronted a new set of concerns no longer connected with the loss of workers to U.S.-bound migration but with the spread of radical ideologies to the ranks of the proletariat. On the political front, the Monterrey elite led efforts to create business associations that would represent capitalists before the emerging revolutionary state (Flores 2000; Rojas and Garza 1985; Saragoza 1988).

Between 1920 and 1940, the city's industry resumed its economic growth as old firms reactivated production and new companies were created. Responding to the underdevelopment and uncertainty of supply chains, these companies undertook a strategy of industrial growth based on vertical integration—creating departments within the original firm—

which provided the necessary inputs to manufacture the final product. These departments eventually became separate industrial establishments that continued to supply the parent firm while allocating part of their output to the larger market. It is also during this period that companies like Cervecería Cuauhtémoc and Vidriera Monterrey began a strategy of expansion by setting up subsidiaries in other parts of the country, notably Mexico City and Guadalajara. During the 1930s, newly formed holding corporations were charged with coordinating the tactics of vertical and horizontal integration of these firms (Flores 2000; Vizcaya Canales 1995).

This process was punctuated by the impact of the Great Depression and the prolonged confrontation of the Monterrey capitalist elite with the succeeding regimes of the postrevolutionary state. At the center of this confrontation was the definition of the bounds of state intervention in private economic activities, particularly the role of the state in capital-labor relations. The conflict between the federal government and local industrialists played out over the issue of labor's political allegiance and control. To counter labor unrest during the postrevolutionary years, Monterrey's capitalist class swiftly moved to create company unions (known in Mexico as *sindicatos blancos,* or white unions) and to implement corporate paternalist labor management practices. As the federal government sought to mobilize the industrial working class behind some of its progressive social and economic policies, including the labor code of 1931, it encountered the opposition of Monterrey industrialists. Local businessmen effectively prevented the penetration of their plants by government-supported unions (also known as *sindicatos rojos,* or red unions) by threatening a citywide lockout and uprooting radical and independent labor leaders, ultimately strengthening their control of workers through a federation of company unions created in 1936 (Rojas and Garza 1985; Saragoza 1988). One of the most important consequences of this experience was the relatively insignificant presence of progovernment unions in industrial workplaces in this city.

## The Import-Substitution Takeoff

After the period of postrevolutionary reconstruction (1920–40), the federal government and local bourgeoisie reconciled, and corporate paternalism and welfare state provisions fused to produce, in Monterrey, an enhanced version of peripheral Fordism under ISI. In this city, then, the ISI model produced not only a protected economy but also a protected urban-industrial working class, which, according to Vellinga, "formed, as a whole, a privileged category in comparison with other proletarian segments of the economically active population" (1989: 116, my translation). Its privileges consisted of relatively high salaries, subsidized housing, health clinics, savings and insurance schemes, and lifetime employment as well as vocational schools and an entire leisure and recreational infrastructure for workers and their families—all part of the Monterrey elite's vision of corporate paternalism first introduced in the early 1900s.

The Monterrey metropolitan economy thrived during the era of ISI. The number of industrial establishments in the state of Nuevo León grew from 1,310 in 1940 to 5,839 in 1970, representing an annual increase of 151 throughout the period. Ninety-two percent of the existing firms in 1970 were concentrated in the Monterrey metropolitan area. Similarly, the number of people directly employed in industrial manufacturing expanded from 14,557 in 1930 to 145,705 in 1970 (Vellinga 1989). During the ISI era, the city consolidated its position as the second-most-important industrial center of the country. In fact, Monterrey's industrial product grew at higher levels than the national rate, allowing the metropolitan economy to increase its share of Mexico's industrial output and overall GDP. The city's contribution to the country's industrial GDP expanded from 7.2 percent in 1940 to 10.4 percent in 1970. Proving a key feature of the Monterrey urban economy, industrial manufacturing represented an extraordinary 47.3 percent of the total GDP of the metropolitan area in 1970. In contrast, commerce and services remained largely underdeveloped. In addition, Monterrey's pattern of industrial development exhibited concentration on a few manufacturing subsectors, an increasing orientation toward the production of capital goods for the internal market, and the continuing concentration and centralization of capital, manifested in the growing significance of a few large industrial conglomerates (Garza 1995b, 1995c; Sobrino 1995).

By the end of the period, the city's share of the national industrial product equaled the combined manufacturing output of Guadalajara, Puebla, and Toluca, the three most important industrial centers after Mexico City and Monterrey. Between 1940 and 1980, the process of industrial expansion continued to be led by a few corporations, which made up most of the manufacturing production of the city. These corporations were still controlled by the same families who had initiated industrialization in the late nineteenth century and who had concentrated their capital and woven their interests together through intermarriage. During the 1970s, the Monterrey capitalist class undertook a new wave of expansion, diversifying investments and establishing new holding corporations to horizontally integrate and control recently acquired firms. This expansion was financed through reinvested profits, internal transfers of capital, loans from national banks (many of which were owned by these corporations), and foreign bank credit flows, an increasingly important source of financing (Flores 2000; Garza 1995a, 1995b; Vellinga 1989).

In terms of urbanization, industrial development produced two significant consequences: the formation of a metropolitan area and a stream of internal migratory flows that fueled the city's labor market. Starting in the 1950s, the expansion of the central city began to incorporate adjoining municipalities. By 1980, the Monterrey metropolitan area comprised eight municipalities, and its population had reached the two million mark. At the same time, internal migration contributed to the city's population growth. According to the 1960 census, one-third (32.9 percent) of the inhabitants of the metropolitan area had been born in states other than Nuevo León. By identifying different categories of internal migrants, including those from rural Nuevo León, the landmark study of Balán, Browning, and Jelin (1973) established that during the 1960s, 69 percent of Monterrey's adult male population was of immigrant origin. Between 1960 and 1990, as much as 75 percent of out-of-state immigrants to the city were originally from the neighboring states of Coahuila, San Luis Potosí, Tamaulipas, and Zacatecas, confirming the regional pulling effect of the Monterrey labor market. During the 1960s, the predominant source areas of these internal flows were the small towns and rural localities of less than five thousand inhabitants of the sending states, rather than their respective cities. The selectivity and labor market incorporation of immigrants had changed over time. From 1930 to 1965, internal migrants from Monterrey were single, young, and better educated than the average individual in their places of origin. In contrast with migrants from these previous waves, who actually found employment in industry, people who arrived in the city during the 1970s were incorporated into the informal sector of the urban economy (Balán, Browning, and Jelin 1973; Vellinga 1989; Zúñiga 1995).

## From Crisis to Restructuring

The 1980s crisis transformed La Sultana del Norte from a city that had been a magnet for immigration and that offered economic growth and increasingly high standards of living into a source of metropolitan out-migration. The recession affected Monterrey disproportionately when compared to the country as a whole, yet this effect was commensurate with the city's share of the national industrial product, which declined from 10.2 percent in 1980 to 8.8 percent in 1988. Thus, while the country's industrial product grew at an annual rate of 0.8 percent over the 1980–88 period, Monterrey's industrial GDP actually declined at a yearly rate of -1.1 percent. Similarly, while the national GDP grew at an annual rate of 0.9 percent throughout the 1980s, Monterrey's overall GDP only increased at a yearly rate of 0.1 percent during the same period. As internal demand for intermediate and capital goods shrunk with the crisis, the metropolitan economy faced its most evident deficiencies: extreme economic specialization in industrial manufacturing, high concentration in the production of intermediate goods, the overwhelming orientation of this sector to the national market, and the growing dependence of local corporations on foreign bank loans to finance their expansion plans (Flores 2000; Garza 1995a; Garza and Rivera 1993; Vellinga 1994).

The immediate response of local industrialists was to scale back production by streamlining operations, selling and closing down companies, and laying off thousands of workers.[30] Between 1980 and 1988, the number of industrial jobs declined 22 percent, from 195,578 to about 153,250. The examples of important conglomerates in the city illustrate the dramatic impact of the crisis. From 1981 to 1983, FEMSA eliminated 21,393 jobs while ALFA, perhaps Mexico's largest private corporation at the time, laid off 18,143 workers between 1980 and 1984. During the same years, VITRO reduced its payroll by 10,000 employees. According to Flores (2000), in 1997 several of these corporations had still not reached the employment levels they had attained in 1980. The bankruptcy and closing of Fundidora Monterrey in 1986 epitomized the severity of the crisis for the city's industrial economy and labor market. Symbolizing the city's one-hundred-year history of industrialization, Fundidora had provided 11,000 direct jobs and much indirect employment through the small- and medium-size shops that furnished the steel mill with components for maintenance and repair work. As a result of the severe economic downturn and of its impact on the local labor market, in the 1980s Monterrey experienced its lowest rate of demographic growth of the twentieth century, 2.5 percent, second only to the population increase of the revolutionary decade. Population growth due to immigration reached a low 0.53 percent between 1980 and 1990, suggesting that the city was attracting few internal migrants (Flores 2000; Garza 1995a; Garza and Solís 1995; Vellinga 1994; Zúñiga 1995).

The initial effect of the crisis was the massive unemployment of male workers who, once laid-off, had to face two circumstances: shrinking employment opportunities in industrial manufacturing and an under-developed informal sector that could not absorb, even temporarily, the surplus labor force. The absence of such a sector can be explained by the dominance of big industry and formal labor markets in the city's economy, in contrast with urban areas such as Guadalajara, Puebla, and León, where informal employment had been intrinsic to development based on small-scale businesses and traditional craft activities (Aguilar Barajas 1993; Morris and Lowder 1992; Pozos Ponce 1996).

Working-class households responded by incorporating more family members into the labor market and by conducting income-generating activities in the service sector of the urban economy. Women began to participate in growing proportions in the economically active population. The rate of female labor market participation increased from 25.3 percent in 1978 to 33.2 percent in 1989, with twenty to twenty-four year old participation expanding from 38.2 percent to 53.7 percent during this period. Older men (65 years of age and older) also increased their labor market participation, from 28.6 percent in 1978 to 38.2 percent in 1989. At the same time, the proportion of men in the city's employed labor force declined by 27.1 percent while the participation of women grew by 39.1 percent during this period (Pozos Ponce 1996).[31] Women and young as well as elderly members of urban households entered the labor market as a result of the decline of male employment and the overall impact of the crisis on household well-being. On the other hand, men who had been expelled from industry became employed and self-employed in services, reflecting both a shift in Monterrey's economic specialization from manufacturing to tertiary sector activities and a new structure of job opportunities for the industrial working class (Pozos Ponce 1996).[32]

Still, Monterrey continues to be one of Mexico's most important industrial centers, with manufacturing remaining a key sector in terms of GDP, employed labor force, and number of establishments.[33] The process of deindustrialization that the city experienced between 1982 and 1988 has been followed by the restructuring and reindustrialization of the metropolitan area, largely in connection with the shift from ISI to EOI and the opening and liberalization of the national economy. Monterrey's leading corporations have been at the forefront of these processes, establishing joint ventures and associations with transnational firms through investment partnerships and stock swaps, expanding internationally by purchasing production facilities in the United States and other countries and thus becoming multinational companies, setting up *maquiladora* plants in Monterrey, selling assets to multinational corporations, and exporting an increasing share of their production. These strategies have allowed local firms to obtain access to advanced technologies and foreign markets in industrialized and middle-income countries, to shed companies threatened by global competition, to circumvent the limitations of the internal market, and to lead a renewed industrial expansion in Monterrey starting in the late 1980s and early 1990s (Gutiérrez Garza 1995; Pozas 1993b).[34]

At the end of the study period for this book, restructuring continued in full force in La Sultana del Norte. After the costly modernization drive of the previous decade, in 2005, Grupo ALFA sold its steel-producing branch, Hylsamex, to the Luxemburg-based conglomerate Ternium, which owns plants in Argentina, Venezuela, and now Mexico. According to ALFA's top management, the sale came in the aftermath of a severe price downturn in the global steel industry, which nowadays is clearly dominated by China.[35] In preparation for the sale, Hylsamex transferred the health care provision for its workers from ALFA's private clinics to the government-run IMSS. By the end of 2005, the new Ternium Hylsa had laid off four hundred workers as it restructured operations, merged individual firms, and shut down parts of its manufacturing complex.[36] In 2007, Ternium acquired IMSA, another leading Monterrey-based steel producer, for about 3.2 billion dollars, consolidating a trend in which most of the Mexican steel industry is in the hands of a few foreign-owned multinational conglomerates.[37]

In this context of modernization and globalization, the largest and most modern firms in Monterrey have embraced new forms of industrial organization and a new definition of the labor process, one associated with the use of flexible technologies in the workplace. The effects of this type of restructuring on labor markets, workplaces, and the institutions regulating industrial-labor relations have been discussed earlier this chapter and need not to be repeated here. Case studies conducted in Monterrey have shown that the introduction of flexible technologies is creating more unemployment, weakening worker and union control of the labor process, and changing the system of industrial-labor relations that unfolded during the era of peripheral Fordism. Pozas (1993a), for instance, argues that even the traditional subordination of

the Monterrey company unions to management has been threatened by
flexibility as the new system calls for changes in the way skill and seniority weigh on vertical mobility and job security, replacing the old system
of occupational specialization with one based on task rotation (see also
Palacios 2003). Thus, the flexible use of labor has allowed firms to flat-
ten the occupational hierarchy within plants and lay off the portion of
the workforce that has become redundant, forcing "unemployed blue-
collar workers . . . to accept lower quality jobs in tertiary activities that
[do] not match their now-superfluous industrial skills" (Aguilar 1997:
127). For workers experiencing this downgraded structure of opportunities in the urban-industrial labor market, migration to the United States
has become an ever-present and more appealing alternative.

CONCLUSION

ISI established the foundations of Mexico's development during the
twentieth century. ISI also created conditions for the formation of a
working class, which benefited from the model's urban bias and need
for expanding consumption. For decades, this urban-industrial working
class did not resort to U.S. migration to attain social reproduction. In
fact, it was actively discouraged from participating in the recruitment
schemes which at midcentury channeled millions of rural Mexicans to
temporary jobs across the border. In the past twenty years, the shift
to EOI has prompted the modernization of manufacturing as part of
the creation of an export-oriented and internationally competitive
economy—a process which, in turn, has also involved dismantling the
social, legal, and political institutions regulating workplaces and labor
markets under ISI.

In Monterrey, these transformations have exposed the once protected
and privileged skilled working class to the uncertainties and risks of a
rapidly modernizing urban-industrial economy. As these workers' high
salaries and substantial social wage eroded, migration became a more
attractive alternative. In this context of restructuring and industrial
modernization, some of Mexico's working-class households are now
resorting to U.S.-bound migration to cope with the passing of protections that ISI once afforded them and with the advent of an export- and
free trade–oriented economy and its concomitant institutions, namely,
a flexible labor market and new factory regime. New flows of urban-
industrial sojourners, such as those examined in this book, are not
as much "the migrants of the crisis" (Cornelius 1992) as they are the

migrants of Mexico's restructuring new economy. Just as the country's farmers and peasants used migration—internal and international—to endure the costs of urbanization and industrialization during the 1950s and 1960s, the urban working class is now bearing the brunt of industrial modernization and the creation of a competitive manufacturing sector through migration to the United States.

# CHAPTER 3

# Restructuring and International Migration in a Mexican Urban Neighborhood

Prompted by the impact of economic restructuring, skilled and semiskilled working-class *regiomontanos* have begun to resort to U.S.-bound migration as one of their labor market opportunities. In this chapter, I explain why and how these urban-industrial workers with little or no prior cross-border experience begin their migratory careers. Having identified the structural national and international forces that cause the dislocation of blue-collar families, I now move to show how such causal forces operate at the urban neighborhood, household, and individual levels in La Fama, the working-class district in the metropolitan area of Monterrey where I conducted fieldwork. Because of its social, spatial, and historical makeup, this blue-collar neighborhood is a strategic research site to study the connection between migration and urban-industrial restructuring. Located next to one of the city's heavy manufacturing corridors, which had burgeoned during the ISI period (Rivera 1995), La Fama exhibits a substantial incidence of U.S.-bound migration. The neighborhood also boasts nearly 150 years of industrial experience, which began in 1854 when local merchants established the first of several textile mills that came to populate the region, making La Fama the cradle of Monterrey's industrialization (Rojas Sandoval 1997).

A highly symbolic event occurred in La Fama in 2003 when the textile mill that had operated for nearly a century and a half closed down. The mill, Textiles Monterrey, had been an important source of employment for many households in the neighborhood during the second half of the twentieth century. Some of the men who lived in the vicinity spent their entire work careers at the mill and, upon retirement, passed their posts on to their children. Throughout the 1990s, Textiles Monterrey underwent a process of restructuring and downsizing as management sought to implement a strategy of labor flexibility to cut manpower costs. With the union opposing these measures and calling for a strike, the Textiles Monterrey management filed for bankruptcy, laid off all workers, and closed the factory's doors permanently. But the fortunes of the households in La Fama had not been completely tied to the fate of the mill for quite some time. During the period of ISI (1940–82), the employment prospects of La Fama's residents had become intertwined with the large national and transnational corporations producing for the expanding internal market in Mexico. In the parlance of international migration studies, this is the sending area of the Monterrey-Houston circuit.[1]

The identification and selection of La Fama and neighboring barrios as a source area for U.S. migration was the result of a process of ethnographic discovery and not the result of random choice. As I discuss at length in the appendix, I discovered La Fama by first conducting field research in Houston, identifying and surveying the networks and clusters of Monterrey-origin migrants. My research in the Bayou City suggested the presence in La Fama of a critical mass of individuals with international migratory experience, a precondition I deemed necessary to analyze the causes and social organization of U.S.-bound migration. Indeed, nearly one-third of the households sampled in La Fama have at least one member with international migratory experience. Still, this is not the only kind of migration present in the neighborhood. Like so many other working-class districts in the city, La Fama has been a destination of rural-to-urban flows stemming from localities and states with a long tradition of internal migration to Monterrey, such as Zacatecas and San Luis Potosí.

The individual, household, and community data presented in this chapter show that as family well-being, household reproduction, and stable formal employment have been undermined by economic restructuring, working-class households have increasingly sought to either temporarily or permanently deploy the labor of their members internationally. But international migration is neither an instantaneous reaction nor a necessary response to economic downturns. The strategies of working-class households analyzed here suggest that the choice of migration entails a series of complex steps that cannot be explained by the simplistic notion that people march to the border in response to the devaluation of the Mexican peso and the ensuing increase in wage differentials between Mexico and the United States. Economic crisis and restructuring may be the *efficient* causes that explain the migration of these urbanites but not necessarily the *sufficient* factors that account for why and when a border-crossing move is undertaken. Individuals and families might endure declining real wages, blocked mobility opportunities, shrinking or no access to credit and insurance markets, downward social and occupational mobility, failed small-business ventures, and precarious employment. But even under these circumstances, people may not resort to migration. Recruitment, the presence of pioneer migrants, the availability of facilitating networks, and the pressures of an expanding household are often necessary for migration to occur.

In this chapter, I provide a historical and ethnographic overview of La Fama and the textile mill (the Fábrica de Hilados y Tejidos La Fama de Nuevo León, later renamed Textiles Monterrey) that originally lent its name to the neighborhood. Using survey data from a representative sample of randomly selected households, I present the sociodemographic and employment characteristics of the district followed by the life history sketches of U.S. migration pioneers from La Fama and nearby neighborhoods. I then use the sample's data to identify the major periods and patterns of international migration in La Fama. In the final section, I draw from interviews and ethnographic observations conducted in Monterrey and Houston to show how the economic crises and industrial restructuring of the last two decades have driven working-class households to resort to cross-border migration.

## THE NEIGHBORHOOD OF LA FAMA

Located in the westernmost municipality of the metropolitan area, Santa Catarina, the working-class neighborhood of La Fama, is considered the cradle of Monterrey's industrialization. In 1854, a group of nine local investors, who had accumulated their fortunes through a variety of commercial and agricultural activities in northeast Mexico, established a textile mill, which they called La Fama (Mendirichaga 1995). A pioneer of Monterrey's tradition of industrial manufacturing, La Fama would be the first of three textiles mills founded in the region between 1854 and 1874. The founders of the factory initially invested seventy-five thousand pesos and imported fifty-six modern weaving looms from Britain as well as cotton from Alabama, Louisiana, and Florida. By 1986, both cotton and coal were imported from Texas, but the firm also used fiber produced in the neighboring state of Coahuila (Cuellar 1996; Rojas Sandoval 1997; Tamez 1996).

The township, known as Congregación de La Fama, was actually founded by the textile workers who built their homes around the factory. The rest of the local population was engaged in agricultural activities in nearby haciendas. The textile factory burned down in 1885 but was rebuilt immediately, and by the turn of the century it employed men, women, and children. Local chroniclers describe the mill hands during the 1930s still as "half workers and half peasants" (Cortés García 1991: 10), that is, as factory operatives who would combine their manufacturing jobs with farming in rented and individually owned land and cooperated to purchase water collectively to irrigate their fields. These accounts describe La Fama as a town with a clearly defined class structure: the factory's management, merchants, and landowners were at the top; butcher shop owners and other small business keepers composed the middle class; and self-employed craftsmen and women (blacksmiths, candy makers, bakers), textile workers, and peasants made up the working class (Cortés García 1991). Despite this stratification, social relations were conducted through face-to-face interactions, in sharp contrast with the anonymity that characterizes urban life in modern cities.

Labor unrest during the 1920s and 1930s signaled changing times for La Fama. Textile workers tried to form a union in 1926, but the company attempted to break the movement by firing the leaders. Organizing efforts finally succeeded in 1933 with the establishment of the Sindicato General de División Abelardo L. Rodríguez de Obreros y Obreras de la Fábrica de Hilados y Tejidos de Algodón "La Fama." Although the act establishing the organization shows an all-male roster of union officials, one-third of the founding signatories were women. Notably, the union was not a *sindicato blanco,* or company union, since it was constituted as a local branch of the national textile trade federation, an industry union affiliated with the progovernment Confederación de Trabajadores de México. Put briefly, in the eyes of Monterrey industrialists and their model of corporate paternalism, this was a *sindicato rojo* (red union).

However, a two-year strike that started in 1939 weakened this organization and forced many workers to take on agricultural and craft activities to survive or to look for other mill jobs in the textile factories of the region. The strike ended with a change in the mill's ownership and the arrival of immigrant workers from other textile towns, many of whom were not affiliated with the union. Local historians also narrate the arrival in La Fama of workers who had been deported from the

United States during the Great Depression in what appears to be one of the towns' first documented contacts with U.S.-bound migration.

The 1940s signaled the metropolitan expansion of Monterrey to neighboring municipalities, reflecting the industrial and demographic growth of this city. As part of this pattern of urbanization, by 1948 numerous large manufacturing plants were being established in the proximity of La Fama. This development contributed to the increase of the working-class population in this township and to the creation of other blue-collar neighborhoods in the vicinity. The proportion of the municipal population engaged in industrial activities rose accordingly, from 24.8 percent in 1940 to 50.2 percent in 1960. By 1970, 58.3 percent of the *municipio*'s economically active population was employed in industry (Garza 1995c; Rivera 1995). Nowadays, La Fama has been absorbed into the urban sprawl and is no longer an independent township. New neighborhoods (or *colonias*), highways, and factories occupy the thirteen-kilometer distance between the former textile town and downtown Monterrey. The manufacturing plants that were built on the northern edge of La Fama are part of a larger industrial corridor which unfolded along a highway connecting Monterrey with Mexico City. These plants belong to the old Monterrey holding groups and to subsidiaries of transnational corporations, established there during the period of ISI. More recently, light manufacturing assembly plants have been set up farther along this industrial corridor.

Thus, La Fama is today a predominantly working-class district. Workers' homes are within walking distance or a short bus ride from numerous manufacturing plants, reminding the observer of the social ecology of industrial cities elsewhere in North America and Western Europe. Walking the neighborhood of La Fama, one can see that street names symbolically reflect the dynamics of the larger political economy: *Juárez, Hidalgo,* and *Morelos*—prominent members of Mexico's officially sanctioned pantheon. But also *Concordia* (Harmony), *Progreso* (Progress), and *Unidad* (Unity)—in one section of the neighborhood where houses were built under the auspices of an employer-sponsored worker cooperative. Most of the houses are one- and two-story cinder block buildings, which in many cases have been constructed in stages. Residents have long used end-of-the-year bonuses and remittances to build an additional bedroom or a second story with several new rooms or to adorn the facade with more expensive materials, such as hand-carved stone. The neighborhood also includes a few pockets of impoverished households, typically living in one-bedroom rental homes with

TABLE I. SOCIODEMOGRAPHIC AND HOUSING
CHARACTERISTICS OF LA FAMA RESIDENTS

| | 1990 | 1995 | 1997–98(*) | 2000 |
|---|---|---|---|---|
| *Sociodemographic characteristics* | | | | |
| Women (%) | 50 | 50 | 47.2 | 50 |
| Men (%) | 50 | 50 | 52.8 | 50 |
| Median age | 22 | 23 | 27 | (-) |
| Population 0 to 14 years (%) | 28 | 25 | 23.3 | 25 |
| Population 15 to 64 (%) | 66 | 68 | 69.2 | 67 |
| Population 65 years and older (%) | 6 | 7 | 7.5 | 8 |
| Literacy rate (15 years and older) (%) | 95 | 96 | (-) | 96 |
| *Housing characteristics* | | | | |
| Average occupants per home | 4.7 | 4.4 | 4.4 | 4.1 |
| Homes with sewer connection (%) | 92 | 97 | 98 | 96 |
| Homes with electricity (%) | 99 | 100 | 100 | 100 |
| Homes with piped water (%) | 83 | 90 | 98 | 89 |
| Homes with roofs made of permanent construction materials (%) | 74 | (-) | (-) | 76 |
| Homes with 2 to 4 bedrooms (%) | 65 | (-) | (-) | 62 |
| Owner-occupied homes (%) | 62 | (-) | 67 | 68 |
| Rental homes (%) | 29 | (-) | 21 | 25 |

NOTE: (-) Not available. (*) The sample of La Fama was comprised of 168 households with a total of 759 members residing in the neighborhood at the time of the survey.

SOURCES: XI Censo de Población y Vivienda, 1990; Conteo de Población, 1995; survey of La Fama households, 1997–98; and XII Censo General de Población y Vivienda, 2000.

roofs made of provisional materials, such as metal and cardboard sheets, and sharing one common faucet with several families. The southern edge of La Fama actually includes a small squatter settlement with homes made of wood and cardboard and metal sheets lining mostly unpaved streets. Still, as table 1 illustrates, the overwhelming majority of homes in La Fama are made of permanent construction materials, enjoy basic urban services, and are owner occupied.

Although the barrio is mostly residential, there is some mixed land use on the perimeter of the neighborhood, with a few warehouses, small factories, and cottage *maquila* operations. Every street block is also dotted with many "mom-and-pop" shops that sell sodas and beer, paper and school supplies, groceries, tortillas, and fast food and that generally are quartered in one or two rooms of a family home. There are also many shops that repair cars, clothing and footwear, electronics, and household appliances. There are also schools that offer education, from kindergarten through high school, a clinic, several private physicians

Figure 1. The Plaza del Obrero in La Fama located next to the now-defunct textile mill. Photograph by Rubén Hernández-León.

and dentists, and a variety of recreational spaces, mainly soccer and baseball fields. At the center of La Fama remains a small but well-kept plaza that reminds the observer about the history of this neighborhood as a formerly independent township.

Migration is beginning to leave its imprint on the social fabric and the built environment of the neighborhood. In addition to the automobiles displaying U.S. plates, migrant remittances are fueling the construction of second floors and general remodeling of existing houses. As in many migrant towns in the Mexican countryside, some of these houses remain empty most of the year, as their owners reside in Houston and other cities, or they are inhabited by women and children who await visits from a male breadwinner shuttling back and forth between La Fama and Texas. An even more familiar sight are the vans that deliver door-to-door cash remittances, letters, second-hand goods, and food sent by La Fama migrants based in Houston and the swap meats that migrants set up in their homes during weekends, stocked with clothes, shoes, and used appliances purchased in the United States. Still, international migration is not yet a basic part of the local imagery, as it is in sending areas in western and northcentral Mexico with a long-standing tradition of U.S.

Figure 2. View of a street in La Fama. Second floors are often financed with remittances from U.S. migrants. Photograph by Rubén Hernández-Léon.

sojourning. Drawing from the firmly established ideology of regional exceptionalism, industriousness, and self-reliance (Snodgrass 2003), in some of my interviews old-time residents vehemently denied that the people of La Fama were actively engaged in migration, proudly contrasting that behavior with the "fact" that neighborhood workers found jobs locally. And yet, strolling through the street markets of the neighborhood, where women buy vegetables and groceries and play *lotería* (Mexican bingo), one can overhear housewives discussing the migratory vicissitudes of their husbands. During the long weekends allowed by either Mexican or U.S. holidays, men stand on the sidewalks of La Fama networking and openly discussing employment opportunities *en el otro lado* (the other side of the border).

## "CELEBRATING" RESTRUCTURING?
## THE CLOSING OF THE TEXTILE MILL

The 2003 closure of Textiles Monterrey was a landmark in the neighborhood's one-hundred-fifty-year industrial history. After instigating a long process of restructuring to face up to competition from less expensive

Asian imports, the management announced that the mill was going out of business. The union responded by taking control of the gates that give access to the factory grounds, a move aimed at forcing the administration to use the firm's assets to provide laborers with a one-time severance payment. The firm had introduced cost-cutting measures starting in the early 1990s when technological modernization allowed halving the number of workers. In 1996, soon after the peso crisis and with the opening of the Mexican economy well under way, the company entered a joint venture to produce and export yarn, leaving behind the decades-long manufacture of cotton fabrics. In this context, Textiles Monterrey downsized once again, eliminating sixty additional posts. The shift from cloth to yarn also had consequences for the mill's sister factory, El Porvenir, located in a town some fifty kilometers south of Monterrey. In the past, the La Fama mill produced the raw fabric that was later finished in El Porvenir to then be shipped to garment shops where it would be turned into school and factory uniforms, shirts, and other clothing.[2]

In the late 1990s, the management of Textiles Monterrey had changed its approach to restructuring, from employing technological modernization, creating joint ventures with other textile firms, and changing its products to cutting down labor costs by scaling down benefits, reducing the hours laborers could work, and firing mill hands. A year after the mill closed its doors in 2003, the remaining 222 workers received their severance paychecks.

At the time of its closure, the company was no longer the mainstay of manufacturing jobs for the residents of La Fama. Still, Textiles Monterrey had been an important source of employment during the second half of the twentieth century and a symbol of the former township's industrial history and identity. It was not uncommon for men and women in the neighborhood to spend entire work careers at the mill and have their children join the factory during adolescence. Even though this was an established practice in many plants in the city, for these textile workers it became a necessity. Since the mill had a red union, many of the offspring of these laborers would not be hired by local firms under the control of company unions (*sindicatos blancos*). An interview with Pablo Gómez, a union leader who worked in Textiles Monterrey for forty years illustrates this dynamic:

> This was an all-family factory . . . the union would take only family members. But since this was a red union and the factories that were in the vicinity of La Fama were white unions, they didn't want to have anything to do with red unions. So our children who wanted to look for new horizons in

Figure 3. The partially bulldozed textile mill would give way to a walled-in housing complex aimed at middle-class buyers. Photograph by Rubén Hernández-Léon.

> other factories [were asked]: "Listen, where does your father work?" "Well, in Textiles Monterrey." "What kind of union is that?" "Red." They would hand in the application but [management] wouldn't call them. So, they couldn't get anything, which forced people and all of us to create a shield, that nobody but our children and relatives were hired.

By November 2004, a few months after the workers had received their severance payment, bulldozers were razing the mill's main building. Not long after the demolition was completed, construction began for a new housing development surrounded by a perimeter wall. Across from this area sit the remains of the old mill, built in the nineteenth century, which had been used for many years as a warehouse and sales office for the uniforms made with Textiles Monterrey's fabric. Inside this facility lie the ruins of the aqueduct constructed in the 1850s to provide water and power for the original factory. The union hall is located behind this structure. Money earned by renting the hall for dances, weddings, and *quinceañera* celebrations supplemented the union's finances, especially during the previous year, when the firm and workers were in a standoff negotiating the terms of the severance compensation.

That same month, during a cold and rainy week, a festival celebrated the one hundred fiftieth anniversary of the founding of the mill. The festivities included cultural activities, professional wrestling matches,

Figure 4. The commemoration of the one hundred fiftieth anniversary of the founding of the textile factory took place at the union hall, capping the activities of the La Fama Antigua Festival. At the event, organizers recognized former mill workers. Photograph by Rubén Hernández-Léon.

athletic competitions, street fairs, and an employment fair. The organizers set aside the last evening of the week-long celebration for a final event at the union hall to honor retired and former workers of Textiles Monterrey. Preceded by the performance of several high school folk dance troupes, the mayor, union representatives, and other local dignitaries led a special ceremony recognizing and awarding medals to the men and women who had worked in the mill for fifteen, twenty, and thirty years. A few of them, quite elderly, had trouble getting onstage to receive their award. The union hall was full, and there were dinner platters and drinks for sale provided by nearby restaurants. A dance with live music was to follow the award ceremony. Although the event evidenced the sense of solidarity and community built around the mill and the neighborhood, the atmosphere was not truly festive. As he made reference to the closing of the factory and to the fact that mill workers were now *former* workers, the master of ceremonies argued that "this [was] not the moment to be sad" and reminded the audience of the festival's motto: "la alegría que nos une" (the joy that brings us together). He repeated this slogan several times throughout the evening. At the back of the room, several men stood and chatted throughout the event. As I talked to them, the dominant theme of our conversations was how

Figure 5. Banner advertising a job fair as part of the La Fama Antigua Festival. During the fair, former mill workers were turned down by potential employers because of age and prior membership in a red union. Photograph by Rubén Hernández-Léon.

difficult it was to find a new job comparable in wages and benefits to the one lost. Because most of these men were in their fifties and had been members of a red union, most local firms would simply not hire them. Many of them had submitted applications to the companies attending the job fair but had been told right away that nobody would employ men their age.

Still, a few had found employment in local factories as janitors and drivers, jobs that not only provided lower wages but also were an insult of sorts to these highly skilled industrial workers. These men had attended vocational schools early in their careers, becoming trainees for a few years to then accumulate decades' worth of on-the-job experience. As I talked to them and continued to observe the ceremony, it was clear that they took great pride in their problem-solving skills. Luis, a fifty-three-year-old, prematurely white-haired welder, gave me a lengthy and detailed description of his work at Textiles Monterrey, highlighting how he was able to solve different kinds of technical problems and adapt imported machinery to local specifications. Luis also used the plant's scrap metal to make knives, which he sold to neighbors and friends. Like many other workers, he was unemployed and was eating away his severance compensation while earning a few pesos doing odd jobs in the neighborhood. He was still years away from retirement and had to use part of his severance to contribute to social security until the age of sixty, when he would be able to receive payments from it. At the event, I also found out that the union was selling its assets, including the big hall where the ceremony was taking place. Union leaders were hoping to divide the money from the sale among those workers who were active at the time of the mill's closure and to give a small sum to the retirees as well. The retirees, in turn, were legally challenging this procedure, claiming a higher stake in the union's assets. There was a certain irony in the fact that the last deed of the seventy-year-old organization, established during the height of postrevolutionary, government-sponsored unionism in this company union city, was one of in-fighting for the spoils of restructuring.

## LA FAMA: SOCIODEMOGRAPHIC AND LABOR MARKET CHARACTERISTICS

From a demographic point of view, La Fama is an aging neighborhood. According to my household survey, 44 percent of the domestic units are in the dispersion stage of the life cycle, in which children leave the parental home to establish their own households.[3] Mexican Census Bureau data from the two census tracts that encompass La Fama actually show that between 1990 and 2000, the neighborhood lost 912 residents, while the average number of occupants per home declined from 4.7 to 4.1 during the same period (see table 1). From the standpoint of type of family arrangement, 60 percent of the families in La Fama have a nuclear structure (parents and children); 33 percent have a complex structure, indicating the presence of extended kin in a multigenerational (grandparents and grandchildren) or lateral sense (siblings and cousins of the head and spouse). The rest of the families are single-parent and single-individual homes.

Like the rest of the Monterrey metropolitan area, La Fama has been a destination point of internal migratory flows stemming from the towns and rural areas of several states in northeastern and northcentral Mexico. According to the survey I implemented in the neighborhood, the majority of household heads (n = 168) were born in the rural localities of Nuevo León, San Luis Potosí, Zacatecas, Coahuila, and Tamaulipas and even in farther Durango and Guanajuato, states that have long functioned as worker source areas for Monterrey's metropolitan labor market.[4] Only slightly more than 40 percent of sample householders were born in Monterrey.[5] Not unlike the social ties that now connect this neighborhood with Houston, these internal flows have been organized by social networks channeling migrants from specific villages and towns in the above-mentioned states to La Fama. This explains the mutual origins of many of the neighborhood's current residents. Many of those born in the state of Zacatecas come from the village of Pedregoso, in the municipality of Pino. A sizable group of residents traces its origins to the town of Parras in neighboring Coahuila. Others have migrated from towns like Villa de Santiago, Nuevo León, some fifty kilometers south of Monterrey. The men and women who emigrated from these villages and towns had different reasons to move to Monterrey. Those from Pedregoso left because of the collapse of rain-fed agriculture, whereas those from Parras, an old textile town, were recruited to work in the mills of La Fama and La Leona (see below). Villa de Santiago was also a mill town, and the owners of the textile plant there were also the founders of La Fama, explaining the circulation of workers between the two places.[6]

Rural to urban migration is indeed a central experience of most households in La Fama, as 63.5 percent of the heads and 62.7 percent of the spouses reported having conducted at least one internal migratory move (survey of La Fama households, 1997–98). In many cases, such move has been a single trip to permanently settle in Monterrey. In a few instances, migration to this city took place through a series of steps in which an individual or a couple moved from a small town or village to a regional urban center and then to the metropolitan area. Several cases in the sample drawn from La Fama illustrate this process; a first, short move from rural localities like San Martín Chalchicoutla or Vanegas, San Luis Potosí, to the state capital was followed by a permanent migration to the Monterrey metropolitan area.

What are the labor market characteristics of households in La Fama? Nearly a third (31.6 percent) of household heads works in manufacturing, and the overwhelming majority of them occupy skilled posts (see table 2). The statistics underestimate the true prevalence of skilled manufacturing occupations among household heads because older heads who are now retired have taken low-pay service jobs. The skilled manufacturing jobs that household heads tend to hold are as industrial welders, machinists, maintenance mechanics, and operators of textile and other types of heavy machinery. Because of skill and seniority, some of these workers have reached supervisory positions within the shop floor. The mostly male household heads owe these jobs less to formal training— their median education is only eight years—than to their arrival in

TABLE 2. SOCIODEMOGRAPHIC CHARACTERISTICS OF LA FAMA RESIDENTS AGED FIFTEEN AND OLDER

| | Household head (n = 168) | Spouse (n = 134) | Male children 15 and older (n = 220) | Female children 15 and older (n = 188) | Current residents 15 and older (n = 582)* | All individuals 15 and older (n = 887)† |
|---|---|---|---|---|---|---|
| *Place of birth (%)* | | | | | | |
| Monterrey | 41.1 | 40.3 | 80.9 | 73.4 | 55.5 | 60.7 |
| Rural Nuevo León | 11.3 | 9.7 | 3.2 | 5.9 | 7.4 | 7.2 |
| Rural San Luis Potosí | 10.1 | 8.2 | .9 | 2.1 | 7.2 | 6 |
| Rural Coahuila | 6.5 | 9 | 3.6 | 4.3 | 7 | 6.2 |
| Rural Zacatecas | 11.3 | 8.2 | 3.6 | 5.9 | 6 | 6 |
| Rural Tamaulipas | 3 | 6.7 | 2.3 | 3.7 | 3.1 | 3.3 |
| *Place of origin (%)* | | | | | | |
| Monterrey | 58.9 | 53.7 | 93.2 | 90.4 | `5.2 | 75.3 |
| Rural Nuevo León | 7.7 | 6.7 | 1.4 | 2.7 | 5.2 | 4.4 |
| Rural San Luis Potosí | 8.3 | 4.5 | .9 | 2.1 | 5.5 | 3.9 |
| Rural Coahuila | 3.6 | 6.7 | 1.4 | 1.6 | 4.1 | 3.9 |
| Rural Zacatecas | 6.5 | 6.7 | 2.3 | 1.6 | 2.6 | 3.8 |
| Rural Tamaulipas | 1.8 | 6.7 | .9 | 1.6 | | 2.1 |
| *Internal migration (%)* | | | | | | |
| Yes | 63.5 | 62.7 | 17.9 | 29.4 | 46.4 | 41.6 |
| No | 36.5 | 37.3 | 82.1 | 70.6 | 53.6 | 58.4 |
| Median years of education | 8 | 6 | 9 | 10 | 9 | 9 |
| Mean age | 44 | 41 | 23 | 23 | 38 | 36 |

Occupations (%)

| | | | | | | |
|---|---|---|---|---|---|---|
| Skilled manufacturing | 25.8 | .7 | 29 | 6.1 | 17.9 | 16.9 |
| Unskilled manufacturing | 5.8 | 2.2 | 5.3 | 2.2 | 4.7 | 4.3 |
| Construction | 3.9 | 0 | 4.3 | 0 | 1.7 | 2.1 |
| Transportation | 8.4 | 0 | 7.7 | 1.1 | 3.4 | 4.6 |
| Skilled technicians | 3.9 | 1.5 | 2.4 | 6.6 | 2.8 | 3.5 |
| Teachers and professionals | 4.5 | 3 | 6.8 | 2.8 | 2.9 | 4.1 |
| Skilled white collar | 3.9 | 2.2 | 4.8 | 12.2 | 4.7 | 5.7 |
| Small merchants | 3.2 | 4.5 | 3.4 | 1.1 | 2.2 | 2.7 |
| Small business owners | 4.5 | .7 | 2.4 | 1.7 | 1.7 | 1.9 |
| Domestics and unskilled assistants | 17.4 | 12.7 | 15.5 | 12.2 | 16.9 | 14.9 |
| Housekeeper | 3.2 | 67.2 | 1.9 | 43.6 | 25.9 | 27.2 |
| Retired | 6 | 0 | .5 | 0 | 2 | 1.6 |

SOURCE: Survey of La Fama households, 1997–98.
NOTE: *This includes individuals who are current household residents regardless of relationship to the household head (e.g., parents, uncles).
†This includes current residents aged fifteen and older and individuals (largely children and siblings of the household head) who have moved away and are no longer residents of the neighborhood.

Monterrey during the expansion years of the urban-industrial economy.[7] Family connections have also allowed younger generations of workers access to certain skilled jobs, as fathers have passed their posts onto their children. The labor market trajectories of these workers have been rather stable, and many of them have spent most of their active years with one or two companies. In the case of those who worked at Textiles Monterrey, it was not unlikely to find individuals who had spent thirty to thirty-five years with the company. This stability was no accident; to the urban proletariat, these types of jobs offered a family wage and benefits that included end-of-the-year and productivity bonuses, paid vacation, modest retirement and pension schemes, health insurance, and low-cost owner-occupied housing.

Still, not all household heads are employed in manufacturing, as a significant proportion of them (17.4 percent) hold jobs in unskilled services (i.e., janitors, domestic workers, night watch attendants, and gardeners). Smaller numbers are employed in transportation (8.4 percent), in construction (3.9 percent), as teachers and professionals (4.5 percent), and as small business owners (4.5 percent). The employment patterns of the mostly female spouses reflect gendered aspects of the factory regime and household reproduction during ISI. An obvious characteristic of the spouses is that most of them are housekeepers dedicated full time to child rearing and other domestic activities. They are basically excluded from skilled factory work and marginally employed in unskilled assembly-type manufacturing (2.2 percent). Their main avenues for labor market participation have been the unskilled service occupations (12.7 percent), chiefly as domestic workers. The median education of these women only reaches the complete elementary school cycle of six years. In the context of limited human capital and gender-segregated occupations—there are no women in construction or transportation—a significant course for women's employment has been self-employment in retail. Thus, 4.5 percent of the spouses have set up small, independent retail operations like grocery stores and stationery shops.

A comparison of household heads and spouses, on the one hand, and their male and female offspring ages fifteen and older, on the other, reveals continuity and change (see table 2).[8] A first relevant yet expected difference is the percentage of children born in the Monterrey metropolitan area, which in the case of males is essentially double the proportion of their parents. Compared to heads and spouses, the median years of education is higher for both men and women. In the offspring cohort, however, females have one more year of median education than males but the same median age. Regarding occupations, men display a relatively consistent pattern across generations while women exhibit significant transformations. Males maintain skilled manufacturing as their most important occupational niche, with modest increases in the teachers and professionals (6.8 percent) and skilled white-collar (4.8 percent) categories. Females have increased their labor market participation, and less than 44 percent of them are full-time housekeepers. In fact, 12.7 percent of these women have made inroads into skilled industrial occupations as skilled manufacturing operatives and technicians (6.1 percent and 6.6 percent, respectively), whereas 12.2 percent hold skilled white-collar jobs.

## INTERNATIONAL MIGRATION PIONEERS FROM LA FAMA

Labor migrations usually begin with one person, a family, or a small group of individuals who, through recruitment, unforeseen dislocation, and even chance, make the first move abroad. By identifying the pioneers of migration in a community, the researcher may grasp the historical origins of a flow and the social construction of networks over time. Pinpointing the pioneers of a flow does not guarantee, however, an understanding of the structural conditions that make migration a mass movement. Through my fieldwork in Monterrey and Houston, I identified a set of pioneers and their children from La Fama and neighboring districts who have personally facilitated the migration of fellow urbanites.

### Elena Lerma

The Lermas are originally from the textile town of Parras, in the neighboring state of Coahuila. They migrated to Saltillo to work as weavers and then were recruited to labor in the textile mill of La Leona, near La Fama. Elena's mother and her brother were the first to migrate to the United States in 1914. The uncle had enlisted with Venustiano Carranza's army during the Mexican Revolution but deserted in the neighboring town of Icamole. To avoid the reprisals of the revolutionary army, he and his sister (Elena's mother) decided to escape by train to Laredo, Texas, leaving their parents behind and hence joining the thousands of Mexicans who migrated to the United States during the 1910s fleeing the violence of the civil war.

Elena was born in 1921 in Austin, Texas. In this state, her mother had met her husband, a man from the Mexican central state of Aguas-calientes. The family did ranch and railroad track work in Texas. Elena was sent back to Mexico in 1931, at the age of ten, to live with her grandmother in San Pedro Garza García, one of the municipalities that nowadays comprise the Monterrey metropolitan area. San Pedro and La Fama are close to each other and have had a long-standing relation-ship as neighboring townships. Today, both places have been engulfed by urban sprawl. Elena grew up, married, and began to raise a family in San Pedro until her husband died in 1965. As a single mother of ten children, Elena decided to return to the United States to work to provide for her youngest offspring. Five of them stayed in San Pedro in the care of her oldest daughter when Elena left for California to work. After a few weeks, these children joined her near San Jose, where she had found a job. In 1974, they moved to Houston, where one of her children found a factory job after experiencing employment problems in California. Elena agreed to move to be closer to the family's hometown. She subsequently moved to Laredo, but her grown-up children remained in Houston, except for one of them who still lives in Monterrey. The role that her adult children have played as social capital, supporting the migration of friends and neighbors between Monterrey and Houston, is analyzed in chapter 4. In her case, a combination of civil war–driven dislocation, the accident of birthplace, and personal circumstance placed her in the unexpected role of immigrant pioneer.

### Raúl Treviño

Raúl Treviño also opened up cross-border migration from San Pedro Garza García to Houston. In 1968, Raúl, one of his brothers, and sev-eral neighbors and friends from this *municipio* were recruited to work in Los Angeles for a company that produced the landing gear for air-planes. The company had posted an ad in a local paper offering jobs and U.S. residency to machine-tool operators and was interviewing potential recruits at a hotel in downtown Monterrey. Even though Raúl was only twenty-three, he had already accumulated several years of experience in neighboring factories as machinist after completing a technical degree in a vocational high school. He applied for and got the job. According to him, the technical knowledge that he had gathered in Monterrey was crucial to his success in the U.S. labor market. This knowledge allowed him and fellow machinists from San Pedro to secure better-paid posi-tions than recruits from elsewhere in Mexico. Although the job in Los

Angeles offered good working conditions and a high salary (the plant was unionized), Raúl decided to leave his post after six months and move to Houston to be closer to his girlfriend and family in Monterrey. He worked in Houston for thirteen years, between 1969 and 1981, when this city "became a technology-distribution center for the world's oil and gas market system" (Shelton et al. 1989: 24). The boom of the Houston economy offered plenty of job opportunities for Raúl and his brothers, some of whom migrated directly from Monterrey. Despite earning lower wages compared to his California job, Raúl benefited from the growing demand for skilled labor in the Houston economy during this period. He worked in several tool and die shops that produced parts for the oil-technology industry, and even though at the outset of his stay in Houston he was making an hourly wage of only $2.50, by the end of his sojourn, he was earning $14 per hour.

Despite his economic success, Raúl decided to return to Monterrey in 1981. The purpose of his migration—an objective shared by his brothers—had been to establish his own machine-tool shop back home. Thus, he had always viewed his migration as a temporary experience and had not established roots in Houston: His wife and children remained in Monterrey, and, notwithstanding multiple opportunities, he had not purchased a home in the United States. Like many Mexicans, the sole aim of Raúl's migration had been to raise the necessary capital to set up his own independent operation, a goal difficult to realize in the country of origin given the lack of access to capital markets (Massey and Espinosa 1997). Besides accumulating savings, Raúl also learned how to operate new types of machines and developed expertise in quality control. By returning to Monterrey during the early 1980s, Raúl and his brothers avoided the downturn of the Houston economy, which by mid-decade raised unemployment figures beyond Great Depression levels (Shelton et al. 1989). Back in Mexico, the situation was not necessarily better. Throughout the 1980s and 1990s, Raúl and his brothers had to face successive economic crises that threatened to shut down their shop on several occasions. They have managed to stay in business for more than twenty years, producing parts and repairing machines for several companies in the metropolitan area. At the time of my interview with Raúl in 2000, they were about to move from a mostly residential neighborhood to an industrial park in response to the economic success and expansion of their operation. Neither Raúl nor his brothers have returned to the United States.

Still, as a trailblazer of U.S.-bound migration, Raúl contributed to support the migration of relatives, friends, and neighbors from San Pedro and La Fama. When he arrived in Houston in 1969, Raúl first lived in Magnolia, the historic Mexican settlement in this city. A year later, he decided to move to Summerland, a predominantly white neighborhood in the northwest section of Houston. This section was closer to work, and, according to him, it was more peaceful than Magnolia. This move opened Summerland as a new settlement for the arrival of migrants from San Pedro and La Fama to Houston during the 1970s and 1980s.

### Juan González

His neighbors consider Juan González the first international migrant in El Tambo, a section of La Fama. Juan is originally from Concepción del Oro, Zacatecas, a town in a historic region for U.S. migration. His first move across the border took place in 1959 when he traveled from Concepción del Oro to Chicago. His brother had been there since 1950, working in the furniture factory where Juan had also found employment as a carpenter's assistant. After six months, he was spotted, detained, and deported to Mexico by the INS. He returned to his hometown and did not attempt to migrate again until 1959; this time he was recruited as a bracero and sent to Donna, Texas, to work in agriculture. At this time, Juan's wife and in-laws moved from Concepción del Oro to La Fama. Thus, instead of returning to his hometown, once he fulfilled his bracero contract he returned to Monterrey. This phase of Juan's migratory career reflects the experience of many international sojourners who moved from rural localities to the United States but who, upon return, resettled in Mexico's large urban centers. As the following section illustrates, during the 1950s and 1960s, in the larger binational migratory system, Monterrey functioned as a receiving center for returning braceros (see also Zúñiga 1993). In this city, Juan sought to learn a skilled trade, becoming a precision welder, which allowed him to work in different textile and petrochemical plants near La Fama. In 1969, he obtained a visa to work legally in the United States and, despite the reportedly high wages he was making in Monterrey, he immediately moved to Chicago, leaving wife and children behind. Three months later he sponsored them to join him in the United States. In Chicago, he worked for five years as a welder in a company that produced metal fences. Later on, he found employment with International Harvester, a manufacturer of agricultural equipment, earning as much as $20 an hour. His eldest son, Javier, also became a welder and worked in the same company.

However, both Juan and his son were laid off from Harvester when the company faced a protracted strike and financial problems in the early 1980s. Being the first one who lost his job, Javier decided to relocate to Houston, where he had already worked as a welder in different factories. Juan and his wife followed him in 1982. They arrived in the Bayou City, nonetheless, at a time when a severe downturn had begun to affect the local economy. Although he managed to get a job as a welder, skilled posts were scarce, and eventually Juan had to work in asbestos removal, an important source of employment for *regiomontano* migrants arriving in Houston during the 1980s. Juan and his family's secondary migration from Chicago to the Bayou City played a crucial role in supporting the migration of many other La Fama residents.

## PERIODS, PATTERNS, AND TRAJECTORIES OF INTERNATIONAL MIGRATION IN LA FAMA

Migration to the United States became a more common practice among the residents of La Fama during the 1980s and the 1990s, the period when Mexico's urban-industrial economies went through a profound process of restructuring. My survey of households (n = 168) indicates that, by early 1999, U.S.-bound migration was a prevalent experience in the neighborhood: One-third (33.1 percent) of households had at least one member with U.S. experience, and nearly 11 percent of all individuals fifteen years of age or older (n = 887) had conducted at least one U.S. trip.[9] By all accounts, migration exploded during these two decades, as the number of first U.S. trips tripled relative to the previous period. In addition, nearly 50 percent of these trips had occurred since 1987, and one-third of all sojourners had began their migratory careers in 1994 or later. Following Massey et al.'s (1987) categorization, nearly two-thirds (64 percent) of all sojourners were active migrants: They had conducted their most recent U.S.-bound move within three years of the start of this study or were still abroad at the time of the survey's implementation. I now turn to the analysis of La Fama residents' patterns, periods, trajectories, and destinations of U.S. migration.

### Sociodemographic Characteristics of Migrants

Several sociodemographic indicators point to the distinctively urban origin of the migratory flow stemming from La Fama. At the time of the survey, 70 percent of migrants with at least one U.S. trip were men, while

nearly 30 percent were women. Thus, the proportion of female migrants
in this urban neighborhood is higher than the rates registered in rural
communities in Mexico (Jones 1995; Massey et al. 1987). Moreover,
men and women were equally represented among active and inactive
migrants (see table 3). Indeed, data collected in La Fama and Houston
show that women migrate not only as part of a process of family reunification (usually following males) but also as household heads responsible for the sustenance of their children. As the case of Elena Lerma,
above, illustrates, some of these women became widows or were left
by their husbands and had to resort to migration to meet the needs of a
household still in the early stages of the domestic life cycle. Several cases
indicate that women may also migrate together with men and, in some
instances, independently of them. In addition, my fieldwork on both
poles of the migratory circuit suggests that women are also a source of
networks for male migrants, namely, that some of these migrants have
access to contacts and information about the U.S. labor market through
their spouses' families—an occurrence that can be associated with the
exogamic marriage behavior common in urban settings.

The following vignette illustrates the case of Josefina, a woman from
La Fama who independently migrated to the United States. Josefina was
abandoned by her husband when he decided to migrate to the United
States in 1960. He returned to Monterrey in 1973, only to die that same
year. His death did not represent a financial problem for the household
since he had not sent remittances or supported the family in any other
way during his stay in the United States. Josefina had long been the
household head and had provided for her six children through her job as
a cook in the canteen of a local factory. However, in 1975, she lost the
job that she had held for twelve years. She used the severance money to
make the down payment on a lot in La Fama. When she could not find
a new job, Josefina decided to migrate to the United States. During the
next ten years, she moved back and forth between La Fama and Dallas,
Texas. There, she held jobs as a cook in various restaurants and cleaned
offices as a part-time employee, working as many as twelve hours a day.
She used her U.S. earnings to pay off the lot, build a house, and finance
the college education of one of her children. Josefina did use network
contacts to undertake migration. Her late husband's daughter (from a
different marriage), living in Dallas, was her primary source of support.
This woman provided her with shelter and helped her get someone else's
papers to cross the border and work in the United States.

As table 3 indicates, 70 percent of U.S. migrants in La Fama are

TABLE 3. SOCIODEMOGRAPHIC CHARACTERISTICS
OF LA FAMA MIGRANTS (N = 96) (*)

| U.S. migrants | % | (n) |
|---|---|---|
| Men | 71 | (68) |
| Women | 29 | (28) |
| Active migrants | 64 | (61) |
| Inactive migrants | 36 | (35) |
| Place of birth | | |
|   Monterrey | 52 | (50) |
|   Border region (**) | 16 | (15) |
|   Historic region (***) | 32 | (31) |
| Place of origin | | |
|   Monterrey | 70 | (67) |
|   Border region | 10 | (10) |
|   Historic region | 20 | (19) |
| Internal migration | | |
|   Yes | 46 | (44) |
|   No | 54 | (52) |
| Mean education (years) | 7.5 | |
| Mean age | 39 | |
| Mean age at first U.S. trip | 26 | |

NOTE: (*) Individuals 15 years of age and older. (**) Tamaulipas, Coahuila, rural Nuevo León, and Baja California. (***) San Luis Potosí, Zacatecas, Guanajuato, and Durango. (-) No cases were found.
SOURCE: Survey of La Fama households, 1997–98.

urbanites from Monterrey, either by birth or by "adoption."[10] The rest claim as their place of origin the rural localities of states such as Zacatecas, San Luis Potosí, and Guanajuato with a long-standing tradition of internal migration to Monterrey. Some of the individuals in this smaller group include migrants who moved to the United States from a rural locality but who resettled in La Fama (or the larger Monterrey metropolitan area) during or shortly after their return to Mexico—a fairly common behavior for bracero sojourners. Over half of all U.S. migrants (54 percent) identified in the sample do not have any internal migratory experience, while nearly 46 percent do (see table 3). The latter include those who have migrated internally during childhood as a result of their family's decisions and strategies and those who have migrated within Mexico during adulthood. U.S. migrants have a mean of seven-and-a-half years of schooling (s = 4.26) and a mean age of thirty-nine years (s = 15.09). These sojourners are on average twenty-six years old at the time of their first U.S.-bound trip. The survey also showed that over one-fourth of male U.S. migrants are skilled manufacturing workers (28 percent), followed in significance by construction laborers (14 percent).

Women are primarily housekeepers (58 percent) and low-paid, unskilled service employees (19 percent).

## Frequency and Duration of Migration

Migration is never the outcome of personal and household motivations exclusively. Instead, the frequency and duration of migration reflect the circumstances in which the overall social process takes place. In the Mexico-U.S. case, for example, the increasing trend toward settled migration has mirrored changes in labor market incorporation of immigrants who progressively left seasonal agricultural employment and moved to year-round urban jobs. This trend also reflects the effect of profound policy changes, such as the amnesty and legalization programs of the IRCA in 1986 and the change in border enforcement tactics that made the old back-and-forth movement of undocumented migrants' trips more costly and dangerous (Eschbach et al. 1999; Singer and Massey 1998; Massey, Durand, and Malone 2002). U.S.-bound migration from La Fama is too novel to attempt a typology, however provisional, of migrants based on frequency and duration of sojourning. The relative novelty of migration in this neighborhood can be gauged from the fact that more than 75 percent of U.S.-bound sojourners had conducted only one migratory trip with a median duration of twelve months. Since, as mentioned, one-third of U.S. migrants have undertaken their first trip during and after 1994, as Mexico was fully immersed in its process of restructuring and in the midst of another economic crisis, it is reasonable to argue that these individuals have most of their migratory careers ahead of them.

Still, there are emerging features that differentiate this urban-origin migration from the rural sending communities studied elsewhere in Mexico. For instance, there are few recurrent and temporary migrants in La Fama. Instead, more than one-fifth of all migrants have spent at least three consecutive years in the United States in their most recent trip, a duration that researchers have associated with patterns of settled migration (Massey et al. 1987). Although such duration suggests connections among urban origins, employment in year-round labor markets, and spending long periods abroad, in the post-IRCA era, lengthy stays in United States have become a feature of Mexican migration in general (Massey, Durand, and Malone 2002).

Another distinctive characteristic of the flow from La Fama is the local residents' use of legal documentation to cross the border and access the U.S. labor market. On their first trip, these migrants have often used tourist visas (44 percent) to enter the United States, documentation that is not meant to be used as work permit. Still, these are valuable documents because they allow the individual to cross legally into the United States, hence avoiding the much riskier and traumatic entry without inspection, which, in this portion of the border, involves swimming across the Rio Grande, walking the deserts of south Texas, hiding in freight trains, and procuring the services of a smuggler (Eschbach et al. 1999). Access to this type of visa is largely determined by social class: Skilled industrial workers are normally able to demonstrate that they own a house and receive a regular paycheck, therefore satisfying the bureaucratic requirements established by U.S. consular authorities. Although about the same proportion of migrants from the neighborhood have conducted their first cross-border trip without papers (46 percent), use of legal documents set these workers apart from sojourners coming from Mexico's rural interior, whom these industrial operatives define as the true *mojados* (wetbacks), or "illegals."

Stressing this distinction and aware of the harsh conditions associated with undocumented crossing, several interviewees in La Fama and Houston argued that had they not been able to cross the border legally, they would not have moved to the United States. Still, adding the tourist visa and the undocumented border-crossing categories together shows that on their first trip, 90 percent of these migrants have entered, worked, and remained in the United States without proper documentation (n = 89; survey of La Fama households, 1997–98). Since legal status changes with time and U.S. experience, it is worth noting that by the most recent trip, the proportion of legal migrants from La Fama had increased from a mere 2 percent in the original migration to almost 21 percent. Still, the large proportion of "wet" and "dry" undocumented workers, even after two or more U.S.-bound trips have taken place, evidences that this migratory flow is still in its early stages of development.

### Periods and Trajectories of Migration

Despite the fact that sizable U.S.-bound flows stemming from La Fama are relatively novel, as part of the larger Monterrey metropolitan area, the neighborhood has long been intertwined in the evolving Mexico-U.S. migratory system. Figure 6 charts survey data collected in La Fama showing varying incidences of U.S. sojourning according to the period of migration, with each period displaying distinct migratory trajectories, changing source areas, and changing destinations. Each of these three Mexico-U.S. migration periods is defined by dominant migratory policies and patterns and a distinct social organization of migration (Durand 1998).

Not surprisingly, the data from La Fama show few instances of U.S.-bound migration in the first of these phases, corresponding to the Bracero program (1942–64), during which only 12.4 percent of all individuals with U.S. experience conducted their first migratory trip.[11] These were the years of Monterrey's greatest growth under ISI, when the city attracted rather than expelled workers. In addition, the migratory trajectories of these individuals were typical of the Bracero era, when rural Mexicans were recruited to conduct seasonal work in U.S. agriculture: They began by migrating from small towns and villages in Mexico to locations in the southwestern United States, made return trips to their communities of origin, and finally settled in Monterrey. The trajectory can be described as a rural Mexico–U.S.–Monterrey path. This trajectory illustrates the role that temporary U.S. agricultural employment played in financing what ultimately were rural to urban moves *within* Mexico. The qualitative data collected in the neighborhood reveals how these rural-origin migrants used their U.S. earnings to purchase urban lots and homes in Monterrey.

La Sultana del Norte, like several other urban areas in Mexico, also hosted a center for the recruitment of braceros. Even though the program explicitly sought to hire people of rural background (Durand 1998), it is likely that a few native or adopted *regiomontanos* were recruited to work in the United States. A respondent from La Fama commented that local construction and teamster workers would sign up as U.S.-bound braceros. As a truck driver who transported construction materials himself, he noticed how the city experienced a shortage of these kinds of laborers during the bracero recruitment season. Still, it is probable that these were recent arrivals to the city or seasonal workers who commuted between temporary urban jobs and agricultural activities in the region's rural localities rather than long-term urbanites.[12]

Lasting from the end of the Bracero program to the beginning of the 1980s economic crisis in Mexico, the period from 1965 to 1982 has been characterized as the era of undocumented migration (Durand 1998; Massey, Durand, and Malone 2002). For this period, the survey I conducted in La Fama uncovered a dominant trajectory of Monterrey-U.S.-Monterrey migration, with Monterrey functioning as the start and return place of U.S.-bound sojourning. In contrast with the previous period, most

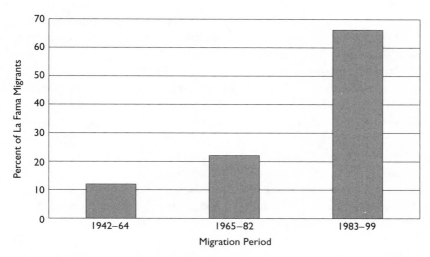

Figure 6. Distribution of U.S. migrants in La Fama (first trip only) by period of migration (n = 96).

first U.S. trips taking place during this stage actually begin in the city and not in a rural locality (and do not involve any prior internal rural-urban migration), strongly suggesting that the flow from La Fama and neighboring districts is a post–Bracero era stream. As the case of pioneer migrant Raúl Treviño illustrated above, at least a portion of this migration was connected to the recruitment of skilled industrial workers conducted by U.S. companies in Monterrey in the late 1960s and early 1970s.

Workers I interviewed in Monterrey and Houston provided repeated accounts of the recruitment schemes targeting skilled manufacturing operatives. According to these accounts, Houston- and Los Angeles–based manufacturing companies contacted firms, managers, and workers in Monterrey offering visas to skilled industrial operatives interested in U.S. employment. Individuals also found out about these recruitment opportunities through ads posted in local newspapers or by word of mouth from conversations with fellow workers and supervisors. Although a first wave of recruits traveled with work visas and resident documents, subsequent waves did not enjoy such benefits. Some informants claimed that, in a manner characteristic of many recruitment schemes, agents enticed workers to migrate illegally by telling them during interviews that the company had exhausted its available visas but that plenty of jobs were available if the person managed to get to the United States on his own. In sum, this small cohort of recruited workers became the pioneering wave of the much larger migration that ensued later on that had Houston as its main destination. Still, only 22 percent of all international migrants identified in La Fama conducted their first U.S. trip during this phase.

In the aftermath of the economic transformations taking place in Mexico, during the most recent period (1983–99), migration from La Fama to the United States virtually exploded: Two-thirds of all migrants conducted their first U.S. trip during this phase—a threefold increase from the previous period. In contrast to the path that emerged in the previous phase (Monterrey-U.S.-Monterrey), migrants appear to be spending longer periods abroad (more than three years) and, in some cases, settling permanently at their destination. To restate a point: In this period, which extends to the present, the trend toward settlement may be an unintended consequence of the border enforcement strategy that keeps undocumented sojourners from moving back and forth between the two countries and forces upon them longer stays in the United States. Thus, target earners from La Fama whom I first met in 1996 in Houston were still working in that city in 2003, unable to obtain legal status and to travel to see family back in Mexico yet clinging to the same job in an apparent pattern of settled migration. I come back to this issue in the next chapter.

Across these three different periods, the most important destination for La Fama migrants has been Texas, not California, which over time has been consistently less significant and has even declined as receiving area. This is to be expected given Monterrey's geographic proximity to Texas, which lowers the cost of international migration, and the historical ties linking the city and its region with the borderlands. Migratory flows between northeast Mexico, with Monterrey as its regional capital, and south Texas predate the Bracero era. Historical research has shown that migration from Nuevo León and Texas started as early as the mid-nineteenth century when the U.S.-Mexico war redefined the location of the international boundary. Between 1848 and 1920, rural *nuevoleoneses* crossed the border by the thousands to escape peonage and indebtedness, while others were attracted by Texas's higher wages and plentiful jobs. The state's growing economy incorporated Mexicans not only as ranch hands but also as craftsmen and haulage contractors. Later, railroads and recruiters contributed to enlarge the stream north (González Quiroga 1993, 2001; Mora-Torres 2001). As I noted above, the Mexican Revolution forced rich and poor residents of Nuevo León to seek refuge in Texas. By 1930, according to Arreola (1993), many

TABLE 4. SELECTED MIGRANT CHARACTERISTICS
BY PERIOD OF MIGRATION (FIRST TRIP)

| | 1942–64 | 1965–82 | 1983–99 |
|---|---|---|---|
| Monterrey born (%) | 25 | 28.6 | 65.6 |
| Monterrey as place of origin (%) | 33.3 | 66.7 | 78.1 |
| *Main trajectories (%)* | | | |
| Rural-U.S.-rural | 33.3 | 4.8 | 1.6 |
| Rural-Monterrey-U.S.-Monterrey | 25 | 9.5 | 1.6 |
| Monterrey-U.S.-Monterrey | 33.3 | 52.4 | 54.7 |
| Monterrey-U.S. | 0 | 0 | 31.3 |
| *Main destinations: states (%)* | | | |
| Texas | 81.8 | 75 | 82 |
| California | 9.1 | 15 | 4.9 |
| *Main destinations: city or region (%)* | | | |
| Houston | 9.1 | 30 | 51.6 |
| Dallas–Fort Worth | 0 | 15 | 8.1 |
| San Antonio | 9.1 | 0 | 6.5 |
| Rio Grande valley | 45.5 | 10 | 4.8 |

SOURCE: Survey of La Fama households, 1997–98.

Mexican Americans in south Texas could trace their origins to the rural localities of Nuevo León and other northeastern states.

However, the La Fama household survey shows that specific destinations within Texas have shifted throughout the three migratory periods, reflecting the occupational transitions immigrants have undergone over time, namely, from seasonal agricultural jobs to urban, year-round employment, as well as the changing origins of migrants who seek destinations and labor markets that accommodate their urban-industrial background. While the Rio Grande Valley was originally the leading destination of the contemporary stream during the 1942–64 period, the valley has given way to Houston as the top destination of the flow from La Fama nowadays: More than half (51.6 percent) of sample migrants conducting their first U.S. trip during the most recent period (1983–99) selected the Bayou City as their target area (see table 4). I corroborated this fact by asking my respondents in La Fama about the destinations of kin and nonkin contacts (neighbors and coworkers) with U.S. migratory experience. Once again, Houston emerged as the foremost destination in the United States across all kinds of kin and nonkin contacts, followed by Dallas–Fort Worth, San Antonio, the Rio Grande Valley, the Chicago metropolitan area, and, to a lesser extent, Los Angeles. The rise of the Monterrey-Houston international migratory circuit, with its density of exchanges, social networks, and mobility of people, goods, and ideas, is by no means a conceptual artifact. Instead, it is grounded in the structural economic transformations affecting working-class *regiomontanos* and on the real critical mass of individuals and households from La Fama and the larger Monterrey area making Houston their home away from home.

## ECONOMIC RESTRUCTURING
## AND INTERNATIONAL MIGRATION

Why has U.S. migration become a widespread social behavior among the residents of La Fama?[13] Restructuring in Mexico transformed migration to the United States from being the experience of a few into a reality for many. International sojourning has become one of the opportunities for industrial, working-class households of La Fama in numerous, complex, overt, and subtle ways but should not be conceptualized as the only response to restructuring. Other responses include employment in the growing informal and service sector economies, work in the new and also increasing *maquiladora* industry in Monterrey and other cities of northeast Mexico, and even perhaps securing a much-coveted yet increasingly scarce job as a skilled industrial operative, technician, or low-level white-collar worker in a large manufacturing firm. As I show in the next two chapters, actual migratory behavior is mediated by varying levels of migration-relevant cultural, social, and human capital accumulated in households and communities (see also Massey and Espinosa 1997; Zúñiga 1992), along with institutionalized practices, state-sponsored schemes, and privately operated channels, such as recruitment programs and migration industry services (see also Durand 1998; Hernández-León 2005). In the rest of this section, I illustrate how international migration is now built into this opportunity structure. I include cases of individuals and households who, at the time of fieldwork, had no migratory experience but for whom migration has become a looming possibility.

For an initial cohort of industrial workers, incorporation into the binational labor market took place within the context of crisis, deindustrialization, and mass layoffs that occurred in Monterrey throughout the 1980s. Members of this cohort did not make an immediate run for the border, nor were they able to afford long periods of idleness in a country that does not have unemployment insurance. Instead, they experienced downward occupational mobility and periods of employment instability as they probed the local labor market for jobs with pay and benefits similar to those they had lost. This process often involved stints in the service sector and in low-skilled manufacturing, either as self-employed or wage workers. Regaining access to manufacturing jobs was blocked not only by the glut of skilled operatives in the local labor market but also by the labor control strategies of many Monterrey-based corporations, which discriminated against workers over forty and those who had labored in so-called red or militant union *(sindicatos rojos)* shops, such as the union of Textiles Monterrey.

In many households in La Fama and nearby blue-collar neighborhoods, the effect of an economic crisis was first experienced through the job loss of the family head. Such job losses occurred as firms downsized—not as a result of technological or organizational restructuring but as an outcome of financial constraints brought out by the crisis. A job loss caused household budgetary problems derived less from the temporary unemployment than from the frequently ensuing downward occupational mobility of the main breadwinner. My survey provided multiple instances of households in which, in the aftermath of an economic downturn and job loss, the head had to take lower paying and sometimes precarious employment.

This was the case for Nicolás Torres, who lost his job in a tire and plastics plant in 1985 and could not find similar work afterward. His employment trajectory included work in textiles and automobile manufacturing. To make ends meet, Nicolás had to sell food as a street vendor. Even though at times he would earn more money than he had working in a factory, there were days when, after long hours of walking the streets with his food cart, he would go back home empty-handed. His wife, Lilia, had completed a degree in social work at the state university but could not find work because she was already married and employers would give preference to single women. She ended up working in a toy store, placing merchandise on the shelves. Unable to find a stable manufacturing job that paid a family wage, Nicolás and his wife decided to go to Houston. In contrast with her husband, who had no migratory social capital of his own, Lilia had multiple contacts in the United States. Her uncle, Juan González, was one of the migrant pioneers in La Fama, and Lilia's family network extended all the way to Chicago, where she still had relatives. After spending two years in the Bayou City, where he worked as an industrial welder building highway bridges and oil platforms, Nicolás and Lilia moved to Chicago, where they still live. In the case of urban households like Nicolás and Lilia's, migration was less a risk-management behavior, which implies some anticipation of future probable (or structural) scenarios (i.e., crop failure) (Massey and Espinosa 1997; Massey et al. 1993) than a strategy to remedy losses inflicted by an economic downturn. In the urban context, for them, U.S. migration was a crisis-management behavior.

In contrast to the sudden and relatively short-term effects of a crisis, restructuring has had protracted consequences, changing and downgrading the structure of opportunities available to skilled manufacturing workers in Monterrey. Instead of the lengthy job tenure that characterized the employment careers of previous generations, for example, workers have had to confront instability associated with layoffs from long-held posts and an overall low quality of offerings in the labor market. Employment instability and downward occupational mobility, with their concomitant negative impact on wage and benefit levels, affected the ability of household heads and their spouses to accumulate capital to make long-term investments, such as buying a house or paying for a child's technical or university education. For industrial workers, especially costly yet highly significant investments, like the purchase of a home, had been possible in part because both state and private-sector firms used formal employment to channel access to housing programs, such as the government-managed National Institute Fund for Workers' Housing (Instituto del Fondo Nacional para la Vivienda de los Trabajadores, or INFONAVIT, in Spanish). As I show below, in addition to disrupting household asset accumulation, unstable employment careers threatened access to these programs and compelled workers to come up with alternatives to replace them. After enduring these experiences, in some cases for months and even years, many of these mostly male workers have ended up migrating to the United States.

My fieldwork in La Fama and Houston identified multiple variations of this story, which I now illustrate with several vignettes. Pedro Solís worked for fifteen years at Fundidora Monterrey, the steel mill that symbolized the city's history of industrialization.[14] By the time the mill was closed in the mid-1980s, Pedro had become a quality-control supervisor. After a year of working as an auto parts salesman while also looking for a job commensurate with his skills and earnings expectations, his wife, in-laws, and Pedro himself decided that it was time for him to look for work in Houston, where his brother-in-law lived and would help him locate a job. In contrast to other workers who were able to transfer their skills to industrial settings there, Pedro experienced downward occupational mobility, finding employment as busboy in a restaurant, a job that he kept nonetheless for more than five years. According to him, in Houston he crossed paths with many former fellow workers from Fundidora. They were working in construction, restaurants, carpentry, and even agriculture. Some had migrated alone and were sending remittances while others had moved with the entire family. By the mid-1990s, when he returned to Monterrey, he had become unemployable from the standpoint of the hiring policies of most large manufacturing firms in Monterrey: He was more than forty years old and had worked in a red union shop. At the time of the interview, Pedro was working evenings and nights as cab driver and was thinking of returning to Texas, possibly relocating his entire family there this time. In his own words, going back to the United States was motivated by the fact that "in Monterrey [he had] no future."

The case of Teresa and her husband, Ricardo, illustrates the effects of unstable employment. Both of them began to experience increasingly precarious employment soon after they married in 1993. His work as a furniture upholster in several factories became scant and poorly paid. There were days when he would simply come home early and stay idle because there was no work. Teresa also went through a similar situation. Employed as a pieceworker in a print shop making cards, the workload started to decline, and, as a result, her income dropped dramatically. Because of these changing circumstances, Teresa and her husband could barely pay the rent and the installments on the refrigerator. They began to depend on her family and on neighbors for cash and groceries. Teresa's father, living in the United States, even bought her husband tools to set up his own upholstery business. After two years, Teresa's husband decided to leave for Houston, where her father and other relatives resided. (Two of his siblings, experiencing similar circumstances, have since migrated to Dallas with the support of a distant relative.) Teresa followed him a few months later. He currently works in a furniture factory in Houston, a job he got through one of her brothers. During my interview with Teresa, she attributed the decision to leave for the United States to her husband's difficulty finding stable employment with a family wage and benefits, such as end-of-the-year and productivity bonuses and health insurance.[15]

The survey in La Fama also captured a few instances of households in which, at the time of the interview, heads of households and spouses were actually considering or planning U.S. migration. Just as in the cases where a migratory trip had already occurred, these individuals and couples were responding to situations of unstable employment, downward occupational mobility, job loss, and declining income. One example illustrates this scenario. In this case, Lucía, a seamstress who had completed high school, was seriously thinking about moving to Houston when her household was randomly selected to participate in the survey. Her husband, Ernesto, had lost his job as a laboratory technician in a private hospital in 1996, a career that he had pursued for twenty years. He was now working as a supervisor in a powdered milk processing plant, a job that paid significantly less than the previous post. After nearly two years at the new job, because he was over forty, he had lost hope of finding employment as a laboratory technician again.

Lucía's work career had been punctuated by four pregnancies and childcare responsibilities when the kids were young. In the past, her salary as a secretary and then as a seamstress had supplemented her husband's earnings. As a result of the household's substantial decline in income, Lucía and her husband had to borrow money to pay for utility bills, food, and repairs of her sewing machine and even had to wait before being able to buy much-needed prescription glasses. This situation forced her two oldest children (sixteen and seventeen) to enter the labor force to pay for the cost of high school and to contribute to the household income pool. At the time of the interview, it was clear to Lucía that she would need to work in the United States for her children to attend college in Mexico. According to her, the question was not the availability of employment in Mexico. There were actually plenty of jobs, but they were poorly paid and required long hours of work. Lucía viewed migration as an alternative to these persistent circumstances, blocking what she defined as her family's "progress." Lucía's experience of downward mobility was compounded by a sense of relative deprivation. The visits of her sister and family, residing in the United States, provided evidence that that her nephews and nieces were enjoying a more nutritious diet than her children in La Fama. In Lucía's own words, compared to her sister's offspring, her kids "looked all skinny."

But not all who have been through the experiences described above are considering U.S.-bound migration. The example of Jaime illustrates how migration only becomes a viable alternative to local conditions if members of the household have access to the social capital of a cross-border support network, a topic I examine in detail in the following chapter. Having lost his job of twenty-two years in 1996 as a maintenance mechanic in a steel plant and approaching the age of fifty, he had to take a job as a night watchman for a year before he was able to find employment at a harness-making *maquiladora* plant. Laid off from the steel firm, he lost food vouchers subsidized by the company and other benefits. Still, because most of his children were young adults and had moved away or were living at home and contributing to the household budget, Jaime did not have to bear the pressure of providing for a large and expanding family. Moreover, he had purchased his home through a cooperative in 1980 and did not have anymore payments to make. But what really prevented him from seriously considering the possibility of looking for work in the United States was the fact that neither he nor his wife had the necessary human and social capital to undertake migration. Neither their parents nor their siblings nor any other close relative had ever worked in the United States. Even though they were aware of the migratory experience of many neighbors, Jaime and his wife did not seem to have a close relationship with any of them. At some point during the interview, Jaime plainly stated that the reason he had not considered going to the United States was because, "in all truth, [I] don't know anything about it." The lack of migration-relevant human capital was also the reason why, in a similar case, a male interviewee who had lost his job of twenty years as a production supervisor in a car filter plant decided against U.S. sojourning. As the respondent put it, "I have never traveled and never been anywhere else [but Monterrey]."

In addition, not everybody perceived migration through a negative lens. My data also include cases of young workers who were developing conscious and active strategies to take advantage of the wage differential between Mexico and the United States, combining the remaining benefits of formal employment at home with informal labor via migration. The case of Juan Luis illustrates this point. After losing his job as an industrial drafter, he was forced to take jobs in Monterrey as a chauffer, a courier, and a construction worker, low-paying and precarious posts. To continue making payments on his house and to otherwise provide for his young family, Juan Luis started to work in construction in Houston and Charlotte, North Carolina. After several trips, he realized the advantages of combining temporary stints in construction in the United States with formal employment in Monterrey, regardless of pay and contractual conditions. A job in Mexico's formal sector would allow him to keep health insurance coverage for his family through the system of government-run hospitals and to hold on to his government subsidized house (acquired through INFONAVIT). Clearly, displaced workers such as Juan Luis were learning to use the remnants of peripheral Fordism, combining them with migratory stints in the United States, to face the consequences of industrial restructuring.

The experience of Rafael, a machinist and production supervisor in a car battery manufacturing firm, presents yet another set of responses to economic restructuring. In the early 1990s, his company was bought out by a large Monterrey-based corporation, which quickly began to reorganize and automate production. The new management computerized the entire production system and began to close and downsize different departments in the plant, cutting as much as 50 to 80 percent of the original personnel. The most senior workers were immediately laid off so the firm could save on the federal labor code–mandated severance compensation. With the introduction of new technology and a new line of plastic products, the old equipment became redundant, and most of it was sold or destroyed. This process unfolded over a period of two years, after which Rafael was also laid off. He was able to find work in a local small machine tool shop but could not support his family with the reduced income and lack of benefits provided by the new job.

Rafael decided to move to Houston, where he found work in a computerized machine tool shop, thus successfully transferring many of the skills that he had acquired through years of vocational school and on-the-job training. Even though Rafael had a tourist visa that allowed him to cross legally into the United States, he had to borrow somebody else's employment documents to be able to work at the shop. Although Rafael's wife, Mireya, had actual migratory experience of her own, she and the children remained in Monterrey, where he visited them every two weeks. Rafael has continued to go back and forth between Monterrey and Houston for nearly ten years using his tourist visa and a six-month permit he obtains at the border that allows him to travel inland. I accidentally met Mireya during the medal award ceremony honoring the workers of Textiles Monterrey in November of 2004. I asked her about Rafael's continued shuttle migration. She said that his plan was to soon stop working in Houston to establish a carpentry shop in La Fama. Unclear as to when this would happen, Mireya added that because of his back-and-forth sojourns, Rafael had completely missed seeing his young children grow up.

The last two cases, illustrating the nexus between restructuring and international migration, touch directly on the experience of Textiles Monterrey. At the time I was implementing my household survey in La Fama during the late 1990s, young textile workers were leaving the mill to migrate to Houston as a response to the company's restructuring process, which combined measures such as reductions in benefits, employee layoffs, and production stoppages. For these young workers, the Fordist system of Textiles Monterrey offered benefits that increased the earnings and consumption capacity of their households. However, the system also entailed a strict linkage between seniority and access to the top and better-paid job categories within the firm, which in turn created bottlenecks for the internal mobility of younger workers. The case of Rodrigo, a young Textiles Monterrey operative, illustrates this situation and the dilemmas it posed for workers. Rodrigo had worked seventeen years in the mill, the same place where his father had labored for more than forty years. Unlike some of his fellow workers, Rodrigo was never laid off. However, his earnings and standard of living sustained a consistent decline as management cut back on a variety of important benefits, such as end-of-the-year and vacation bonuses as well as the number of hours employees could work.

Rodrigo unsuccessfully looked for jobs in other large manufacturing firms located near La Fama, such as Vitro, John Deere, and Caterpillar, all well-known among local workers for their high wages and comprehensive benefits. He also undertook at least three trips to Houston in 1997 and 1998, probing employment opportunities there, especially in construction. Even though at first he used his wife's kinship network, he subsequently resorted to his contacts with friends and neighbors from La Fama to find lodging and work in Houston. During one of his trips back home, Rodrigo decided to give up his job at Textiles Monterrey. He also used some of these return trips to probe employment conditions in local *maquiladoras,* notorious for their low wages, limited benefits, and lack of opportunities for internal mobility. I interviewed Rodrigo on several occasions at his in-laws' place in La Fama, where his wife and children were staying during his stints in the United States. During one these interviews, he reflected on the appeal and quality of jobs, such as the one he had quit at the mill, for the people of his father's generation. Rodrigo reasoned that "now everything [was] changing; the things that used to have great value no longer exist." At the time of our last contact, he appeared to have developed an active strategy of combining construction work in Houston with *maquiladora* employment at home. Longing for a stable job and disliking the separation from his wife and children, he experienced this new world as a loss in occupational status and as a step back in his quality of life.

As opposed to Rodrigo, who still faced the financial challenges of a young family and a work life ahead of him, the case of Pablo Gómez

provides an example of how restructuring and, in this instance, the closing of Textiles Monterrey were also launching skilled industrial workers into U.S. migration at the dusk of their careers. Union leader and
veteran electrician at Textiles Monterrey, Pablo not only lost his job of
forty-two years with the closing of the factory but also the certainty of
a modest yet secure retirement pension. One of the benefits that the job
provided upon retirement was a pension jointly paid by the IMSS and
a union trust fund to which the firm's owners also contributed, each
source providing 80 percent and 20 percent of the funds, respectively.
At the age of fifty-eight, Pablo was forced to use his severance money
to make monthly contributions to his social security account until he
reached sixty, when the IMSS portion of his retirement would kick in.
According to him, since the closing of the factory meant that no more
contributions would be made to the trust fund, the union would dis-
tribute the remaining moneys by paying a lump sum to both retired and
active workers who were laid off.

When I first asked him if he had ever worked in the United States,
Pablo replied with a straight "no." During the same conversation, a few
minutes later, he mentioned a recent two-month stint in Iowa, facilitated by his daughter, who had moved to the Midwest after marrying a
Chilean man she had met on the Internet. After learning of her father's
travails as a result of the factory closing, she prompted Pablo to visit her
in Iowa, telling him, "Vente para acá, aquí hay trabajo" (Come, there's
work here). With his tourist visa in hand, Pablo and his wife were able
to travel to Iowa without any complications. In Iowa, he worked for
his son-in-law, who owns a small business providing general maintenance services to apartment complexes and single family homes. Pablo
did yard work, water pressure cleaning, and house painting as well as
small electrical tasks. His son-in-law paid him $2000 after two months
of labor. He returned to Monterrey to settle and finalize the sale of the
union hall. Together with other union leaders, he organized the medal
award ceremony in honor of the workers of Textiles Monterrey, ending
the La Fama Antigua festivities.

Like most of the now-unemployed former mill operatives, Pablo
could not find a stable job commensurate with his qualifications. He bitterly complained about the age discrimination he and his fellow skilled
coworkers encountered in the local labor market. Age and participation
in a so-called red union shop narrowed the prospects of these proud,
skillful operatives to menial tasks, such as sweeping factory floors,
which represented an insult of sorts to their experience and problem-

solving capabilities. At the time of our second and last interview, Pablo confirmed that he was planning to go back to the United States soon.

## CONCLUSION

The neighborhood survey, interviews, and ethnographic observations I conducted in La Fama confirm that in the cradle of Monterrey's indus-trialization, restructuring is fast turning U.S.-bound migration into a common strategy skilled and semiskilled industrial workers and their households deploy to deal with the effects of employment instability, the downgrading of the manufacturing labor market, and the changing regime of industrial-labor relations. By the late 1990s, one-third of the households in the neighborhood had at least one member with experi-ence in the United States. Intimately associated with the highly symbolic closing of Textiles Monterrey in 2003, the stories of Rodrigo and Pablo illustrate how restructuring was launching individuals young and old into employment careers involving work and residence in the United States.

Although sizable migration from La Fama to the United States is a recent phenomenon, I have identified three distinct phases in this neigh-borhood's connection with the larger Mexico-U.S. migratory system. Each phase has been characterized by its own migratory patterns, dura-tions, and specific destinations. The first such phase dates back to the years of the Bracero program, when men returning from agricultural work in the Southwest decided to settle in the Monterrey metropolitan area instead of returning to their communities of origin in the country-side. By purchasing a lot or a house in La Fama, these men typically used their U.S. earnings to finance a rural-to-urban migration within Mexico. The second phase unfolded during the late 1960s and 1970s, when U.S. firms tapped the Monterrey labor market and its ample pool of skilled manufacturing labor, recruiting workers for jobs in the aerospace and oil industries (and their ancillary branches) located in Los Angeles and Houston. The pioneer migrants from La Fama identified in this study are both former *braceros*–turned-urbanites and recruited industrial workers who first moved to California and Illinois and later relocated to Texas. Unsurprisingly, geographic proximity has turned this state into the most important destination of migration from La Fama over time.

Starting in the 1980s, restructuring became the single most important force propelling workers to the international labor market. During the present phase, Houston has clearly emerged as the flow's most important destination and settlement area, establishing what I have called the Monterrey-Houston connection—a binational, intermetropolitan migratory circuit linking Mexico's third-largest city with the third-largest concentration of Mexican immigrants in the United States.

I now turn to describing how this circuit was created, what kinds of bridges contribute to funnel people through the circuit, and the types of occupational and social experiences *regiomontano* immigrants have endured in Houston.

# CHAPTER 4

# The Monterrey-Houston Connection

*The Social Organization of Migration
and the Economic Incorporation
of Immigrants*

In this chapter, I move from the causes and structural forces that have uprooted skilled industrial workers to the social organization of international migration in the Monterrey-Houston intermetropolitan circuit. As I analyze the kinds of networks and social capital these urbanites use to migrate to the United States and specifically to Houston, their most important destination, I also offer a window into a variety of border-spanning social contacts and activities immigrants and their families and friends undertake, thereby linking Monterrey and the Bayou City. In addition, this chapter undertakes a second analytical task: uncovering the types of jobs *regiomontano* workers obtain in Houston's labor market and determining the effect that their urban-industrial extraction has had on their occupational incorporation in the United States.

The fact that networks and social capital sustain and contribute to diffuse migratory behavior is a well-established finding of Mexico-U.S. migration studies (Massey et al. 1987; Massey, Goldring, and Durand 1994; Rouse 1989; Wilson 1994). However, since most studies have focused primarily on the migratory flows arising from the country's rural areas, the existing knowledge of the social organization of international migration stemming from Mexico's urban and metropolitan areas is quite limited. Available studies suggest that because of an advanced social division of labor, anonymity and heterogeneity, and lack of economic cooperation across households, large cities are not fertile grounds for the development of migratory social capital, especially strong nonkin social ties (Flores 2001; Fussell and Massey 2004; Roberts, Frank, and Lozano Ascencio 1999). Twenty years ago, the seminal *Return to Aztlan* (Massey et al. 1987) demonstrated that urbanites countered this socio-logical reality by accessing, through kinship, networks and social capital originating in towns and villages with a long-standing tradition of U.S.-bound migration. This landmark study demonstrated, albeit indirectly, that even though city migrants did not rely on their own urban-grown support network—drawing instead from family and rural origin ties—their migration was neither atomized nor unstructured.

Ten years of fieldwork on the Monterrey-Houston connection con-firm the centrality of networks in the social organization of migration in La Fama and of kinship ties as the most important source of contacts, information, and support for cross-border migration. However, I also encountered a different set of findings, namely, that the men and women of this barrio *also* use the social relations established in the urban neigh-borhood as a means to sustain U.S. migration. In contrast with previ-ous research, I discovered that the residents of La Fama often activated their ties with fellow neighbors to cross the border, find shelter, and obtain a job in the Houston labor market. In La Fama, then, the ques-tion is not whether residents were able to establish networks rooted in the city to support their sojourning in the United States. The evidence shows that they did. The question is what kind of context and social relations allowed for the rise of networks that were grounded in the urban neighborhood and were not dependent on rural connections. The answer has to do, in part, with the residential and employment stability of the households of La Fama, a characteristic generally shared by the industrial working class in Monterrey. Having lived for decades side by side and close to common workplaces, individuals and families devel-oped relationships going beyond the uniplex relation of *vecinazgo* (being a neighbor). They had attended the same public schools, played in the same soccer clubs, and worked in the same factories.

Without reaching the multiplexity and strength of *paisano* (rural hometown) networks, in which people are connected by blood, eco-nomic cooperation, and residence, the social ties created by La Fama urbanites generated opportunities for migration for an ever-increasing number of people, many of whom had no prior personal or family cross-border experience. Reminding us about the capacity of weak ties to reach beyond small, closed groups, argued by Granovetter (1973), neighborhood-based networks contributed to the diffusion of migratory behavior by expanding the social infrastructure that sustains and makes migration a collectively organized and durable social process.

For more than twenty years now, these networks have channeled La Fama migrants to specific neighborhoods and jobs in Houston. Compared to the networks and the migratory history of western Mexico, dating back more than a century, the ties connecting Monterrey and Houston are rather young. As I demonstrated in the previous chapter, pioneer immigrants first arrived in Houston during the late 1960s and early 1970s, with the bulk of migrants moving there during the 1980s and 1990s. Nonetheless, immigrants from Monterrey have established a branch community in the northwest section of the Houston metropolitan area, where individuals and families from La Fama and surrounding neighborhoods have concentrated, showing how settlement at the destination is mediated by social networks.

Still, migrant networks cannot entirely account for why and how Houston became the most important destination of the flows originating in Monterrey. Even though Mexicans have long been part of Houston's urban-industrial development (Shelton et al. 1989), the Bayou City did not become an important destination for *regiomontano* migrants until the mid-1970s, when the city emerged as a global center for the oil extraction and oil technology industries. Thus, in addition to early active recruitment, Houston's momentous economic growth during the oil boom of the 1970s was a key force attracting immigrants from Monterrey. Notably, many of these newcomers were able to transfer their industrial manufacturing skills and experience to the Houston labor market, which was dominated by the needs of oil-related industries. Having received technical education in Monterrey's ample vocational and trade school infrastructure and after long years of on-the-job training, these predominantly male workers have been incorporated into skilled, nonseasonal urban occupations, often as machinists, establishing niches in several manufacturing industries. These technical skills have allowed workers to be less dependent on strong and closed ties and to establish yet another kind of weak tie network based on occupational contacts with fellow machinists, mechanics, precision welders, and even the owners and supervisors of the workplaces that employed them.

However, skilled *regiomontanos* also toiled in unskilled occupations, particularly in the unstable and dangerous removal of asbestos, a job that became available in the 1980s when labor demand in the oil industry plummeted due to the worldwide decline in oil prices. Despite profound changes in Houston's urban economic specialization, which have reduced the importance of the oil industry and its branches in the metropolitan labor market, *regiomontanos* have continued to find employment in the oil tools and technology, maintenance, and extraction industries, where they use a combination of technical skills and networks to leverage better wages and conditions.

I begin this chapter by presenting a review of Houston's contemporary political economy and the role of Mexican immigration in this city's urban-industrial development. I then turn to the social networks that sustain migration between Monterrey and Houston, revisiting the experience of immigrant pioneers from La Fama to assess the role that these individuals, their families, and their neighborhood institutions have played in articulating cross-border support ties. The last two sections of the chapter analyze the occupational incorporation of *regiomontanos,* focusing on machinists and other skilled workers, on the one hand, and asbestos removal laborers, on the other; and the contours, determinants, and limits of immigrant transnationalism and border-spanning social activities and linkages in the Monterrey-Houston migratory circuit.

## THE POLITICAL ECONOMY OF HOUSTON AND MEXICAN IMMIGRATION

Established in the 1830s by northern capitalists as a real estate venture, Houston functioned during the nineteenth century as a commercial and banking center for the Texas agricultural economy. With a sizable black population to serve as cheap labor, Houston did not begin to attract Mexicans in significant numbers until the turn of the century. The discovery of oil in the surrounding region in 1901 signaled the start of a process of industrialization that soon transformed Houston into "a major oil and gas city" (Shelton et al. 1989: 11; see also Feagin 1988). Houston's political economy became quickly intertwined with Detroit and the automobile industry and with New York City, where financial decisions about oil investments were made. At the same time, large oil corporations began to dominate the business by buying up smaller companies and expanding to a variety of oil-related sectors besides extraction. The development of an infrastructure to process and transport oil and oil products required increasing numbers of workers, and hence the city began attracting Mexican laborers. The Mexican Revolution, however, was an additional factor explaining the arrival of individuals and families who were fleeing widespread violence south of the border.

Thus, between 1910 and 1920, Mexicans started to settle in the periphery of the downtown area and to establish two distinct *colonias,* the Second Ward and Magnolia. The second of these settlements, Magnolia, originally a neighborhood of European immigrants, evolved around the construction and the industries and commerce of the Houston Ship Channel. Laborers from the northeast and north-central Mexican states of Nuevo León, Coahuila, Tamaulipas, San Luis Potosí, and Zacatecas resided in these areas, which nowadays make up the historic Mexican American districts of the city (De León 1989; Feagin 1988; Rodríguez 1993; Shelton et al. 1989).

The *colonias* maintained a strong sense of cultural and ethnic identity due to intense contacts with the homeland and the social and economic barriers erected by the Anglo establishment that isolated Mexicans and segregated them to the lowest-paid jobs. In this context, educational opportunities were restricted, and social mobility was limited to the bounds of the ethnic and immigrant enclave. Nonetheless, the Mexican *colonias* evolved their own community institutions (newspapers, cultural and mutual aid associations, churches, and schools), businesses (grocery and drug stores, barber shops, bakeries, cafés, and doctors' and dentists' offices), and even an internal stratification system with laborers, merchants, and a few professionals providing services to local residents. Needless to say, Spanish was the lingua franca of these settlements. Meanwhile, immigrants from Mexico and Mexican Americans from other parts of Texas continued to arrive in Houston. According to De León (1989), by the 1920s, people from the core region of migration in Mexico (Guanajuato, Jalisco, and Michoacán) were present in the *colonias.* The Mexican origin population in Houston expanded from 6,000 in 1920 to 15,000 in 1930, reflecting a pattern of broader demographic and industrial growth affecting this city. During the same period, Houston's total population more than doubled, increasing from 139,000 to 292,000 (De León 1989; Rodríguez 1993).

The 1930s signaled a new era for the Mexican settlements of Houston as the generation of the children of immigrants began to consider itself American (rather than Mexican) and to show an orientation toward U.S. mainstream institutions. De León (1989) calls them the Mexican American generation. According to Rodríguez (1993), this shift in orientation also marked the transformation of the *colonias* into inner city barrios inhabited by a minority population and incorporated as such into the larger urban political structure. The markers of this transformation were the increasing use of English, the celebration of American festivities, and the introduction of mass consumerism into the economic life of the barrio. During the 1930s and 1940s, Mexican Americans founded new political organizations that sought to establish alliances with Anglo leaders. These developments also indicate the emergence of clear and yet fluid divides between Mexican Americans and Mexican immigrants (De León 1989; Rodriguez 1993).

The continued discovery of oil fields in east Texas saved Houston from the worst effects of the Great Depression. The city's role as a major port for shipping oil and commodities such as cotton and lumber strengthened, and, by the 1940s, Houston surpassed New Orleans as the most important gulf seaport, actually becoming the sixth largest of such facilities in the United States. During this period, the Gulf Coast emerged as the most important oil-refining region of the nation, with more than one-third of the country's total refining capacity. The eras immediately before and after World War II were also characterized by the flow of substantial federal resources into the Houston economy. During the Depression years, federal investment helped to erect the city's infrastructure of roads, schools, and government buildings and to make improvements to the ship channel. During and after the war, government money was invested in the petrochemical industry, which first produced aviation oil and synthetic rubber and then made asphalt and plastics. Major oil and gas pipelines channeled these raw materials from east Texas to the Northeast (De León 1989; Feagin 1985; Shelton et al. 1989).

Although Mexicans in Houston did not experience the massive deportations that their compatriots did in cities like Los Angeles during the Depression, they did suffer forced repatriations, poverty, and ever-increasing social exclusion and discrimination. The estimates reported by De León (1989) suggest that Mexican immigration to Houston slowed down during the immediate post–World War I period—a development resulting perhaps from the effects of the crisis and the repatriations. During the 1940s and 1950s, Mexican demographic growth in Houston took place by means of the internal migration of rural Mexican Americans to this city as part of a process of urbanization of the Texano-Mexicano population. Thus, 1950 census data indicate that five of every six Spanish-surnamed residents of Harris County were U.S. born. Furthermore, the 1960 census revealed that only about 13 percent of the county's Mexican inhabitants were foreign born (De León 1989).[1]

Houston continued its rise as a national and international oil center benefiting from the postwar demand for petroleum and oil products, such as asphalt, plastics, and jet fuel. Despite the antistate rhetoric of its growth coalition that construed an image of a "free enterprise city," Houston received substantial federal aid. A prime example of this support was the creation of the National Aeronautic and Space Administration (NASA) complex in this city in the 1960s. During this decade, the restructuring of the oil industry had a significant impact on Houston as big corporations relocated subsidiaries and administrative headquarters and increased production there.[2] This attracted large numbers of both white-collar and blue-collar workers to the city. As a result, Houston's population grew from 600,000 in 1950 to 938,000 in 1960, and further to 1.2 million in 1970. A rapid increase in undocumented Mexican migration to Houston ensued during the late 1960s and 1970s, responding not only to this city's economic boom and its transformation into the global center of the oil industry but also to the end of the Bracero program in 1964 (which closed the avenue for legal migration) and the general trend of migrants to move from rural to urban employment in the United States (De León 1989; Durand 1998; Feagin 1987, 1985; Shelton et al. 1989).

By the 1970s, many different sectors of the oil industry were concentrated in Houston, from subsidiaries and units of large corporations in charge of exploration, discovery, and extraction of petroleum and gas to transportation businesses, producer services firms (law, accounting, and marketing), refineries, and petrochemical companies. By this time, "Houston had evolved into the oil-technology distribution center for the world's oil industries" (Feagin 1985: 1219). Two particular branches of the oil technology sector were housed in this city, namely, "oil-tool companies manufacturing machinery, drilling equipment, and construction equipment; [and] metal fabrication companies making pipe, storage tanks, and oil rigs" (Shelton et al. 1989: 20). These are branches that incorporated many skilled industrial workers originating in the Monterrey metropolitan area.

In Houston, the 1970s were a golden era. As the global city of the oil industry, Houston benefited from the increase in oil prices and the demand for petroleum-related technology and services in key producing areas of the world.[3] Indeed, oil prices increased from $3.39 a barrel in 1971 to $31.77 a barrel in 1981 (Feagin 1987). As a consequence, industrial and financial firms concentrated their investments in oil-related projects, further deepening the economic specialization of the metropolitan area. Thus, while other cities were experiencing the effects of the recession of 1973–74, Houston was undergoing an economic boom and multiplying its links to other cities and regions of the world (Feagin

1985). The demographic growth of the city continued unabated, and by the early 1980s, Houston had reached a population of 1.7 million, while the metropolitan area had climbed to 3 million. The number of Latinos in the metropolitan area increased from 212,444 in 1970 to 424,903 in 1980, while various estimates put the early 1980s undocumented Mexican population between 80,000 and 150,000 (De León 1989; Feagin 1987; Rodríguez 1993, 1987).

As much as it accounted for its success, Houston's structural position in the world economy also explained its coming crisis. Feagin has best summarized this structural position, contending, "As a leading center for the operation, production, and technological diffusion of the U.S. and world oil industry, Houston [was] probably the largest metropolitan area directly and massively affected by investment and production shifts in the world oil-market system" (Feagin 1985: 1221). Such a shift occurred in the 1980s, when the world price of oil started to drop from a high of $34 (in November 1981) to $16 in 1985–86. All sectors of the Houston economy were affected—from oil extraction and refining to retail and real estate. Moreover, industrial production and oil refinery use declined while unemployment rose well beyond the national average. By the end of the crisis in 1987, Houston had an unemployment rate of 10 percent and had lost 200,000 jobs. In the context of an excess capacity accumulated during the boom years, the restructuring strategy deployed by oil and petrochemical corporations included mergers, shutdowns, and cutbacks as well as concentration in the production of higher value added chemicals. While the Anglo white-collar workforce fled Houston, the central city's Latino population continued to grow from 281,331 in 1980 to an estimated half million by 1989. The 1990 census reported more than 700,000 Latinos in the metropolitan area (Hagan and Rodríguez 1992; Hill and Feagin 1987; Shelton et al. 1989).

The economic boom of the 1970s and early 1980s was accompanied by massive investments in real estate, particularly in the construction of office buildings. Surplus capital from the national and international financial sector and the oil and gas industry was the primary source of these investments. According to Feagin (1987), more than 80 percent of all office buildings in Houston were constructed during the 1971–87 period. As oil prices declined dramatically and the urban economy entered its most severe crisis in 1982, the overproduction of office space and other real estate developments became evident, resulting in high vacancy rates and bankruptcies (Feagin 1987).

The economic downturn also propelled the out-migration of Anglo white-collar employees who lost their jobs in the midst of the crisis. Their flight evidenced that overproduction had occurred not only in the office building sector but also in the housing sector, specially in the construction of apartment complexes destined for white middle-class consumers. In Houston's Westside, apartment complex owners and managers turned to new Latino immigrants arriving during the 1980s, hoping to attract them as tenants. Targeting a lower-income immigrant tenant population, owners slashed rents, posted signs in Spanish, hired Spanish-speaking staff, and offered free English classes. Many of these new renters were refugees and economic migrants from Central America who were fleeing civil wars and political violence in countries like El Salvador, Guatemala, and Honduras. These newcomers helped diversify the Latino population in Houston, which had been traditionally dominated by Mexicans. As Rodríguez (1987) has noted, Central Americans were incorporated into the low-paid occupations of the service industry and not in the declining heavy manufacturing sectors of the metropolitan economy. Central Americans settled in traditional Hispanic neighborhoods but also established their presence in areas that were new to Latinos, such as in the above-mentioned apartment complexes of the Westside. As the urban economy recovered in the late 1980s, owners moved to restructure their tenant population by raising rents and evicting units with families (Hagan 1994; Hagan and Rodríguez 1992; Rodríguez 1987).

Mexican immigrants continued to arrive in Houston during the 1980s and 1990s, working not only in industrial plants but also in construction and the service industry (i.e., cleaning, retail, restaurants). Rodríguez (1993) has noted the large number of single Mexican women who migrated to this city and who joined the ranks of the low-paid workforce in services, such as office and household cleaning. Immigrants settled in the traditional Latino neighborhoods of the Eastside (Magnolia and El Segundo Barrio), where an entire spatial and economic ethnic enclave made their presence less conspicuous. Their arrival also helped expand the economic base of the enclave, as newcomers demanded an array of products and services. Over the past twenty years, new arrivals established residence in *ethnoburbs* (Li 1998), that is, sections of the metropolitan area with an increasing Latino and Mexican population but where other national and ethnic groups were also present. This was the case of Summerland, located in the northwest section of the city, where many immigrants from La Fama and Monterrey have settled.

The Immigration Reform and Control Act (IRCA) of 1986, which offered amnesty to those immigrants who had been continuously in the United States since 1982, also affected recent Mexican immigration to Houston. More than ninety thousand undocumented Mexicans sought to legalize their status through IRCA. Even though IRCA offered obvious benefits to the newcomer population, it also restricted—through employer sanctions—the labor market possibilities of recent arrivals, further marginalizing them (Rodríguez 1993). But as Hagan and Baker (1993) observed, by creating a sizable legal and permanent population, IRCA's amnesty program enhanced the social capital available to future entrants and therefore provided the basis for the continuation of migration. This has certainly been the case for Mexican immigrants in Houston. By 2000, Harris County had the third-largest concentration of foreign-born Mexicans in the United States with nearly four hundred thousand, trailing only the counties of Los Angeles and Cook (Chicago) (U.S. Census Bureau 2005).

Still, despite their economic contributions and demographic weight, Mexicans in old and new settlements in Houston lacked sufficient political representation and strong organizations facilitating political mobilization and were largely excluded from mainstream political institutions. In contrast with Mexican immigrants in Los Angeles and Chicago, in this "corporate-dominated city in a right-to-work state" (Meyerson 2004: A10), immigrants could not count on the powerful and well-organized Latino-led labor movement present in Southern California or the network of hometown associations and Democratic machine politics characteristic of the Windy City (Cano 2002; Meyerson 2004; Rodríguez et al. 1994).[4] Houston has only been marginally integrated into the diaspora politics of the Mexican government. Absent from this city's landscape are the state federations that have been at the center of immigrant activism in major U.S. urban areas in recent years. Cano (2002) attributes this absence to the fact that most Mexican immigrants in the Bayou City come from nearby border and northern states, such as Nuevo León, Tamaulipas, and San Luis Potosí, and to Houston's own proximity to the border, a geographic marker that increases the mobility and floating component of the Mexican immigrant population. In sum, Houston does not have the network of binational organizations present in other important centers of the Mexican diaspora in the United States.

Today, Houston remains the global city of the energy industry—still home to many of the top producers of oil and oil-related commodities and operators of crude oil pipelines—but the city's economy is less dependent on the fortunes of the petroleum world market. Houston boasts a less specialized economy. A recent *Los Angeles Times* article reported that oil-related employment in the Bayou City declined from 150,000 jobs in 1982 to the current 105,000. At the same time, a more diverse urban business base now includes information and high-tech industries and professional and medical services (Calvo 2005: C1).

## SOCIAL NETWORKS OF URBAN MIGRANTS: KINSHIP AND NEIGHBORHOOD TIES

*Regiomontanos* are not concentrated in a single area or neighborhood of the Bayou City. In fact, I found these immigrants settled in different sections of the Houston metropolitan area: in the historic Mexican neighborhood of Magnolia, employed as precision welders in the nearby ship channel; in the northeast section of the city, working as aviation mechanics at the George Bush Intercontinental airport; in the northwest Houston transition ethnoburbs abutting I-10, living side by side with Koreans, Vietnamese, and white residents, where they formed roving crews of asbestos removal laborers but also worked as machinists in the many small machine tool shops dotting the area's industrial parks. Such a pattern of dispersal comes as no surprise given that this flow originates in different neighborhoods and sections of Monterrey, one of Mexico's largest cities. Thus, this migratory stream is not organized through a single network of extended family members and *paisanos* but by multiple social networks, many of which—it is safe to argue—are simply not linked to each other.

### Fathers and Siblings

Still, networks have played a fundamental role in the social organization of the Monterrey-Houston connection in anticipated but also unsuspected ways, challenging the prevailing findings of the Mexico-U.S. migration scholarship. In La Fama, I asked respondents of my survey about the most important sources of assistance utilized by household heads to migrate internationally. As expected, family members and relatives residing in the United States topped the list across different types of assistance: offering general economic support, providing room and board, and finding work on behalf of newcomers. In fact, La Fama households could draw from an extensive pool of migration-specific human and social capital, gauged from the proportion of kin with U.S. experience. As shown in table 5, among households with at

TABLE 5. THE SOCIAL CAPITAL OF LA FAMA
HOUSEHOLDS WITH U.S. EXPERIENCE

| Relatives and nonkin with U.S. experience (%) | Household head (n = 58) | Spouse (n = 56) |
|---|---|---|
| Father | 33.3 | 21.4 |
| Mother | 10.5 | 14.3 |
| Grandfather | 5.3 | 5.4 |
| Grandmother | 5.3 | 1.8 |
| Sibling | 47.4 | 35.7 |
| Spouse of sibling | 28.1 | 21.4 |
| Spouse of child | 14 | 12.5 |
| Uncles and aunts | 28.1 | 21.4 |
| Cousins | 33.3 | 26.8 |
| Nephews and nieces | 29.8 | 19.6 |
| Neighbors | 57.1 | 57.1 |
| Coworkers | 14 | 3.6 |

NOTE: The percentages in each kin and nonkin category reflect the existence of at least one individual with at least one past or ongoing U.S. trip.
SOURCE: Survey of La Fama households, 1997–98.

least one member with cross-border migratory experience, one-third of the household heads (33 percent) had a father who had worked in the United States. Similarly, in nearly half of these households (47 percent), the heads had at least one sibling who had migrated across the border. Uncles, aunts, or cousins who had lived abroad also appeared as prominent potential sources of migratory social capital.

Even though my fieldwork in Monterrey and Houston confirmed the claim of the contemporary scholarship on Mexico-U.S. migration about the role of kinship ties as the fundamental source of support for sojourning, these urban settings contained significant surprises. Because of the emerging nature of this flow and the impact of restructuring on younger cohorts of industrial workers, siblings appeared to be a more significant source of migratory social capital, a trend that the above-mentioned figures already suggest (see table 5).[5] In a number of cases in La Fama and Houston, the migration of a brother or a sister had sparked the sojourning of other siblings and only later the cross-border move of the father, reversing the order in which migratory behavior is known to spread in rural contexts with older and more established flows. This is not to argue that such order was entirely reversed in La Fama. More often than not, the father's migration preceded the sojourning of sons and daughters. But in several instances, fathers had briefly worked in the United States under the auspices of the Bracero program and had returned to Mexico to settle in Monterrey. Their U.S. experience had taken place a long time ago—thirty or forty years before their children's own sojourning—and could hardly be used as active and useful migratory social capital. In contrast, the presence of families with a large number of siblings who had lived and worked in the United States without parental antecedent was highly conspicuous in this neighborhood as well as in Houston.

## The Role of Women

Women's involvement in the networks connecting La Fama and Houston deserves particular attention. As I mentioned in the previous chapter, women constitute 30 percent of the U.S. migrants identified in the neighborhood. Still, the qualitative as well as the survey evidence suggest that women played an important role as purveyors of social contacts for men, primarily spouses, who lacked migration-specific human and social capital. A relatively evident explanation for such a role has to do with the still emergent nature of this migratory circuit: Given the absence of widespread and long-established networks, some men resorted to contacts provided by women. The fact that women possessed their own set of contacts to relatives and friends with migratory experience can be easily gauged from table 5.

Described at length in the previous chapter, the case of Pedro, the quality control supervisor who lost his job with the closure of Fundidora Monterrey, clearly illustrates his dependence on his wife's migratory support networks. During my interview with him, sitting inside the taxi he was driving upon his return to Monterrey, Pedro described in detail how after looking for a job similar in salary and benefits to the one he had lost, he, his wife, Lupita, *and* her parents jointly decided that it was time for him to try his luck in Houston. In addition, *her* brother would host Pedro and help him find a job. Needless to say, what is noteworthy in this account is Pedro's complete reliance on his wife's contacts, who were involved in every step of his migratory process, from decision making to arrival and job search at the destination. It is not difficult to grasp how such dependence on her networks provided Pedro's wife a measure of social control upon his expected behavior—to work hard and send money home—especially since his spouse and children were to stay behind. In other words, relying on his wife's networks prevented Pedro from becoming a *desobligado,* that is, someone "who clearly and repeatedly has stopped fulfilling his familial responsibilities" (Durand 1994: 307–308, my translation).

The conspicuous role of women as sources of networks for men stems not only from the scarcity of migratory social capital but also from the exogamic marriage practices that prevail in urban settings, which contrast with the endogamy of rural communities. Here, it is worth taking a brief detour to explicitly compare and address the relevance of exogamic versus endogamic marriage for network formation, an issue that the scholarship on Mexico-U.S. migration has largely ignored, even in the prolific vein of studies of rural contexts as source areas for migratory streams. This literature has long identified two types of networks as the basis for the social organization of migration in small towns, ranches, and hamlets, namely, kinship and *paisano* (hometown) ties. In practice, however, these two kinds of networks may be difficult to differentiate because men and women often marry *within* the hometown. With each new marriage, kinship and *paisano* ties become increasingly intertwined, reinforcing each other.

I observed these dynamics not in Monterrey, but in a small town one hundred miles southeast of the city. This town—I shall call it El Naranjo—has a long history of U.S.-bound migration. There are groups of Naranjenses all over the United States, with new destinations in Georgia and Virginia. As I followed and interviewed Naranjenses in one of these new destinations—a suburb of the Atlanta metropolitan area—I noticed the constant repetition of a handful of last names among the respondents. As I reconstructed family trees with the help of female interviewees, I realized that marriages had occurred between twice-removed cousins and occasionally even between first cousins. More important from an ethnographic point of view, Naranjenses had developed their own folk categories to distinguish those who were kin from those who were not, suggesting widespread endogamy. Naranjenses spoke of various individuals, saying *son de la gente* (they are of the people) to signify *de nuestra gente* (of our people). The strong ties that people had with each other, capable of supporting and spreading migration, derived from the multiplex quality of such connections: People were *paisanos* and *parientes* (relatives) and cooperated on a variety of economic activities, such as agriculture and production of traditional crafts.

I use the case of El Naranjo not as an in-depth case study but rather as a point of reference to advance my interpretation of what I see as distinct in the urban environment. In La Fama, I did not find a persistent pattern of endogamic marriage—not even among those whose lives were closely connected by virtue of their long ties to the neighborhood and the factory. Although there were a number of families who had been in La Fama for generations, most people had settled there because they had been recruited as textile workers from other regions of Mexico or because of straightforward internal migration. In this neighborhood, as it is in urban contexts in general, the norm was exogamy. And even though exogamic marriage did not lead to the formation of strong, multiplex ties, it did facilitate the spread of migratory social capital via *parentesco político,* creating links between different tightly knit family groups in a way that is similar to what Granovetter (1973) characterized as the bridging capacity of weak ties.

## Neighbors as Sources of Weak Ties

In La Fama, the ties that residents have sustained with each other for years as neighbors proved to be a key source of migratory social capital. In contrast with the prevailing notion that urbanism is not conducive to the formation of social networks capable of sustaining and diffusing migratory behavior, in La Fama, neighbors supported each other's migratory endeavors in different ways. As table 5 suggests, people were aware of the migration of fellow neighbors and, I should add, of the U.S. destinations they had chosen. Still, it was my ethnographic fieldwork in Monterrey and Houston that uncovered the depth of friendship- and neighborhood-based networks in the social organization of this migratory circuit. The in-depth interviews and life histories I conducted with pioneer migrants revealed how their assistance had played a crucial role, supporting and virtually allowing for the sojourning of other La Fama residents. This was the case of Juan González, considered by his neighbors to be the first U.S. migrant from the section of La Fama known as El Tambo. As described in the previous chapter, after settling in La Fama, Juan moved to Chicago and later on to Houston. In these two cities, Juan's home provided shelter to numerous neighbors from La Fama and nearby barrios. According to him,

> When we arrived in Houston [coming from Chicago in 1982], all of a sudden there were groups of six or eight people, or at the very least three. They were from here [La Fama], and they would bring their friends crossing through the desert. Upon arrival they would come straight to our house; we were acquaintances, the closest from this whole area [in La Fama]. They would arrive and *it was impossible not to give them shelter there,* right? So they could sleep in the living room, a few here and few there, and we also fed them. With the help of God, we were able to give them food while they would find work and contribute some money. Once they had money, three or six of them would get together to rent a small house and so on. . . . All

the folks, all the people from La Fama, many, many, not only a few, many of them stayed in our house while they were looking for a job, and they would stay for some fifteen days. (Emphasis added.)

Juan's description of the assistance he provided to acquaintances and neighbors from La Fama is a classic example of the types of support migrants receive from other network participants. In addition, his statements shed light on the sense of obligation he felt toward neighbors and friends, clearly expressed in his assertion that "it was impossible not to give them shelter there, right?" Needless to say, Juan has also provided assistance to many of his relatives who migrated to the United States.

A similar sense of obligation and expectations was expressed by other members of this neighborhood-based network in more casual circumstances and yet in the same direct way as Juan. During one of my visits to La Fama, someone mentioned that a fellow neighbor had purchased a home in Houston, an occurrence rare enough to make it worthy of local commentary. Later that day, I met the new homeowner's brother, Beto, chatting with friends outside his mother's home. He confirmed that his brother had just purchased a house in the Summerland area of Houston, adding without pause: "Ahora la raza ya tiene a donde llegar" (Now the crew has a place to crash).

Support from friends and residents from La Fama and surrounding barrios was also channeled through local neighborhood institutions, particularly soccer clubs. Studies such as *Return to Aztlan* (1987) have noted the role of Mexican soccer clubs and leagues as spaces for networking and information exchange among immigrants in U.S. urban centers. In Monterrey, where the soccer club is not an ethnic institution as much as it is a neighborhood association, the clubs received invitations from Houston teams led by immigrants from La Fama to play in special tournaments celebrated during Mexican national holidays. These invitations would be used by the organizers to obtain tourist visas at the local U.S. consulate. Once in Houston, visiting club players would be hosted by friends and former neighbors from La Fama. When some of the guests decided to stay and try their luck in the Houston labor market, they could normally count on the assistance of their hosts to provide them with lodging and tips about potential jobs. Still, even if the visitors returned home, the trip to Houston provided networking opportunities that could be capitalized on later.

Raúl Treviño, one of the pioneers showcased in the previous chapter, began organizing these matches between neighborhood soccer clubs from

La Fama and its vicinity and *regiomontano* clubs in Houston as early as 1973. He was joined in this activity by Abelardo Lerma, a son of Elena Lerma, the female pioneer of this migratory circuit also documented in chapter 3. Abelardo owned a hardware store and had a life-long interest in amateur sports. Although moving to Texas was always a possibility—his mother was a U.S. citizen—he never left Mexico, perhaps because of a disability caused by a childhood bout with polio. For years, Abelardo would charter a bus to travel to Houston. The players, visas in hand, had no trouble crossing legally into the United States. In the Bayou City, Raúl and his brothers happily awaited their visitors, many of whom were former classmates and childhood friends. Inevitably, a few players would stay and not return to Monterrey. Although some were responding to their friends' invitation to stay, others had obviously planned the move beforehand. Thus, the soccer clubs—a truly neighborhood institution in the working-class districts of Monterrey—became a vehicle for many to cross the border legally through their regular visits to play in Houston.

The case of Rodrigo once again illustrates this phenomenon. During his stints in the United States, Rodrigo worked with a contractor he actually met at one of the soccer tournaments in the 1980s. Just like Raúl and Abelardo, Rodrigo and a friend organized such tournaments once a year, typically during Mexican Independence Day (September 16). Invitation in hand, the two of them would assemble a team, rent a van, and head for Texas. The connection with the contractor continued through the reciprocal visits of Houston-based teams to La Fama. Rodrigo did not seize on this contact until his future as a Textiles Monterrey worker started to look shaky in the late 1990s. When he decided to make the move and try his luck in Houston, he called on his friends and acquaintances in the Bayou City, who found him a job and welcomed him with a cookout!

Notably, this phenomenon did not develop in La Fama and nearby barrios alone. According to the testimonies of several interviewees, people from other *colonias* in the metropolitan area arranged similar schemes. In these other neighborhoods, some organizers had begun to charge money to those individuals who wanted to make the trip and be included on the team roster. According to Abelardo, the whole thing had become a form of *coyotaje* (human smuggling), a realization that prompted him to discontinue this activity, given the obvious potential legal problems. Rodrigo provided similar reasons for ceasing his involvement in the organization of the trips. Still, the participation of soccer clubs in binational amateur tournaments continues, and it has even become a regular feature of urban districts in Monterrey with a tradition of U.S. migration.[6] More important, the example of the soccer clubs illustrates how networks and institutions established in the midst of an urban neighborhood were transformed by friends and *vecinos* into social capital that reduced the cost of migration and diffused migratory behavior. Once restricted to the neighborhood, these ties evolved into a translocal network embedded in a binational context, facilitating travel and border crossings and entry into the U.S. labor market.

## The Strengths and Weaknesses of Neighborhood Weak Ties

These ethnographic findings beg two questions: What accounts for the capacity of neighborhood ties to sustain international migration in La Fama? And, are the ties between *vecinos* (neighbors) the urban equivalent of rural *paisano* networks? I contend that both residential and employment stability were fundamental conditions for neighbors to develop a nexus with many of the characteristics often attributed to *paisano* ties: trust, reciprocity, and a sense of obligation. The anonymity and heterogeneity historically associated with urbanism were the exception rather than the norm in La Fama. It is worth recalling, as shown in chapter 3, that the barrio had little internal differentiation and was highly homogeneous, particularly in terms of occupations. In La Fama, people had lived side by side for decades, often attending the same primary and middle schools, working in the same factories under lifelong tenure systems, and joining a handful of neighborhood sports clubs. In other words, well before migration to the United States had begun, residents were connected to each other through multiple social ties, confirming what Balán, Browning, and Jelín (1973: 321) had identified in their landmark study on internal migration and social mobility, namely, that "it is the neighborhood rather than the entire city that represents for nearly all Monterrey families the meaningful unit of social interaction."

La Fama residents also displayed a strong identification with their neighborhood's history and local institutions. For instance, they were keenly aware and proud of La Fama's unique history as the cradle of the region's industrialization. Skilled workers like Pablo Gómez, the union leader introduced in chapter 3, were history aficionados, or *cronistas* (chroniclers), as they saw themselves, writing and publishing an array of booklets about the mill and its workers and management, prominent baseball and soccer clubs, and anecdotes and funny stories about local characters. These amateur *cronistas* often received support from municipal authorities, the staff of the city archive, and full-time cultural activists to help publish these booklets. As figure 3 illustrates, the neighborhood's annals were not only recorded in such booklets but also displayed in the murals that dotted the streets surrounding La Fama's plaza. These murals evoked the nineteenth-century stone aqueduct, built to bring water to the original textile mill. Although the aqueduct was destroyed, three of its arches remained, becoming an emblem of sorts for local residents.

Still, these neighborhood networks did not possess the same qualities attributed to strong *paisano* ties. In the urban barrio, in contrast with small rural settings, people were neither economically interdependent nor did they marry *within* the neighborhood. Barrio networks and exogamic ties proved effective at making migratory social capital available to individuals and households without U.S. experience yet lacked the enforceable trust and solidarity that rural networks—bounded by *paisanaje*, kinship, and economic cooperation—possessed. As a result, exercising social control upon individual behavior was a difficult undertaking, while withdrawing support from fellow residents in the context of migration was not met with the harsh penalties found with closely bounded groupings. The case of Lino illustrates these arguments. Lino left for Houston in 1983 when he lost his job as the barman of La Atarjea, La Fama's most popular cantina, located within walking distance of the mill. In Houston, Lino worked in construction, regularizing his immigration status through IRCA and quickly sponsoring the migration of his family and his siblings. Although not a pioneer of the circuit, Lino took pride in the shelter and clothing he provided his fellow neighbors from La Fama as they arrived in the United States. Still, he also made clear that he had literally kicked out of his home young men from the barrio who were disrespectful and had abused his hospitality. In these cases, he would hand them a change of clothes and show them the door. The fact that he would do this without any fear of social reprisal suggests that the weak ties that connected Lino and these new arrivals did not provide additional sanctions to enforce expected codes of conduct and solidarity.

Despite these characteristics, which evidence the limitations of urban-based networks, kinship and neighborhood ties combined proved very effective in channeling sojourners from La Fama to Houston's Summerland district. Thus, although *regiomontanos* in general were dispersed throughout the metropolitan area, migrants from La Fama and surrounding neighborhoods formed their own daughter community (Massey et al. 1987) in Summerland. In doing so, they were not only supporting the cross-border migration of fellow friends and neighbors but also concentrating social resources and actively constructing the U.S. destination of their intermetropolitan migratory circuit (Massey, Goldring, and Durand 1994). In Summerland, immigrants congregated in a series of apartment buildings and single-family homes. The area's main thoroughfare was dotted with remittance and transportation operations, including the courier vans specializing in servicing the Monterrey-Houston circuit (see chapter 5). Once in Summerland, women worked in a range of low-skilled, low-paying jobs, from stocking shelves at Wal-Mart to cleaning offices and houses and serving lunches at school cafeterias, whereas men joined the machine tool shops located near this district or the roving asbestos removal crews that labored all over the country, experiences to which I now turn.

## THE LABOR MARKET INCORPORATION OF 'REGIOMONTANOS' IN HOUSTON

The findings of fieldwork I conducted in Houston, primarily in Summerland but also in historic Mexican neighborhoods such as Magnolia and El Segundo Barrio (the Second Ward), mirrored much of what I detected in Monterrey regarding the causes, characteristics, and social organization of migration in this binational circuit.[7] Immigrants from Monterrey did not come from the ranks of the urban poor in that city. Instead, they belonged to the ample skilled and semiskilled working class that powered the industrial life of La Sultana del Norte. Just like the people I surveyed in La Fama, those I interviewed in Houston had worked in formal sector manufacturing pursuits at home, enjoying access to social wage benefits such as public and private health services, small loans, and low-cost owner-occupied housing. Their median education was equivalent to a middle school diploma—higher than the average Mexican immigrant—and was often accompanied by formal training in the vocational and technical schools that have long supplied industrial firms in Monterrey with much-needed skilled operatives. Employment stability had also characterized the occupational careers of *regiomontanos* before moving to the United States.

The interviews and ethnographic data I collected in Houston on the migratory patterns of sojourners from Monterrey were consistent with what I discovered in La Fama. Needless to say, to argue that Houston is the primary destination of immigrant *regiomontanos* borders on tautology, since this datum is based on observations gathered exclusively in the Bayou City. Still, the migratory histories of my interviewees confirm the direct connection that exists between Monterrey and Houston—one that is not mediated by staging areas or first arrivals in other urban or rural labor markets (i.e., the Rio Grande Valley, San Antonio, Dallas). Taking the Bayou City as the vantage point confirmed that the Monterrey-Houston connection is an entirely post–Bracero program phenomenon, maturing over the past twenty years as a result of economic transformations changing the face of urban-industrial Mexico. The urban-origin migrants that populate this circuit are not recurrent sojourners. They had undertaken one or two cross-border trips, often using tourist visas to gain entry into the United States and settling more or less permanently in Houston. Over time, some of those who overstayed their visas and those who were entirely undocumented obtained legal permanent residence, mainly through marriage and the provisions of the 1986 IRCA. More recent arrivals remained undocumented. In Summerland, the role of kinship- and neighborhood-based networks in the social organization of immigration is readily observable. In this district of the expansive Houston metropolitan area, family members reside within a few minutes' drive or even walking distance of each other, and single friends from the old neighborhood room together in bachelor apartments, following the spartan lifestyle not uncommon among target earners.

What were the occupational experiences of these urban-origin migrants in the Houston labor market? How did the urban-industrial background of individuals and households figure in their incorporation into the local economy? The incorporation of these urban-origin migrants into the Houston labor market conforms yet also challenges the hypothesis that newcomers are generally employed in a secondary sector of low-skilled, low-wage, unstable jobs (Piore 1979). In Houston, *regiomontanos* were employed in an array of occupations and industries, some of which are typical of those open to an immigrant workforce in a dual labor market, or what Harris (1995) calls the "sweated trades in the developed countries": waiters, cooks, and busboys in restaurants; domestic and home care attendants; laborers in construction and asbestos removal; low-skilled operatives in food processing and light manufacturing assembly plants; janitors and office cleaners; low-wage white-collar and service employees, such as security guards and cashiers; and teamsters and drivers in moving and transportation companies.

However, working-class immigrants from Monterrey had also devel-

oped a niche in the skilled trades of the oil tools and oil extraction industry of the Houston region. These were jobs that by all measures were
high-skilled, well-paid, nonseasonal posts. Such positions were also
highly segregated by sex, as women were for the most part absent from
these occupations. The demand for workers and pay in such jobs were,
nonetheless, largely determined by the cycles of the oil industry.[8] It was
during the boom period of the late 1960s and 1970s that *regiomontanos*
were first recruited into these expanding sectors of the petroleum business. Their networks quickly replaced formal recruitment in extending
the presence of workers from Monterrey as machinists, precision welders, industrial maintenance mechanics, and oil pipe repairmen.

The dramatic drop in oil prices during the early 1980s not only displaced thousands of native-born (both white and black), highly skilled
service workers (Hagan and Rodríguez 1992) but also some of the high-
skilled technical and blue-collar operatives from Monterrey. Those who
lost their jobs or who could not find employment encountered different
alternatives. Some returned to Mexico and waited for an upturn in the
Houston economy, while others found work in the asbestos removal
industry. This activity is unstable and dangerous indeed but offers wages
that are twice as high as the salaries paid in other unskilled occupations
of the service sector.

Despite the ups and downs of the metropolitan economy and the
restructuring that followed the 1980s crisis in Houston, Mexican immigrants have increased their presence in skilled and semiskilled manufacturing occupations. Using census data from selected industries, table 6
shows how, in two decades, Mexican immigrants have more than tripled
their participation in Houston's heavy manufacturing complex, from
4 percent in 1980 to 13.3 percent in 2000. In the metal industries sub-
category in particular, the group's percentage contribution grew from
6 percent in 1980 to 22 percent in 2000. Similarly, an analysis of the
1997 American Community Survey (Capps 1999) shows that 23.3 percent of Mexican immigrants in Harris County (which contains the city
of Houston) and neighboring Fort Bend County were employed as precision production, craft, and repair workers. Moreover, 13.7 percent were
occupied as machine operators, assemblers, and repairers. When classified by industry, 12.5 percent and 5.8 percent of Mexican immigrants
worked in durable and nondurable goods manufacturing, respectively.
Taken together, these industrial categories are only surpassed by construction (22.3 percent) and retail trade (20.4 percent) (Capps 1999).
In sum, these aggregate level data also suggest that Mexican immigrants

TABLE 6. PARTICIPATION OF MEXICAN
IMMIGRANT WORKERS IN MANUFACTURING IN
THE HOUSTON METROPOLITAN AREA,
1980–2000, BY PERCENTAGE

| Industry | 1980 | 1990 | 2000 |
|---|---|---|---|
| Metal industries | 6 | 17 | 22 |
| Machinery, except electrical | 4 | 7 | 11 |
| Electrical machinery | 2 | 5 | 7 |
| Average | 4 | 9.7 | 13.3 |

SOURCE: Census of Population and Housing, 1980, 1990, 2000 (United States), Public use microdata sample: 5-percent sample.

have made significant inroads into skilled manufacturing occupations and industries in Houston.

The fieldwork conducted in Houston also included ethnographic observations of two occupational niches created and reproduced by the networks of migrants from La Fama and Monterrey more generally. The first of such niches is located in the above-mentioned oil tools, technology, and service industry. What accounts for the formation of this niche? It developed through the initial arrival of a few pioneers during the late 1960s and early 1970s in response to active recruitment. As I described earlier, these pioneers became the foundation for the subsequent migration of relatives, friends, and neighbors from Monterrey. Ultimately, niche occupational incorporation cannot be explained solely on the basis of either the demand for skilled workers or the operation of networks. In addition to these networks, what made niche incorporation possible was the fact that *regiomontano* migrants possessed the industrial background and skills that allowed them to take on jobs as machinists, precision welders, sheet metal workers, and industrial maintenance mechanics. In fact, a distinct feature shared by many of my interviewees in Houston was the accumulation of long years of on-the-job training and experience in some of the largest and most technologically advanced industrial firms in Monterrey. Moreover, several machinists had actually received several years of formal training in technical and vocational schools in that city. The availability of a skilled industrial workforce south of the border was by no means an accident. In need of such a workforce, the Monterrey industrialists had invested much effort in establishing technological institutes and vocational schools, an effort epitomized by the founding of the Instituto Tecnológico y de Estudios Superiores de Monterrey (popularly known as Tec de Monterrey) in

1943. Although Tec de Monterrey is nowadays devoted to the education of business leaders and has expanded to the rest of Mexico and to other countries in Latin America, its original purpose was to produce the technical cadres and skilled labor force that industry needed.

Two vignettes selected from my Houston fieldwork illustrate the background and skills of these industrial workers now turned international migrants. Paco had completed formal studies as an automotive mechanic in Monterrey and had also accumulated many years of experience working for John Deere, where his job was to redesign agricultural machinery imported from the United States to adapt it to Mexican norms and systems. Prior to his job at John Deere, he had apprenticed at Chrysler in Mexico, where he had won a worldwide contest on auto mechanics. Despite these outstanding qualifications, Paco worked in a small auto repair shop in Summerland, his job mobility hampered by his undocumented status.

Much older than Paco, Ramiro was a machinist from La Fama who had completed a post–high school technical degree and had worked several years in local industries in Monterrey. His previous experience with manual, electrical, and fully computerized lathes allowed him to take on a job as a machinist in Houston, where he designed and produced high and low pressure valve parts for several oil companies and NASA. Still, most of his work consisted of programming numeric control machines. When I asked Ramiro about the single most important problem he faced at work, he paused for a moment and replied, "Trigonometry!" According to him, maintaining an adequate level of knowledge in trigonometry was necessary to solve most programming issues. Skills such as these explain the capacity of these manufacturing workers to create and maintain their own niche in the Houston labor market. It is worth noting that these immigrants had also developed weak ties based on occupation, which allowed them to exchange information about pay and other conditions across workplaces in Houston. This was particularly the case among machinists, who would move from one shop to the next on the basis of a salary increase and conditions that allowed them more control over the work process. Still, mobility and salary were also determined by legal status. Regardless of skill, operatives who lacked work and residency papers received lower wages and enjoyed fewer opportunities than their counterparts who were documented.

In some cases, these skilled industrial workers from Monterrey had colonized entire small manufacturing shops in Houston, ranging from the less to the more technically sophisticated companies, which used fully computerized machines. Early in my fieldwork in the Bayou City, I visited one of these shops, interviewing several operatives. In this workplace, machinists still used the less technologically advanced electromechanic lathes. Although the firm employed a truly small number of workers (there were three onsite during my visit), it is worth noting that all of them were part of a preestablished network of friends who not only shared a common place of origin in Mexico but had also attended the same machinist training school in Monterrey.

But not all the *regiomontano* industrial workers were able to find jobs in Houston that corresponded with their occupational background and skill levels. The second occupational niche, the asbestos removal business—an industry representative of the secondary labor market that typically incorporates most immigrants—reflected this reality. This industry rose as an alternative for a growing number of immigrants from La Fama and surrounding districts migrating in the 1980s and 1990s as the cycles of boom and bust forced the diversification of the Houston economy, making it less dependent on oil-related employment. Compared to other unskilled blue- and white-collar jobs, asbestos removal offered relatively high salaries. On occasion, asbestos laborers could even get a higher hourly rate than a skilled manufacturing worker, but these situations were rare. In 1999, *regiomontano* asbestos laborers were making $10 per hour, and by 2003, they made $13.50 per hour. Although workers used disposable protective suits and followed detailed safety protocols at jobs sites, asbestos removal presented serious health risks, such as lung and other types of cancer.

Viewed from the labor supply side, the business was organized through typical subcontracting arrangements in which a contractor assembled a crew that was then taken to different sites for work. Although Houston was the home base of these crews, they were also hired to remove asbestos almost anywhere in the United States, including other states in the South and places as far as the upper Midwest. This arrangement offered additional advantages for workers, such as higher hourly wages and paid room and board. Still, work was always temporary and had a seasonal component, with lower demand during the winter months. Asbestos removal was also segregated by ethnicity, with African Americans and Mexican immigrants making up most of the workforce. Mexican Americans and white Americans generally participated as supervisors. Migrants from La Fama and nearby neighborhoods in the Monterrey metropolitan area had also developed networks that channeled newcomers into this industry.

It is evident that due to the hazardous nature of the job, its lack of appeal to the native labor force (particularly whites), and the dominance of subcontracting, asbestos removal companies were very open to hiring undocumented workers, a fact that turned this activity into an easy gateway to the Houston labor market. Prospective laborers had to obtain a variety of falsified documents in addition to work and residency papers, including health assessments and certificates on how to handle hazardous materials. According to my observations and interviews with *regiomontano* migrants in Houston, these practices seemed more prevalent among asbestos removal workers than among machinists, welders, and other skilled manufacturing operatives. But as the province of undocumented workers, asbestos removal sites were also a frequent target of immigration enforcement and raids, which resulted in *regiomontano* laborers being deported from workplaces as faraway as South Dakota. By the middle of the current decade, as asbestos was effectively removed from buildings and other sites in most of the United States, jobs were becoming scarce and workers were moving to other types of jobs, especially in construction.

The evidence collected in Houston suggests that immigrants from Monterrey, and La Fama in particular, have become incorporated into a variety of industrial sectors and occupational niches. Most notable is their participation in the high-skilled occupations of the industrial manufacturing sector and the oil tools, technology, and maintenance industry. First attracted by the boom in the petroleum industry during the 1960s and 1970s and then propelled by industrial restructuring during the 1980s and 1990s at home, migrants from Monterrey have become part of the industrial working class of the Houston metropolitan area, transferring their technical know-how acquired in manufacturing settings south of the border.

## THE MONTERREY-HOUSTON CONNECTION: TRANSNATIONAL COMMUNITY OR SEGMENTED IMMIGRANT POPULATION?

Is the Monterrey-Houston international migratory circuit an instance of a transnational community? Should the heightened levels of cross-border contact, frequent trips, and binational social networks connecting Houston and Monterrey be interpreted as evidence of immigrant transnationalism? In some respects, the Monterrey-Houston connection is a poster child for both elite and grassroots transnationalism. The two cities are linked by a highly developed communications and transportation infrastructure. Several toll roads and highways connect Monterrey and Houston via the border cities of Laredo, McAllen, and Brownsville, Texas. Dozens of bus companies service the two cities every day. In late 2005, ten nonstop flights departed the Houston Intercontinental Airport for Monterrey daily. The *regiomontano* industrial elites and the city's upper middle class are frequent consumers of Houston's medical, professional, and commercial services, including its shopping centers and amusement parks. By the same token, physicians with practices based in Houston fly their patients to Monterrey to perform procedures not yet approved by U.S. authorities. Monterrey-based corporations have established branches and have acquired manufacturing facilities in Houston, while business leaders and officials from the Bayou City often conduct trade missions to La Sultana del Norte. Houston corporations also conduct head-hunting activities in Monterrey, which is northern Mexico's most important university center and home to the country's largest private university system—the Tec de Monterrey. It is not uncommon to find engineers and professionals recruited in Monterrey working for Houston-based firms, a trend bound to increase as a result of NAFTA and the exchange programs established by leading universities of these two cities (Greater Houston Partnership 2000).

The ease of the Monterrey elite and middle class in straddling the border, moving back and forth between countries, contrasts with the difficulties encountered by working-class *regiomontanos*. To be sure, the mostly working-class individuals and families from La Fama and other Monterrey neighborhoods who have migrated to Houston have developed an intense social field linking these two major cities of Mexico and the United States from below—to use Guarnizo and Smith's (1998) characterization of immigrant transnationalism. But while their networks effectively link and bridge these two cities across the international boundary, the border and, in this sense, the state loom larger than ever in their sojourning. Whereas the people of northeast Mexico moved back and forth across the border with relative ease during the late nineteenth and early twentieth centuries, from the 1920s (a decade that includes the forced repatriations of Mexicans, preceded by the creation of the Border Patrol in 1924) to the present, the trend has been one of increasing curbs to immigration, hardening of the international boundary, and asserting state power and control over cross-border population flows in general (González Quiroga 1993, 2001; Mora-Torres 2001; De León 1989). Although the U.S. government has been a major actor in these historical trends, the Mexican state has also sought to control emigration, establishing guest worker programs and criminalizing undocumented migration and the use of Mexico's territory as a staging area for clandestine entry into the United States by nationals of other countries (Hernández 2002).

The migration of *regiomontano* urbanites is firmly nested in and shaped by these sociohistorical forces. Thus, there is little in this migratory circuit that is *trans,* or beyond, the national and the nation-state. On the contrary, state institutions are present and engage migrants at every step of the social and political process of migration—with the host state erecting numerous barriers to entry and long-term immigration (Zolberg 1999). The reality I observed in this binational circuit is not of migrants transcending the national but one of migrants challenging the receiving country's consistent effort to keep them out. Such uneven confrontation—what Rodríguez (1996) has called the "battle for the border"—has had long-lasting consequences for sojourners and their families, even when migrants can make it past the U.S.-Mexico border and when dependents have decided or have been forced by circumstances to remain in Monterrey. The most important of these consequences is the dispelling of the notion of a transnational community. Even when looking exclusively at the migrants from La Fama and their daughter settlement in Houston's Summerland district, it is obvious that this otherwise highly homogeneous group (in class and occupation) is stratified by migratory legal status. As Menjívar (2006) has also argued in the context of Salvadoran and Guatemalan flows, such differentiation, imposed by the host state in the context of immigration, determines both the kinds of exchanges and the activity patterns individuals and families can sustain across borders and the experiences of incorporation (and nonincorporation) into the United States they endure. Instead of members of a transnational community, then, *regiomontano* workers have become part of a segmented immigrant population.

## Citizens and Residents

Immigrants with U.S. citizenship and legal permanent residence engaged in frequent and diverse transborder contacts with the relatives, friends, and neighbors that remained in Monterrey. Taking advantage of the relative proximity between the two cities, these individuals and their families traveled the little more than four hundred miles separating the metropolises as often as two to four times a month—usually during weekends. Still, a more common pattern was one of a handful of trips scattered throughout the year. Visiting aging parents and young families left behind; attending family events, such as weddings, *quinceaños* (sweet fifteen celebrations), baptisms, and funerals; seeing doctors and dentists; and conducting informal business activities, like bringing used clothes and other goods to sell in local flea markets and in private homes, were all reasons to travel to Monterrey. On any given weekend, walking the streets of La Fama, I observed the makeshift businesses migrants set up in the front rooms and porches of their homes, stocked with clothes, shoes, and used appliances, including refrigerators and stereo systems, originally purchased in Houston. Neighbors and passersby would stop to inquire about the price of these items. The neighborhood flea markets also had stands displaying similar merchandise.

Thus, men and women holding U.S. residency and citizenship documents sustained the most varied and frequent types of contacts, traveling with ease between Monterrey and Houston, taking advantage of the proximity and the sophisticated communications and transportation infrastructure connecting these cities. Hence, those sanctioned by the U.S. and Mexican governments to cross the border—bearing the most "national" of documents, passports and visas—were the most "transnationally" oriented migrants. Through their frequent presence in Monterrey, Houston-based individuals and families managed to participate and include relatives and friends in functions and activities that not only contributed to reproduce their networks but also allowed them to assert their newly found social status derived from migration. Many of the immigrants in this cohort had moved to the United States during the early days of the Monterrey-Houston flow and had benefited from the sponsorship of employers, which enabled them to obtain a green card. Others had immigrated either before or right after the passage of IRCA and had secured U.S. legal residency through its amnesty and Special Agricultural Worker (SAW) programs.

The case of José Lerma, son of pioneer migrant Elena Lerma and brother of Abelardo Lerma, the organizer of Monterrey-Houston soccer tournaments, illustrates this argument. Holding U.S. citizenship and living in Houston with his family, José began collecting recycled baseball items to donate to the baseball junior league in which he played during his childhood in Monterrey. This first venture was motivated by his intention to "repay" the league for the formative experiences of his early years in that city. The success of this endeavor motivated José to suggest to the principal of a local elementary school in Houston where he was a physical education teacher's assistant the idea of a baseball players' exchange between the school's team and the junior league in Monterrey. The exchange incorporated children and adult members of the Summerland district in Houston and La Fama and neighboring districts in Monterrey and included reciprocal visits by each team. When the Texas team played in Monterrey, local families hosted children and guardians in their homes and prepared meals to celebrate their visit while neighborhood newspapers reported on the games against *regiomontano* teams. Even though U.S. citizenship allowed him to go back and forth between Houston and Monterrey, José's transnational activities could not be carried out seamlessly. Several of the primarily Mexican and Central American schoolchildren participating in the program from Houston were undocumented and could not risk leaving the United States. According to José, during the trip to Monterrey, Mexican immigration authorities did not grant entry to a Vietnamese child. Finally, once he lost his job as a teacher's assistant (and in the absence of a Houston-based *regiomontano* hometown association), José also lost the institutional support he needed to organize the baseball tournament, bringing his binational sports and community project to an end.

U.S. citizenship and legal residency allowed Houston families to turn to their relatives in Monterrey for long-term childcare, particularly during the summer school break. For immigrant parents, having their children spend the summer months in Monterrey was part of a strategy to deal with the risks of urban poverty—keeping their young away from gangs, drugs, and violence—and to manage the often difficult process of acculturation to the United States by instigating "Mexican cultural values" among their children. In my interviews, mothers and fathers often expressed concern and even outrage about the fact that their own children could bring charges against them when physical punishment had been used to solve a disciplinary problem at home. In this context, frequent visits to Monterrey and long stays under the supervision of grandparents and other relatives provided the opportunity to reproduce traditional child-rearing strategies and to reassert parental control.

## Tourist Visa and Border-Crossing Cardholders

Contrast this group with those who have moved to Houston seeking employment or reunification with their families in the Bayou City, crossing the border with the help of a tourist visa or a border-crossing card (BCC).[9] According to my neighborhood survey and the ethnographic observations conducted in both cities, this was a large segment of U.S.-

bound migrants in La Fama. While the tourist visa tended to facilitate the border-crossing experience, these individuals had to use false papers or borrow authentic documents from relatives or friends to work in Houston. Even though these individuals did not consider themselves *mojados* (wetbacks), they were fully aware of their precarious status and behaved accordingly. Like undocumented workers who consciously keep a low profile, they followed a well-known daily routine of *de la casa al trabajo y del trabajo a la casa* (from home to work and from work to home) to minimize the risk of getting caught. Still, it is not surprising that a crucial aspect of their experience involved the very act of crossing the international boundary through a port of entry along the Texas-Mexico border.

Rafael and Rodrigo, two young men from La Fama whose reasons for looking for work in Houston were described in chapter 3, used tourist visas to cross the border legally. While Rodrigo had traveled to Houston a handful of times, first as an organizer of soccer games and later as a construction worker, Rafael had kept a job as machinist in the Bayou City for nearly ten years, returning to Monterrey every two weeks to see his wife and children. While holding a tourist visa allowed for this pattern of back-and-forth movement, such a visa did not fully guarantee uneventful admittance into the United States. Coming into the country through ports of entry along the Rio Grande, border crossers were required to apply for a six-month-long I-94 permit allowing them to travel inland. This was often a critical moment in the individual's sojourning experience since it involved several minutes of interaction with a customs or immigration official. A man in the prime of his productive years, such as Rafael, would have to prove that he had a job back in Monterrey and submit upon demand evidence such as pay stubs and utility bill receipts. In addition, he would have to provide material proof that he was indeed a tourist: cash or other means of financial support, an invitation to a wedding or function if that was the stated purpose of the trip, and luggage that matched the alleged duration of the visit. If the applicant seemed hesitant, the official would conduct a highly invasive check of his wallet (or purse in the case of women), emptying its contents while looking for evidence that betrayed his stated intentions: a Texas-issued identification card, stubs, or receipts demonstrating previous presence in the United States. While conducting this check, the official would also verbally probe for clues demonstrating that the individual was lying, taunting him in such a way as to provoke contradictions and mistakes in his account. In this highly unequal interaction, in view of everybody present in the offices of the port of entry, the immigrant would often be infantilized and verbally humiliated—an outcome I observed multiple times during my own coming and going across border cities from Laredo–Nuevo Laredo to Brownsville-Matamoros.

Although seasoned border crossers like Rafael were normally prepared for these eventualities, even experienced sojourners could make mistakes, such as having let the I-94 expire while still in the United States. In short, there was always the possibility of getting caught and, as a result, being denied entry and turned back or, worse, having the actual visa seized and cancelled. Those turned back could try their luck at some other port of entry, especially individuals with the flexibility of traveling in a private vehicle or in one of the many informal van courier services providing transportation to migrants in the Monterrey-Houston circuit. For those crossing the border with a tourist visa, the perils of the migratory journey did not end with a seemingly uneventful passing through the port of entry, particularly when traveling by bus. A few miles inland, at the checkpoints along the main highways leading to Houston, the Border Patrol would still try to purge these busloads of people who, in the eyes of the agents, did not fit the profile of the short-term leisure traveler but instead were actual immigrant workers. Because of these heightened risks, even an uneventful crossing using a BCC was often followed by long periods of immobility, as going back to Mexico and then having to return to the United States would only bring the individual to face-to-face contact with immigration and other border enforcement authorities.

Needless to say, immigrants found creative alternatives, deploying resources from either side of the border to deal with such immobility. During one of my early fieldwork stints in Houston in the mid-1990s, I interviewed Guadalupe, a middle-aged woman who had crossed the border together with her family using a tourist visa. Although she could return to Monterrey anytime she wanted, she was keenly aware of the risk of being detected by U.S. immigration authorities if she attempted to reenter the country. Recently arrived and without credit or cash in hand, she was struggling to purchase the appliances she needed to set up her new household. In charge of domestic chores, her most pressing need at the time I met her was buying a washing machine. Unable to go to Monterrey and bring her own perfectly working household items back, she found out that she could use her Sears credit card, issued in Mexico, to purchase a washing machine in a Sears store in Houston. The appliance was delivered to her apartment in this city, while the sale was billed, in pesos, to her home in Monterrey. In taking advantage of the ubiquity of a multinational corporation, Guadalupe found a practical solution to a problem derived from her own immobility.[10] Still, her experience also illustrates how the state casts its shadow on an immigrant's behavior long after a successful and even legal entry into the country. Here, the true *trans*national actor was not Guadalupe but Sears.

### Resident Undocumented Population

While there was a clear *discontinuity* between citizens and residents, on the one hand, and tourist visa border crossers, on the other hand, there was a kind of *continuum* between border-crossing cardholders and undocumented sojourners. As shown above, a botched encounter with a U.S. government official could turn one of these visa holders into an undocumented immigrant. More important, however, is that legal entry was for many a first step into a clandestine existence in the United States. In Summerland, many people had first entered Texas using a BCC and overstayed their visas. They included unaccompanied male and female target earners who roomed with relatives in the many apartment complexes of the area as well as spouses, children, and even elderly parents joining a head of household who had moved to Houston first. Needless to say, there were some who had never had a tourist visa, having crossed the border clandestinely with the assistance of one of La Fama's local smugglers.

Although a few *regiomontanos* who had migrated during the late 1980s and early 1990s had been able to regularize their status through late amnesty provisions and to apply for legal residence on behalf of family members, many remained undocumented throughout the entire research period (1995–2005). The term *transnational* and its variants do not capture the essence of their social lives, whether viewed from the standpoint of the receiving country or from the perspective of the larger Mexico-U.S. migratory system. These men, women, and children had become part of the resident undocumented population in the United States. What struck me about this segment of the Monterrey origin population in Houston was not their transnational orientation but their social and physical immobility. Immigration and border enforcement policies (the Immigration and Welfare Acts of 1996 and Operation Rio Grande) and global events (9/11 in particular) that ensued during the 1990s and early part of the present decade appeared to trap undocumented immigrants inside the United States, significantly limiting their ability to move and travel—if not impeding their cross-border mobility altogether.

In the absence of a new amnesty or legalization program that could change this situation, over the decade-long study period, conditions only worsened. Replicating border enforcement strategies first implemented in El Paso and San Diego, U.S. officials beefed up policing resources along the urban areas of the Rio Grande in 1997. In addition, the Illegal Immigration Reform and Immigrant Responsibility Act (IIRIRA) of 1996 further criminalized undocumented migration, increasing the penalties for document fraud and unauthorized reentry, expediting removal, and making retroactive a newly broadened definition of aggravated felony—a crime punishable with deportation (U.S. Department of Justice 1997). As a result of these increasingly restrictive policies, in 2003, those lacking papers would pay as little as $35 for a one-way trip by bus to Monterrey but faced a $2000 smuggler's fee to return to Houston (with no successful outcome guaranteed). The smuggling fee was striking not only because of the relative proximity between the two cities but also because it had nearly tripled in less than ten years—up from $700 in 1995.[11] Most of the undocumented could only afford this hefty expense and the risks of a clandestine reentry in the case of family emergency, such as the death of a parent.[12]

The social experience and consequences of membership in this resident undocumented population varied depending on multiple factors, such as gender, marital status, whether the family was divided between Houston and Monterrey or all members lived under one roof in the United States, and the legal status of household members. I frequently encountered both single men and entire nuclear families as part of this resident undocumented population. The case of Teo illustrates the experiences of male target earners who had migrated to Houston, leaving their families behind. Teo was a skilled manufacturing worker with a background as an industrial mechanic and welder in Monterrey. During his first stint in the United States in 1993, he crossed into Texas using a tourist visa, and for eight months he worked removing asbestos in Houston. He went back to Mexico, where he set up his own taco stand, a business that failed two years later. Teo returned to Houston in 1996, again using his BCC. This time he found work in a wrought iron shop, a job in which he could use much of his knowledge as a welder. Teo did not go back to Monterrey to see his family until 2003. But when he tried to reenter the United States, immigration officials confiscated his tourist visa, forcing him to enter clandestinely after paying $2000 to a *coyote*.

Teo's case is relevant because it exposes multiple dimensions of the social life of a resident undocumented individual. Teo is not a regular industrial welder. At the shop where he has worked since 1996, he has become a craftsman, creating many of the wrought iron gates and fences that adorn River Oaks and other highly exclusive neighborhoods in Houston. During one of my visits to his place in Summerland, he showed me a photo album with pictures of his creations, some of which are sold for tens of thousands of dollars. On this occasion, Teo also proudly shared with me photographs of a wrought iron stand he built for a museum exhibit in Amsterdam. The stand would support a projector for a multimedia show using light and photography. Even though Teo had not designed the structure, he had worked closely with the artist and was proud that his creation was showcased in an international venue. Despite this success, he was making $17 an hour at the shop. Teo was planning to establish his own business in Monterrey, saving and investing in tools that he purchased in Houston and shipped to Mexico with the courier vans traveling between the two cities several times a week. He also remitted about $1600 a month to his family in Monterrey.

When I first met Teo in 1996, he was sharing an apartment with other men from La Fama. Many of these men were married, were expected to send their earnings home, and were therefore living a spartan existence in Houston. Their living quarters were always sparsely furnished, with up to ten people cramming into the small two-bedroom apartment. There was never a phone line, so nobody would be left with a costly bill of international long-distance calls—an issue that became less important over time as wireless communications and calling cards became readily available. Residents would come and go, partly as a result of their work in asbestos removal, which took some of them away from Houston for weeks in a row. But in the absence of their wives and children, these men also behaved like unattached males, drinking heavily, especially on weekends, consuming marihuana at least sporadically, and establishing casual sexual relations with women in the neighborhood. Their rowdy behavior often got them in trouble with the managers of the apartment complex, who on more than one occasion forced them to move.

Women were aware of the perils of prolonged exposure to these kinds of conditions. Although I never met Teo's wife, I did interview Nicolás's spouse, Lilia. Nicolás's reasons for migration were showcased in chapter 3. At the beginning of his migratory experience, Nicolás underwent a similar situation to Teo's and the other lone target earners from La

Fama. As soon as Lilia caught up with him in Houston, she decided to move the family to Chicago. She explained the reasons for this move: "The men who have migrated from this neighborhood have not made any progress. People have not made any progress. The ones who leave [for the United States] are males and they do not get settled. A man has more freedom. When they leave by themselves, men just stagnate. They make good money working in asbestos; they make good money but spend it. They face no obligations, unlike married men. That's why it's so important that the couple migrates together, not the man alone."

The concerns expressed by Lilia were obviously not new to people separated by migration. I argue, however, that the restrictive immigration policy and border enforcement strategies in place from the mid-1990s onward actually exacerbated and prolonged separation. In contrast with the Mexican sojourners of the undocumented era of Mexico-U.S. migration, whose border-crossing practices reflected the "revolving door" and "cat-and-mouse" strategies of border policing (Massey, Durand, and Malone 2002), the *regiomontano* migrants, many of whom had entered the United States during the post-IRCA era, could not afford a similar back-and-forth mobility. One direct consequence of this new environment is that while pre-IRCA Mexican migrants were able to spend a three-to-four-month rest period at home with their spouses and children every year, Teo and his fellow undocumented arrivals from La Fama endured separations lasting several years, a pattern that resembles Salvadoran and Guatemalan flows (Menjívar 2006). Thus, in the era of globalization and transnational migrations, these clandestine immigrants had become less and not more transnational than their mostly rural predecessors of the 1960s and 1970s. In addition, an even more stringent set of immigration and border enforcement policies appeared to be leveling out, at least in some respects, Mexican and Central American migrations, despite the distinct causes and geographic characteristics of these flows.

Undocumented families experienced an even more complex situation. In a country where immigration policy depends on the federal government, not on states and localities, and where enforcement is highly concentrated along the border, not in the interior, making it past the international boundary represented for these families the possibility of a progressive integration into the economic and social fabric of their new place of residence.[13] The social lives of these families were not oriented toward a transnational social field: Clandestinely present in the country, they were unable to travel to Mexico; when families were reunited in Houston, household heads had few reasons to remit money to Monterrey. After more than a decade of presence in the United States, many of these families experienced a paradoxical situation. They were clearly not members of the American polity (Waldinger and Fitzgerald 2004), yet their lives by no means entailed a complete underground existence. On the contrary, adults had bank accounts, had taxes withheld from their paychecks, started their own business ventures, paid into Social Security accounts, received Women, Infants, and Children (WIC) vouchers, were credit-worthy customers of car dealerships and department stores, and, in some cases, had even managed to purchase a home. Their children attended public schools and, when born in the United States, were entitled to receive federal and state assistance.

In certain cases, the efforts of these undocumented immigrants to avoid detection led them to deepen their integration into local economic life. This was the experience of Javier Guzmán, a former computer systems supervisor at an auto plant in Monterrey. After twenty-seven years on the job, Javier and his wife and four children moved to Houston in 1988. Having arrived in this city during the implementation of IRCA, which included an employer's sanctions program, Javier soon realized that many firms sought verification of his legal status, a situation also faced by his adult sons. To get around this circumstance, he decided to set up his own business: a used tire recycling operation in which he and his sons could be self-employed—and avoid immigration document inspection. The investments that this venture required, albeit modest (a truck, commercial permits, a few tools) increased, not diminished, Javier's stakes in Houston, providing the means for a deeper incorporation into the United States.

Many of the families who were part of this resident undocumented population were also characterized by the mix of legal statuses of their members. Having moved to Houston first, the adult male members of such families often lacked any type of legal documentation. They had entered the country clandestinely and were holding jobs the same way. Women and children who had later followed the breadwinner using a tourist visa or BCC had also become undocumented after overstaying their visas. In contrast, younger members, whether children or grandchildren of the adult cohabiting couple, having been born in the United States, were American citizens. During the late 1980s and early 1990s, when many Mexican immigrants were readjusting their status under the provisions of IRCA, this blend of immigration statuses was often a temporary situation. But as the avenues for legalization closed, the waiting period of regularization lengthened, and the penalties for clandestine entry and presence increased during the late 1990s, the coexistence of undocumented residents, lawful permanent immigrants, and citizens in the same household became a long-term reality.

This was the case of Marcos and Felipa. He first migrated to Houston clandestinely in 1986, the same year IRCA was passed, and later unsuccessfully applied to regularize his status under the SAW program. Marcos and Felipa married in Monterrey in 1991, and, soon after the birth of their first child in 1993, Felipa and the baby joined Marcos in Houston, using tourist visas to enter the country. Two other children have since been born in the Bayou City and are therefore U.S. citizens. Felipa's undocumented sister and her U.S.-born son recently joined the household. After ten years of laboring in asbestos removal, Marcos moved to more stable yet poorly paid work as a school custodian. I found no trace of a transnational life in Marcos's and Felipa's immigration experience. Unable to travel to Mexico with their undocumented parents and one sibling, their Texas-born children knew only the United States. Despite their clandestine status, Marcos and Felipa paid taxes, contributed to Social Security, and had a bank account. Still, having received food stamps, WIC, and Medicaid during their time in Houston and solely dependent on Marcos's $11.25 an hour job, this family's incorporation resembled the experiences of the working poor in the United States.

But in contrast with the *native* working poor, the resident undocumented population was subject to deportation and, if the circumstances mandated, "voluntary" preemptive self-removal from the country. In 1997, in the context of the climate of fear created by the implementation of the IIRIRA and a series of Border Patrol and Immigration and Naturalization Service sweeps in immigrant neighborhoods in Houston, several undocumented families from La Fama decided to send women and children to Mexico, leaving behind adult men in Texas.

## LEGAL STATUS AND CROSS-BORDER ACTIVITIES: A FAMILY'S EXPERIENCE

The experience of the González family illustrates how the cross-border activities of migrants and their ability to go back and forth between Monterrey and Houston have been affected by the changing legal status of its members and the evolving yet restrictive immigration and border enforcement policies of the post-IRCA era. I met the Gonzálezes during my first fieldwork stint in Houston in 1995, and I kept in touch and visited with them in both cities regularly for ten years. Antonio and Raquel González got married in Monterrey in 1983. Antonio migrated illegally to Houston in 1988, on the footsteps of three of his siblings, after nearly ten years of work experience in different manufacturing firms in Monterrey. He was soon joined by Raquel and their two young children, Laura and Gabriel, all of whom crossed the border using tourist visas. Two more children were born in the United States.

In Houston, Antonio worked in asbestos removal, and Raquel found employment as a babysitter and later in a food-processing plant making sandwiches. In 1993, Antonio became a permanent resident of the United States, through the SAW program of IRCA, although he had never worked in agriculture. It took seven more years for Raquel and the two older children to obtain their green cards. Although Raquel had had a work permit since 1993, she (and her Mexico-born children) could not leave the country unless the immigration authorities granted her a costly special permit. In contrast, Antonio and the two U.S.-born children were able to travel and visit family in Monterrey. When I first met Antonio, Raquel, and their four children, they lived in a small apartment in a complex located on one of the main streets of Summerland, where many former La Fama friends and neighbors concentrated. During my visits to their home, I often encountered newly arrived La Fama sojourners who were being hosted by Antonio and Raquel. Antonio's work in asbestos removal required him to travel to other cities and towns, primarily in the South, with crews made up of men from La Fama and other Monterrey neighborhoods. He often used his own vehicle and charged fellow workmates for the ride to distant job sites.

In early 1997, Antonio was arrested by Border Patrol agents at a checkpoint on I-35 near Laredo, Texas, together with el Güero, a local La Fama *coyote*. They were transporting a group of undocumented workers el Güero had just smuggled. When they were queried by the agents, the undocumented immigrants identified el Güero as the *coyote*. However, since it was Antonio's car that was used in the failed operation, he was charged with a felony and released on bail. He later pleaded no contest to the charges and was sentenced to two years' probation. In contrast, el Güero spent eight months in a county jail near Laredo to then be deported to Mexico. This was a costly incident for Antonio not only because of the legal fees and confiscation of his car but also because of the possibility of losing his permanent resident status. Had this happened a few months later, he would have lost his green card under the provisions of the 1996 IIRIRA, which increased the penalties for human trafficking and accelerated the deportation of so-called criminal aliens. This legislation did not become effective until 1997.

By 2000, Antonio had fulfilled the terms of his probation. That same year Raquel and her two oldest children received their permanent residency documents, ending a long period of what Menjívar calls "legal liminality," namely, a situation in which the immigrant is "not fully documented or undocumented but often straddling both" statuses (Menjívar 2006: 1001). With papers in hand, Raquel immediately visited her parents and siblings in Monterrey. With all the members of the family as either legal residents or citizens of the United States, Antonio and Raquel were able to take advantage of business opportunities requiring the back-and-forth movement across the border. Also in 2000, a popular courier van operation shuttling remittances, passengers, and parcels between Houston and Monterrey closed down after nearly twenty years of providing services to immigrants from La Fama and surrounding neighborhoods (see chapter 5 for a full account). Antonio saw this development as an opportunity to enter the business. Using his old Suburban, he started traveling to Monterrey every weekend, taking with him and his family used goods, remittances in cash, and a few riders. Sometimes, depending on the demand, his oldest son would drive a second vehicle. In my conversations with him, Antonio always downplayed the significance and profitability of this business. However, he told me that he could make $1000 profit per trip, an amount that clearly dwarfed his weekly income based on his $13.50 an hour asbestos removal job. Still, Antonio did not quit his regular job, a move that allowed him to remain relatively inconspicuous as he undertook his cross-border courier enterprise. Antonio's attempt to keep a low profile stood in contrast with the important consequences this business had for his standard of living and his status among immigrants as well as stay-at-home individuals and families from La Fama. He was able to move into a single-family home in Houston in 2002—not too far from the apartment where he and his family had lived for more than ten years.

Being legal residents of the United States allowed the Gonzálezes to celebrate their only daughter's sweet fifteen party, or *quinceañera*, in Monterrey—while earnings from the courier business allowed them to pay for it. For more than a year, as they traveled every weekend back and forth between Houston and Monterrey, Antonio and Raquel also planned Laura's celebration. While Antonio delivered the remittances and parcels to households in La Fama and neighborhoods in the westernmost section of Monterrey's metropolitan area, Raquel and Laura spent time organizing the religious ceremony and ballroom party that, combined, make up the *quinceañera* celebration. While Raquel scouted for the church to hold the mass to give *gracias a Dios* and the ballroom for the fiesta, Laura attended catechism classes with the local priest and practiced the choreography she and her *chambelanes* (male chaperons) would perform at the start of the dance. Laura was a very good student at her school in Summerland, where she earned top grades. Despite her intense transnational existence—attending school in Houston and spending weekends in Monterrey—she had told her parents that she wanted to join the U.S. Air Force after high school, a decision that worried and baffled her parents.

The day of the *quinceañera*, a limousine took Laura to the studio where a professional photographer took her picture and then to Monterrey's Obispado, the historic bishop's building (now a museum) dominating the entire city from the top of a hill. In the courtyards of this colonial-era monument, she was photographed wearing her light pink dress and tiara while holding a bouquet of white roses. She was later driven to the church, where she was the only *quinceañera* celebrated at mass. As Laura and her parents entered the building led by the priest, their expensive outfits could only contrast with the small, austere church surroundings. The officiating priest seemed to pick up on such contrast as he welcomed Laura and his family and apologetically noted the modestly furnished chapel. Laura and her mother wore long dresses, while Antonio and his oldest son wore matching off-white cowboy suits and hats—Antonio's outfit alone costing more than $1000.

At the ballroom, a crowd of relatives and friends applauded as Laura and Antonio danced to an opening waltz, followed by brothers, uncles, and cousins who took turns briefly dancing with the *quinceañera*. Later, Laura changed attire to perform several choreographed pop, techno, and merengue remixes with five *chambelanes*. There were no *damas* (the *quinceañera*'s maids of honor) because most of Laura's female friends lived in Houston and could or would not be allowed to travel to Monterrey. Wearing cowboy hats, baseball caps, and ordinary, working-class clothes, the guests danced away to the rhythm of *cumbias, rancheras,* and *tejano* tunes blasting off the sound system. After dinner, with Laura back in her *quinceañera* dress, a mariachi band entered the ballroom playing songs evoking the relation between parents and daughter. Antonio danced again with Laura and handed her a doll, symbolizing her last childhood present. The rest of the night belonged to the young, who took over the dance floor until the end of the party.

To be sure, the *quinceaños* is a ritual involving multiple meanings, including the control of a woman's sexuality and body in the transition from childhood to adulthood, a socially constructed experience that Napolitano (1997) has called "becoming a *mujercita*" (becoming a little woman). But the celebration also carries meaning as "a demonstration of family status and prestige" (Napolitano 1997: 290). By holding the event in Monterrey, where more than three hundred guests attended the party, Antonio and Raquel demonstrated in front of their working-class family and friends their success in the United States and the economic mobility they had achieved through migration. In this sense, it is telling that Antonio and Raquel did not resort to the system of *padrinos* (godparents) to underwrite the cost of the beverages, the *quinceañera's* dress, the ballroom rental fee, and other items. Raquel's siblings contributed to the celebration with a few hundred dollars, and Antonio's older brother paid for the mariachi band. Antonio and Raquel had come up with the bulk of the more than $10,000 invested in the event, a stratospheric amount for any working-class *regiomontano* (and even middle-class) family.

Their decision to hold the celebration in their hometown and the long and complex planning that led to the mass and party could also be interpreted as an affirmation of their ties to the kinship and friendship networks which originated in Monterrey. However, over the years, these networks had become binational in nature, while Antonio's economic fortunes had become progressively intertwined with them due to his cross-border courier activities. Arguably, Antonio and his wife did not need to use the *quinceañera* as an expressive statement of belonging to such networks. I recognize, however, that Antonio and Raquel could have different motivations for celebrating the *quinceañera* in Monterrey, as opposed to Houston. In my conversations on the topic with Raquel, she argued that the choice had to do with the fact that most of her siblings lived in Monterrey. In contrast, Antonio's own behavior was consistent with a "status and prestige" motivation foretold by his $1000 outfit, including his $600 boots and $100 wallet, both made with crocodile hide.

## CONCLUSION

Monterrey migrants have found in Houston their chief destination in the United States. But this fact is not the result of an accident or the natural outcome of the geographic proximity of these two cities. Responding to Houston's transformation into the global city of the oil industry in the

1960s and 1970s, local firms set out to recruit skilled manufacturing workers in Mexico, finding a plentiful source in Monterrey, the country's premier heavy manufacturing center. In La Sultana del Norte, a mix of kinship- and neighborhood-based networks has facilitated the U.S.-bound migration of new workers from the 1980s to the present. In this city, exogamic marriage appears to be expanding the migratory social capital available to men without prior sojourning experience. Contrary to what the scant scholarship on Mexican cities as sources of emigration has established, in La Fama and surrounding working-class districts, relations of friendship and *vecinazgo* have shown to be capable of sustaining international migration, a quality I attribute to the employment and residential stability and the emerging multiplex nature of ties established between neighbors.

In La Fama, even neighborhood institutions, such as the local soccer teams, have been used to organize and support migration to Houston. Still, despite their emerging multiplexity, these ties cannot be equated with the networks of rural Mexicans, for whom kinship and *paisanaje* (reinforced through endogamic marriage practices) and economic cooperation often overlap. As a result, if the beneficiary of assistance does not abide by certain norms of conduct, the provider of the aid can cut off the favor without fear of substantial consequences. Still, despite their limitations, these networks of friends and neighbors have been effective enough to channel emigrants from La Fama to a distinct number of neighborhoods in the northwest section of Houston and to specific occupational niches in this city's labor market.

Early migrant cohorts were incorporated into an array of oil-related industries dominating the economy of the Bayou City—from extraction to processing to oil tools and technology—which reflected the demands of the Houston labor market and the urban-industrial background of *regiomontano* workers. In these industries, immigrants have labored as machinists, mechanics, and precision welders, creating and maintaining the infrastructure of this nodal center of U.S. and global oil production and management. After the decline in oil prices of the 1980s and the ensuing restructuring of the Houston economy, new waves of mostly undocumented *regiomontanos* found employment in asbestos removal and other construction-related occupations. Despite these transformations, during the 1990s, skilled manufacturing workers from La Fama could still find employment as machinists and industrial mechanics in the Bayou City's large network of small- and medium-sized shops servicing the oil industry and NASA.

In Houston, neither people from La Fama nor immigrants from the larger Monterrey metropolitan area had established any kind of hometown association channeling collective cross-border activities. Correspondingly, neither the Mexican consular representatives nor the state government of Nuevo León were particularly keen on turning the Bayou City into a bastion of hometown politics. In the Monterrey-Houston circuit, cross-border activities were conducted individually and through families, households, and neighborhood-based networks in the form of private social and economic ventures. Still, an array of binationally organized cross-border activities occurred in this migratory circuit: charitable projects and sports tournaments, family celebrations, business enterprises, and cultural and religious exchanges. Although such a lively social field could be interpreted as proof of the existence of some sort of transnational community or of the transnational orientation of immigrants, I argue that the transnational label would mask a broader and more complex reality: The receiving state's immigration and border enforcement policies create an immigrant population segmented along the lines of legal status.

This interpretation is not devised to disprove the transnational approach to international migration—something that clearly cannot be done on the basis of a single case study. Rather, my aim is to argue that the contacts and exchanges that these urban working-class immigrants can effectively sustain with the sending country are largely (but not exclusively) contingent on their legal standing in the receiving polity—the United States. Not surprisingly, those *regiomontanos* who had acquired U.S. citizenship or permanent residence were, in fact, the leading *transnationals* in this circuit. In contrast, those who overstayed their tourist visas and undocumented sojourners were unable to participate in cross-border activities, or, at the very least, effective participation was made difficult. In the context of the hardening of border enforcement and an increasingly restrictive and punitive immigration policy, clandestine immigrants faced mounting obstacles to any cross-border movement. For these newcomers, the result was both social and physical immobility and long-term incorporation into the resident undocumented population in Houston.

These immigrants with their differentiated legal statuses interacted with each other in multiple and complex ways. As the case of the González family illustrates, multiple legal statuses could coexist under one roof for a long time, affecting what specific individuals but also the household as a whole could do. As legal statuses changed over time, new opportunities opened up for some while others saw their chances restricted. Thus, Antonio and particularly Raquel González and her Mexico-born children's acquisition of permanent legal status not only ended a lengthy period of immobility but also allowed them to initiate a business that entailed regular travel across the border, providing services to fellow *regiomontanos* whose undocumented status forced them to stay put. It is to these types of immigration-related services that I now turn.

# CHAPTER 5

# The Migration Industry in the Monterrey-Houston Connection

In this chapter I analyze a different kind of social infrastructure connecting origin and destination in this migratory circuit, namely, the matrix of entrepreneurial activities and services easing cross-border movement and channeling sojourners between Monterrey and Houston known as the migration industry (Castles and Miller 1998). In turning my attention to the migration industry, I undertake two distinct yet related analytical tasks: first, I identify the components and characterize the role of the migration industry in the social organization of international mobility; and second, through the lens of a case study, I tease out the interactions between the migration industry, its entrepreneurs, and its activities, on the one hand, and social and political actors, such as migrants, their social networks, and state institutions, on the other. Making sense of these interactions is vital to understanding, for example, whether entry into the migration industry is contingent on the migration entrepreneur's membership in the social network and the ethnic group he or she serves.

I define the migration industry as the ensemble of entrepreneurs who, motivated by the pursuit of financial gain, provide a variety of services facilitating human mobility across international borders (Hernández-León 2005; see also Castles and Miller 1998). Although the literature on international human mobility has always paid attention to various kinds of migration entrepreneurs, scholars have generally treated the migration industry as a marginal subject and have subsumed it under other actors and structures of the social and political process of international migration, such as coethnic and immigrant networks.[1] More recently, studies of the migration industry have focused on entrepreneurs who facilitate clandestine entry into countries of destination, namely, *coyotes* and other human smugglers, often reflecting the concerns of receiving states seeking to control immigration. Similarly, in response to the growing interest of sending states in extracting benefits from expatriate populations, a growing strand of the literature has started to analyze the remittance industry (de la Garza and Lowell 2002).

In contrast to these prevailing perspectives, I argue that the migration industry comprises a broad set of actors and services that play an active role in every step of the process of migration (i.e., initiation, continuation) and are present in different types of migratory movements (i.e., permanent, cyclical, return). In a sociopolitical context characterized by the restriction and control of cross-border population flows (Zolberg 1999), the migration industry "greases" the engines of international human mobility, providing and articulating the expertise and infrastructural resources that facilitate such mobility and the realization of goals intimately tied to the experience of migration. Migration industry entrepreneurs include moneylenders, recruiters, transportation providers and travel agents, legitimate and false paper pushers, smugglers, contractors, formal and informal remittance and courier service owners, lawyers and notaries offering legal and paralegal counseling to migrants, and, under certain circumstances, promoters of immigrant destinations.

I also contend that the migration industry should be treated analytically, as a distinct actor in the social process of international migration that overlaps the mainstream, ethnic, and immigrant economies and straddles formal and informal sectors of economic activity (Hernández-León 2005). Still, I recognize that often migration entrepreneurs are coethnics with their customers and are able to identify business opportunities by virtue of their membership in immigrant and ethnic social networks. At the same time, nonethnic entrepreneurs might use ethnic and immigrant employees and their cultural and linguistic knowledge to enter the industry and to make inroads into particular business niches (i.e., transportation, remittances, and legal services). These observations, derived from Light's (2005, 2006) understanding of the ethnic and immigrant economies, suggest that migration industry entrepreneurs, their employees, and their activities are often closely connected to their customers via immigrant social networks and social capital.

While some researchers have studied the migration industry as a borderless ethnic economy (see Harney 1977), I contend that international boundaries are not only at the heart of the phenomenon but are also its very raison d'être. Indeed, even though the migration industry does not erase the borders signaling "the geopolitical discontinuity" (Foucher 1991: 38) between countries, it exists and thrives because of its distinctive capacity to span such borders. This suggests that both sending and receiving states play a fundamental role in shaping the contours of the migration industry, the rise and fall of particular types of entrepreneurs and activities, and the social organization of services offered to sojourners and to the employers of immigrant labor. This is not to say that state policies and regulatory regimes completely determine the profile and dynamics of the migration industry. Instead, what I argue is that the intended and unintended consequences of such policies and regulations, including the strategies of both migrants and migration entrepreneurs to circumvent them, effectively influence why certain services become available, under what conditions such services are offered, and who provides them.

Here, I seek to map out in great ethnographic detail the relationships among the migration industry, the sending and receiving states, and the *regiomontano* sojourner networks in the Monterrey-Houston circuit through the case study of a courier service shuttling between the two cities transporting remittances, parcels, and passengers. This venture, identified here by the fictitious name of Transportes García, is one of the many transportation services that exist in the Monterrey-Houston connection and one of the perhaps hundreds that undertake similar operations between the United States and Mexico. These small transportation companies are known in the Monterrey-Houston migratory circuit as *camionetas,* or passenger vans, describing the vehicles used to conduct these transborder activities. A key feature of these operations is the combination of multiple services under one roof: the delivery of cash remittances to the Monterrey homes of Houston-based immigrants; the shipping of parcels containing a wide variety of new and secondhand goods destined for household consumption and for sale at local swap meets; and the transport of small numbers of passengers. Before the advent of inexpensive cellular telephones and international calling cards, the *camionetas* used to carry correspondence between sojourners and stay-at-home members of migrant households and families. In fact, customers would euphemistically refer to the remittances as *las cartas* (the letters), since the cash would be delivered in an envelope that often contained a letter or a brief written message from the sender. On the way back to the United States, Transportes García would bring letters, medications requested by

Figure 7. International calling card advertisement
posted at an exchange booth near La Fama. Such
ads have become visible in recent years. Photograph
by Rubén Hernández-Léon.

those without ready access to health care, and tokens of appreciation for
the money just delivered by the courier, including food and beverages.

In this chapter, I begin by situating Monterrey and Houston in the
larger network of migration industry services available to sojourners in
the Mexico-U.S. migratory system. Partly because of their geographic
location and their salience as major urban centers in their respective
countries, both cities are actual hubs of the migration industry. I then
recount the origins of Transportes García and describe how the courier
business functioned, effectively connecting its binational clientele. In the

following two sections, I examine the relationship of this transport to the social network it primarily served, during "normal" times and then in the context of successive crises that led to the eventual shutdown of this particular operation. I argue that looking at the ups and downs of a specific venture, such as Transportes García, over several years provides unique insights into long-standing questions regarding the relationship between the migration industry and actors germane to the social process of international migration (i.e., immigrants, employers, states, and advocacy organizations).

## THE MIGRATION INDUSTRY IN MONTERREY AND HOUSTON

### Monterrey

In Monterrey, the migration industry is largely invisible. Still, this city—known nationally and internationally for its industrial capitalist trajectory—is a regional service center for the migration industry. Several geographic and social conditions allow for this role, including Monterrey's own proximity and long historic ties to the United States. Only two hours away from the border by car, La Sultana del Norte is the largest urban center in all of northern Mexico, the main transportation hub of the region and a gateway to Texas. For most long distance coach lines heading to and returning from the United States, the city and its bus depot are the obligated stop where vehicles refuel and change drivers and passengers board buses to their final destination in Mexico's interior. Geography has also turned this metropolitan center into a staging area for Central and South American undocumented transmigrants, suggesting that at least some of the services that facilitate these flows are located in this city and its hinterland.

Monterrey is also home to the U.S. Consulate that issues more work visas than any other worldwide—more than 66,000 in 2003 (Hennesy-Fiske 2004). The consular district includes the states of Nuevo León, Coahuila, Durango, San Luis Potosí, Zacatecas, and Aguascalientes, all with a long tradition of migration to the United States. This combination of circumstances makes the city a center for formal and informal recruitment, with agents identifying and processing candidates' applications for the H2A and H2B temporary work visas issued by the U.S. government. These recruiters provide different services to their customers, who include both workers and employers, from transportation to and lodging in Monterrey to assistance with the visa application process at the consulate and transportation to the worksite in the United States—all for various fees (Hennesy-Fiske 2004). Recruiters, or *enganchadores,* may be based in a city or in rural areas of a state with long-established migratory flows, operating from storefront offices or private homes. Some are most likely former participants of the temporary visa programs (Fitzgerald 2006a). Whether based in the city or the countryside, these *enganchadores* appear to have one thing in common: They both search for and sign up potential laborers in rural areas and not in the city itself, suggesting how U.S.-bound rural and urban migratory streams remain separate not spontaneously but as a result of the active involvement of migration entrepreneurs and other actors (see below). Early on in the midst of conducting fieldwork in La Fama, I encountered the presence of recruiters using homes in the neighborhood as part of operations that involved enrolling *ejidatarios* (communal land farmers) from the state of Coahuila for work in agriculture in Tennessee. Notably, these recruiters did not seek to enlist men from La Fama.

The U.S. Consulate in Monterrey also attracts a variety of paper pushers who fill out forms and promise visa applicants a speedy and successful bureaucratic process. These paper pushers are often the subject of police crackdowns but have apparently survived the advent of a system of consular appointments and interviews, which limits the exposure of visa applicants to certain intermediaries. There is also an ancillary industry of false Mexican documents—paycheck stubs, utility bills, social security contributions—which migrants utilize to satisfy their visa application requirements.

Monterrey is also the base for numerous human smugglers, or border-crossing *coyotes* or *polleros,* often seen by scholars as the archetypical figure of the migration industry. The *coyote* is a historical fixture of the northeast Mexico-Texas border, and even though both governments and media have portrayed smuggling as an increasingly complex, multinational enterprise, ethnographic studies suggest that in the case of Mexicans, this branch of the migration industry is still dominated by individuals who are firmly embedded in immigrant networks and who often are little more than experienced sojourners themselves (Spener 2004). Clearly, different types of *coyotes* operate in and around Monterrey, including rural-based smugglers who use the city merely as a transit point as well as those who service the urban networks studied in this book.

I met el Güero, a city-based *coyote* smuggling migrants from La Fama, during the early stages of my fieldwork in Houston, and I stayed in touch with him long after he left the business. In a manner that reveals how

*coyotes* pass as regular sojourners, when I first met him, el Güero introduced himself as a just another La Fama migrant in Houston. I did not
find out about his actual occupation until I started conducting research
in the neighborhood back in Monterrey. During one of my first visits, I
quickly found out that el Güero was in jail in a Texas border city, accused
of smuggling undocumented immigrants. When I interviewed him in his
home more than two years later, el Güero recounted the circumstances
of his arrest. He was leading a group of Monterrey and Mexico City
migrants around a well-known Border Patrol checkpoint on I-35 in south
Texas. To his surprise, the Border Patrol had set up a second checkpoint.
Once the group was detained, one of the sojourners, a man from Mexico
City, got scared and quickly identified el Güero as the smuggler. A few
days later, during court proceedings, el Güero pleaded guilty to charges
of smuggling undocumented migrants and spent eight months in jail near
Laredo, Texas. Since his release, he has returned to his wife and children
in Monterrey and started work as a truck driver.

Although analyzing el Güero's career as both migrant and smuggler is
beyond the goals of this section, it is worth noting that his case is typical
of many migration entrepreneurs, including the transportation business-
man studied in the remainder of this chapter. El Güero was a regular
migrant for many years, shuttling back and forth between Monterrey
and San Antonio and then Monterrey and Houston, working primarily in construction. The opportunity to get started as a *coyote* came to
him when a smuggler asked him to replace a guide who had become
ill. Selecting el Güero to complete the job was by no means arbitrary;
a longtime sojourner of this region, he knew the highways, backroads,
and ranches of south Texas, as he says, "como la palma de mi mano"
(like the back of my hand) (interview with el Güero 1999).

Like many migration entrepreneurs, el Güero was originally a member of the network he served, although he also smuggled individuals
outside this network (such as the migrant who told on him to the Border
Patrol). In his description of the smuggling business, el Güero emphasized the significance of trust between the *coyote* and the migrant, a
quality derived from their common membership in a bounded network
or community (usually the hometown or the *paisano*-kinship network). In this interview and subsequent encounters, he distinguished
between three kinds of *coyotes:* the rural smuggler, who often doubles
as a recruiter and contractor, offering migrants both clandestine border
crossing and work placement services; the urban-based *coyote*, embedded in a social network but often limiting his assistance to facilitating

illegal entry into the United States; and the border smuggler, not connected to the migrant through any particular set of social ties. According
to el Güero, it is the latter type who, absent any kind of trust cementing
his relationship to the sojourner, often preys on his clients, asking them
for advance payment and even victimizing them in transit to their destination in the United States (interview with el Güero 1999, 2000).

Illustrating how state actors might limit the field of action of *coyotes,*
recruiters, and allied intermediaries (Spener 2005), presenting them
with potential "competition," in 2005 the state government of Nuevo
León established the Oficina de Atención al Migrante (Office of Migrant
Affairs). The newly formed agency was charged with recruiting candidates in Nuevo León and other states for the H2B temporary worker
program of the United States. The office thus functioned like most
*enganchadores,* connecting Mexican job seekers with companies across
the border, chiefly in landscaping, hospitality, and reforestation industries, but without charging fees to the workers. The agency's staff holds
information sessions in the state's rural areas, maintains links with similar entities in other states, and helps H2B candidates apply for visas at
the American Consulate in Monterrey. On the demand side, the office
identifies potential employers taking advantage of the state secretary of
economic development's contacts with U.S. firms. These companies pay
for the interview and visa fees and for transportation of the individual
to the worksite in the United States. Still, according to the office's staff,
these same firms are often reticent to offer formal contracts to these
workers (author's notes 2005).

The government of Nuevo León is by no means alone in establishing a
state agency to run this type of mini–Bracero program. In fact, the states
of Jalisco and Zacatecas have implemented similar efforts since 2001
(Fitzgerald 2006a). However, two things are worth noting: first, the
office did not recruit in the city, something that would have infuriated
local industrialists and undermined the grand narrative of Monterrey as
an economic powerhouse attracting rather than shedding workers, and
second, as they conducted information and recruitment drives in rural
areas of the state, the agency's staff seemed quite careful not to step
too hard on the toes of well-entrenched *enganchadores.* Although it is
not clear what kinds of effects local state participation has had on the
activities of recruiters and how the latter have responded to government
intervention in the management of the H2B temporary worker program,
the potential for displacement of private agents was clear. Still, a complete dislocation was unlikely, given that the office's involvement was

reduced to the formal guest worker program and naturally limited by
the number of visas granted by the United States.

As one of the largest metropolitan areas in the country, Monterrey
is home to numerous households receiving remittances from the United
States. The 2000 Mexican census showed that in the nine metropolitan
municipalities combined, there are more than sixteen thousand households that benefit from such cash transfers (CONAPO 2002)—a figure
that places Monterrey above several states in the country in absolute
number of households taking delivery of remittances. More recently,
data from the Banco de México demonstrated that the rate of growth of
remittances in Nuevo León for the 2004–2006 period hovered around
25 percent, well above the national average (PNUD 2007).

While the remittance industry has come to be dominated by electronic
transfer companies (Banco de México 2007), the movement of remittances in kind has emerged as a potentially lucrative market. Interestingly,
Monterrey-based corporations, such as Cemex and Famsa, have flocked
to this new frontier, illustrating how the migration industry as a matrix
of economic activities comprises not only informal (and illegal) services
but also legitimate mainstream firms. The entry of these corporations
into the migration industry matrix stems from three factors, all unfolding in the 1990s: the internationalization of Mexican conglomerates
(Pozas 1993a, 2002); the geometric growth of the Mexican immigrant
population in the United States, which more than doubled during the
decade in question (Grieco 2003); and the inability of increasing numbers of undocumented workers to go back and forth across the border
due to heightened policing of the international boundary (Massey,
Durand, and Malone 2002). Mexico's cement giant, Cemex, has established a subsidiary called Construmex, which allows immigrants to purchase construction materials in the United States that can in turn be
picked up at any of its thousands of retail locations south of the border.
Customers still have to transfer the money through Construmex for a
nominal $1 transaction fee. The firm also offers free construction con-
sulting services to its clients, including planning and estimating building
costs and using designs developed by its own architects. In addition, in
partnership with several developers, Cemex has recently launched a pilot
program offering mortgages to immigrants who want to buy a house in
Mexico (Boudreaux 2003; http://www.cemexmexico.com/se/se_co.html,
accessed December 15, 2005; Reuters 2007).

Similarly, the appliance store Famsa offers its immigrant customers
the possibility of buying all sorts of items (from refrigerators to living

room furniture sets) at any of its U.S. outlets. These items can then be delivered anywhere in Mexico using Famsa's vast network of warehouses and stores, including one strategically located in La Fama's main shopping center. Tellingly, Famsa's sales slogan in the United States is "La Tienda sin Fronteras" (The Borderless Store). Still, rather than erasing borders, Cemex, Famsa, and other corporations, such as Elektra and Telmex, are capturing migrant savings even before they leave the United States by offering the transfer of remittances in-kind while capitalizing on their leading position in the Mexican market. Industry analysts have estimated the value of this emerging above-ground in-kind remittance market at $20 billion (Delaunay 2002).

Finally, as a regional capital of the migration industry, Monterrey has emerged as a transportation hub servicing not only U.S.-bound *regiomontano* migrants but also sojourners from many origins in northeast, north-central, and southeast Mexico. As an important connection of rail lines from the late 1800s onward and a recruitment center for braceros during the 1950s and 1960s, Monterrey had probably performed this nodal function for most of the twentieth century. Today, however, as buses and vans have replaced trains, the city has become headquarters to a number of transportation companies often established by entrepreneurial migrants tapping the needs of fellow international sojourners. This is the case of Autobuses Adame, a bus operation started by a Mexican migrant to service the Monterrey-Houston circuit. Using first his car and later a fleet of vans, Esteban Adame initiated his cross-border venture in the early 1980s, switching to buses ten years later. By the late 1990s, he had opened his own bus terminal in Houston and a similar bus station in Monterrey. He also established El Faisán, a separate bus company that transports passengers from the Monterrey terminal to locations in Mexico's interior. In addition to bus rides, Autobuses Adame offers money transfer and courier services, through which customers can send correspondence and documents to any of its multiple destinations (Moreno 2003)

In early 2003, Autobuses Adame had a fleet of fifty buses, with eleven offices in the United States and eight in Mexico, and provided transportation services to 180,000 people yearly in the two countries. In newspaper accounts, Adame reported annual revenues of $13.5 million from the bus service and $1.5 million from the remittance business (Moreno 2003). My own observations in Texas and Georgia suggest that Autobuses Adame has enjoyed a tremendous expansion as a result of the opening of the southeast as the new frontier of Mexican immigration in the United States. With Houston as its U.S. base, Adame's destinations now include the Atlanta metropolitan area, Nashville, and cities and towns in North Carolina and Virginia, where the company owns terminals or shares bus depots with other firms specializing in the immigrant market (Borden 2004). In one of my last fieldwork stints in Monterrey in early 2006, I found out that Autobuses Adame had established an alliance with Autobuses Ejecutivos and Omnibuses Mexicanos, two firms with a dominant position in the Mexican interstate bus system. This alliance underscores how large corporations are seeking to establish a foothold in the expanding immigrant transportation market (also see Posada García 2005).

Still, coach lines do not have the monopoly on land transportation in the Monterrey-Houston circuit. Courier services, typically using small fleets of vans, compete with bus companies by specializing in particular networks and clusters of neighborhoods of the Monterrey metropolitan area. As the story of Autobuses Adame shows, some of these van operations have been the startup version of current full-blown bus firms. However, the *camionetas* remain a distinct kind of service offered by migration entrepreneurs in this circuit.

## Houston

Over the past twenty years, Houston has emerged as a major hub of the migration industry in the Mexico-U.S. migratory system—a development that stems from Houston's own geographic proximity to Mexico and the city's newly found place as the third-largest concentration of Mexicans in the United States, the distribution center of Mexican labor for the Southeast, and the gateway to the larger eastern seaboard. Needless to say, as the chief destination of U.S.-bound *regiomontanos,* the Bayou City also hosts services and entrepreneurs specializing exclusively in the Monterrey-Houston circuit.

As in the case of cities and towns with sizable immigrant populations across the United States, an array of migration industry services are concentrated in Houston's Mexican neighborhoods. In the Bayou City, no other place reflects this phenomenon more clearly than Magnolia, the historic Mexican neighborhood adjoining the Houston shipping channel. Here, newcomers can locate the services of smugglers, contractors, formal and informal transportation operators, remittance firms, travel agents, lawyers and notaries offering legal and paralegal advice, individuals producing fake papers, telecommunications agencies to stay in touch with friends and relatives across the border, grocers and check-cashing establishments catering to the clandestine segment of the immigrant population, and ethnic realtors offering rentals and homes for sale to both documented and undocumented Mexicans. There are emerging clusters of migration industry services in the more recently established Mexican ethnoburbs of northwest Houston, including Summerland, but they still lack the density of businesses observed in historic neighborhoods.

An area in which the stations and small storefront offices of bus and *camioneta* services are concentrated, Harrisburg Boulevard is the center of migration industry entrepreneurial activities in Magnolia. Many of the transportation services located along this thoroughfare are among the oldest and most established operations in the city. As figures 8 and 9 show, these are "above ground" firms which advertise in local Spanish newspapers and offer multiple services, including transportation, wire transfers, and remittance and parcel delivery in Mexico. An examination of these ads suggests that the overwhelming majority of firms transporting passengers to Mexico use coaches, while businesses offering transportation to U.S. inland destinations utilize vans.[2]

The distinction between bus and van transportation operations and their sharply different destinations reveal aspects of the social organization, division of labor, and geography of this segment of the migration industry. While the highly regulated and expensive-to-operate coach lines appear to focus on the cross-border market, linking Houston to a handful of preestablished locations in Mexico along clearly defined routes (usually reflecting one or more migratory circuits), the small and often informal van operations perform an entirely different function, namely, the distribution of Mexican immigrant workers from the Bayou City to numerous labor markets along the eastern seaboard, the Midwest, and even California. Thus, the vans offer a great deal of flexibility in terms of specific destinations, often advertising the names of states instead of cities and towns (with the exception of large metropolitan areas). To be clear, these van services are not entirely new; on the contrary, for decades, they have offered their services to immigrants toiling in agricultural labor markets in the way of the more informal *raiteros* (ride providers) and *troqueros* (truck drivers) (Griffith and Kissam 1995).[3]

However, two important developments have changed the role of van transportation operations and perhaps have even boosted their numbers.[4] The first of such developments is the rise of new destinations of Mexican immigration, particularly in the northeast, mid-Atlantic, southeast, and Midwest regions. As millions of Mexican newcomers moved to urban and rural destinations in these vast areas starting in the late 1980s, Houston became not only a gateway into the United States

Figure 8. *Camioneta* advertisements from a Houston newspaper. These companies link Houston with destinations in the U.S. interior. Photograph by Rubén Hernández-Léon.

but also an entryway into these regions. As a result, new van companies have emerged, transporting immigrants to a long list of uncharted urban labor markets for Mexicans, including Miami, Atlanta, Durham and Raleigh in North Carolina, Washington, D.C., New York City, and Boston. Needless to say, this transformation has also attracted the participation of a few bus operators, such as the aforementioned Autobuses Adame, and a handful of other firms offering services on both sides of the border (i.e., El Conejo, El Expresso).[5]

A second development has to do with the aftermath of the 9/11 terrorist attacks. *Camionetas* traveling to internal destinations have become a preferred means of transportation for undocumented sojourners who are now forced to avoid the stringent vigilance of airports. Not only are police and customs and immigration agents ever more conspicuous at the country's airports, but since 9/11 and the enactment of the Patriot Act, it is a federal crime to use false documents as proof of identification at airline counters and security checkpoints. Van lines do not ask riders

Figure 9. Bus line advertisements from a Houston
newspaper. Buses link Houston with localities in
the Mexican interior. The firms also offer remittance
services. Photograph by Rubén Hernández-Léon.

for any kind of documentation, nor are they required by law to do so. In
exchange, they charge their customers sums of money that easily dwarf
the cost of airfare. In 2005, a one-way van trip from Houston to Los
Angeles could cost between $350 and $400. These fees reflect less the
cost of long-distance land transportation than the price of special services
van operators offer their customers, such as the significant knowledge
drivers have accumulated about the location of Border Patrol checkpoints on major highways and about the alternative back roads used to
avoid them. Thus, van services specializing in domestic destinations in the
United States appear to assist undocumented immigrants in circumventing
the roadblocks to mobility set up by the receiving state that extend well
beyond the border (see Valenzuela, Schweitzer, and Robles 2005 for a
similar conclusion).[6] Evidently, in the division of labor between buses and

vans, bus companies traveling across the international boundary, through established ports of entry and along major highways, cater to legal border crossers, while van lines specialize in clandestine immigrants who seek a low profile while trying to reach destinations in the U.S. interior.

Van courier services such as Transportes García combine some of the features of both bus and van passenger services. Like bus companies, they specialize in the cross-border market of services; and like their van counterparts traveling to the U.S. interior, they are largely informal operations.

## THE SOCIAL ORGANIZATION OF A MIGRATION INDUSTRY BUSINESS: THE CASE OF TRANSPORTES GARCÍA

### The Origin and Operation of Transportes García

Like many migration entrepreneurs who emerge from the ranks of the newcomer group, Jorge García first got started in the Monterrey-Houston circuit as a regular labor migrant. He arrived in Houston in 1979, following his father and two siblings who had made the trip earlier in the decade. They were part of the flow of skilled and semiskilled industrial workers who started migrating to Houston during the 1970s and early 1980s and who found employment in the city's booming economy in companies specializing in petrochemicals, oil and gas extraction, and oil technology. First recruited by agents of these expanding industries and later displaced by the contraction and restructuring of heavy manufacturing in Monterrey, these workers had already acquired the necessary skills to become machinists, industrial welders, and maintenance mechanics in the Houston metropolitan economy back in Monterrey. Thus, after several years of employment in a machine repair company servicing textile factories in Monterrey, Jorge García moved to Houston to work a numeric control machine in a shop that produced turbines for NASA.

Jorge's remittance transportation business practically began as an extension of his frequent visits to Monterrey. The relative geographic proximity of Houston and Monterrey made it possible for him to travel home regularly, leaving Houston on Friday night and returning Monday morning. The frequency and regularity of his visits quickly became public knowledge among *regiomontano* migrants settled in the northwest Mexican ethnoburbs of Houston where he lived. These migrants started to finance Jorge's gasoline costs in exchange for the transport and delivery of packages to family members in Monterrey. Soon after initiating these exchanges, he became aware of the lucrative business prospects that this activity held, including the perceived benefits of self-employment. Transportes García began operating as such in 1982. However, Jorge did not leave his salaried post right away: For four years he combined his job as a machinist with his emerging transportation business until the latter absorbed most of his time. The growing success of this small company allowed him to quit the shop and work full time in the transport of money and correspondence. The evolving infrastructure of Jorge's company reflects the origins and development of his business over more than fifteen years of operation. His first trips were made in his own car until he purchased two vans. These more spacious vehicles provided him with the opportunity to not only transport money and correspondence but also parcels and, to a lesser extent, passengers. In 1997, Jorge replaced his old vans with two recent models he used to do the traveling between Houston and Monterrey. At that point, the old vans were kept in Monterrey and used exclusively for the delivery of remittances and other items in La Sultana del Norte.

One of Houston's local neighborhood parks was Transportes García's first center of operation. Here, Jorge collected and organized envelopes with money, correspondence, and packages with a variety of items that Monterrey migrants were sending to their families. After seven years of having utilized the park as a site for his activities, two policemen forced him to leave the park area. It is worth noting this encounter with agents of the receiving state, who clamped down on the operation's obvious informality and partly chartered the small firm's resulting step. Following this forced removal, Jorge decided to lease a small office located at the back of a Mexican restaurant on one of the main streets in northwest Houston, paying $350 for monthly rent. After operating out of this space for a few years, Jorge had to move the business to a similar locale in a small commercial strip along the same avenue and then again to another shopping center near his house. The reason for these moves was basically the same: Both the back of the Mexican restaurant and the commercial strip where the business was located did not have the capacity to accommodate the flow of customers and vehicles stopping by the office during the days the *camionetas* were set to leave for Monterrey.

Jorge García's passenger vans used to make two trips between Houston and Monterrey every week. Every Friday and Monday afternoon, families and single men gathered in the small office and parking lot to drop off the money to be remitted to their relatives living in the Monterrey metropolitan area. Others stopped by to leave a parcel or to ask why a particular item had not been delivered back home. According to Jorge, the Friday trip was the more important of the two conducted every week because of the many persons who received their paychecks and were ready to send part of their salary to Mexico on that day. Inside the office, in Houston, Jorge, his wife and oldest son, a niece, a brother-in-law, and two to three assistants worked on the recording and organizing of the shipments. Thus, the business was fundamentally a family operation. Jorge, his wife, and his niece personally handled the money and correspondence.[7] The employees were in charge of placing boxes, packages, and bags in the van and a small trailer, and one of them was responsible for driving the vehicle. It is worth noting that these assistants were all from the same neighborhood where Jorge grew up in Monterrey, once again pointing to the significance of the urban barrio in the organization of networks and contacts that support city-origin migration from Mexico to the United States.

The system used to ship the money deserves a detailed description since it illustrates significant aspects of the informal nature of the operation and its significance as an example of the migration industry facilitating the movement of cash, goods, and people in the Monterrey-Houston circuit. The money handed in by each customer was counted by Jorge and his wife and placed in an envelope. A letter or brief written message frequently accompanied these cash remittances. Once the envelope was sealed, the address of the person receiving the shipment in Monterrey would be written on the outside as well as the dollar amount to be remitted. Jorge and his wife did not extend any receipts to their clients, although his niece registered the names of the sender, the beneficiary, and the total sum in a logbook. Again, the sender did not keep any receipt or slip acknowledging the shipment. When the delivery person arrived at the home of the recipient in Monterrey, he required the customer to count the money in front of him to make sure that the figure written on the outside of the envelope matched the actual cash amount. Then the recipient was asked to sign the front of the empty envelope, which served as proof that the money had arrived safely in the hands of family members in Monterrey.

Thus, the *camionetas* traveled the highways that connect Houston and the capital of Nuevo León every Friday and Monday night. The trip would take approximately ten hours, but sometimes the border checkpoints could add two or three additional hours to the journey. Jorge used to make one of the two weekly trips, while his assistants were responsible for the other one. Upon arrival in Monterrey the following morning, the passenger van proceeded to the Mexico "office" of the small company, a house that Jorge bought for his father to spend the last days of his life in under the care of his sisters. The second fundamental phase of the small transportation business was conducted here: Another brother-in-law, a sister, and a nephew were in charge of delivering the envelopes with money, letters, and parcels. They were also responsible for classifying the shipments according to their destination in the metropolitan area. Nevertheless, some clients would prefer to go directly to the house to pick up *las cartas* from Houston. The delivery would begin once the envelopes and parcels had been classified and placed in the older vans. The actual delivery routes of Transportes García evidenced that this small company specialized in distinct migratory networks located in two metropolitan municipalities. Of the two-van fleet dedicated to the distribution of shipments to the nine Monterrey municipalities, one was solely used for the delivery of packages in two of these municipalities while the other was utilized to transport items to the remaining metropolitan districts. In other words, this *camioneta* business catered to clusters of households and neighborhoods, connected to each other not by accident but as a result of the strong and weak ties channeling migrants to the Bayou City in the first place.

How much money in cash remittances did Transportes García move between the two cities, and how many households and families did it serve? According to Jorge, his small transportation company mobilized some $40,000 from Houston to Monterrey every week. His clients in Houston remitted an average of $200 per *carta,* with the *camionetas'* two weekly trips making a minimum of two hundred deliveries. The number of deliveries, however, is not commensurate with the total number of families and households using this service. Jorge García's clientele was composed of regular as well as more occasional customers. Regular clients, those who would send money every week, were most likely members of *casas divididas* (divided households), where an immigrant breadwinner had left behind his or her dependents in Monterrey, usually a spouse, children, and, in some cases, aging parents who relied on the income remitted from Houston.[8] Most of those who sent cash intermittently were individuals who had immigrated with their entire nuclear family. This type of customers remitted $50 a month on average, sometimes responding to an emergency occurring within the extended family or to some other special occasion. The total amount of money the *camionetas* moved reached as much as $60,000 during particular times of the year. For example, in April and May, larger sums would be sent home

because migrants remitted their tax refunds to Monterrey. Another reason for the increase in remittances during the month of May was the
celebration of Mother's Day in Mexico. Similarly, December was a peak
time for remittances because of the Christmas holiday.

Participant observation I conducted at the home office in Monterrey
and during the vans' delivery trips throughout the metropolitan area indicates that families received anywhere between $70 and $400 from their
relatives in Houston. There was little difference in service costs for varying amounts of cash delivered: Clients in Houston would send up to $300
for a $10 fee; up to $500 for $12; up to $700 for $15; and up to $1,000
for $20. However, the most important features of the service, from the
point of view of migrants, were that the funds were delivered the next day
in cash (and in dollars) and that they arrived directly to the family home
in Monterrey. Thus, cost was one of the obvious differences between this
small transportation company and wire-transfer services such as Western
Union. In 1998, sending $500 to Mexico through Western Union could
cost between $70 and $80, considering fees and the hidden costs of an
unfavorable exchange rate (see García, Levander, and Sandoval 1998).

Even though the movement of remittances in cash was the main line
of business of Transportes García, the transport of items and merchandise used in daily household consumption was also an important part
of the operation. These goods were actually remittances sent in kind.
Shipping *paquetería* (parcels) was less profitable for Jorge and considerably more troublesome than transporting cash remittances (see below).
However, this activity had great significance for the material and symbolic reproduction of the Monterrey-Houston migrant circuit. In any
given trip, the *camionetas* carried an average of forty *paquetería* deliveries. In Monterrey, an array of goods ready to be distributed throughout
the metropolitan area littered the front of the home base, the sidewalk,
and the street and occupied much space in the vans and trailers used to
transport these items: clothes and shoes; coolers full of chicken, milk,
and orange juice; bags of tortillas; television sets; toys; bicycles; chairs;
lamps; air conditioners; stereos; and car tires.[9] Other types of items were
present as well: heaters, refrigerators, living room furniture, and washing machines and dryers. On the way back to Houston, the van would
take a variety of items that family members in Mexico had sent to their
relatives in the United States. Aside from correspondence, food, flour
tortillas, medicine, Mexican beer, and local soft drinks were the articles
most frequently shipped to Texas.[10]

In the eyes of those who sent and received these objects, whether in Houston or Monterrey, the items not only possessed discrete and material value (for immediate or long-term household consumption or productive or leisurely utilization) but were also endowed with symbolic meaning. To me, the presence of some of these items among the *paquetería* cargo of Transportes García was at first puzzling. For instance, some immigrants in Houston sent corn tortillas to Mexico. In turn, some people in Monterrey sent locally produced Coke and other bottled soft drinks to the United States. When these sodas were consumed, the crate with empty bottles would make a trip back to Monterrey for refill. Once these bottles were exchanged for full ones, the *Cocas, Joyas,* and *Topo Chicos* began their journey back north aboard the *camionetas.* These seemingly misplaced and redundant objects (i.e., U.S.-made tortillas in Mexico, Mexican soft drinks in the United States) provides symbolic continuity to a population that inhabits a discontinuous geographic space, establishing links between families, households, and groups of friends of distant cities located in two nation-states. Because individuals conduct social interactions through objects and artifacts (Boruchoff 1999), sending goods (even if they were of little monetary value) allowed persons living and working in one place to assert a symbolic presence in another while claiming participation in the daily lives of distant family members. Thus, the shipping of a secondhand stove or a bundle of used clothes to Monterrey allowed a person to contribute to the daily reproduction of a family back home, while the sending of local foods and beverages to Houston permitted the expression of gratitude. The case of Transportes García shows how the migration industry not only facilitates human mobility across borders but also helps realize material and symbolic goals associated with international migration.

Jorge's *camionetas* also transported passengers back and forth between Monterrey and Houston. Eight or nine people would make the one-way trip in the van. These clients were usually residents of the two neighboring metropolitan municipalities in which the small company specialized. The transportation of passengers was a facet of the business that Jorge had tried to develop in the past with little success. A few years back, he had purchased a minibus but was forced to sell it because he could not make his insurance payments. As explained above, small, informal businesses like Jorge's compete with larger, "above-ground" companies that concentrate on the passenger market and on routes connecting Houston and other cities in the United States with cities and towns in Mexico's interior. These companies utilize large coaches instead of vans, offering daily departures to multiple destinations. However,

most of them are still located in Magnolia, the historic Mexican neighborhood in Houston, far from the area where Jorge operated and where
many recently arrived Mexican immigrants have settled, effectively shel-
tering Transportes García from direct competition.

Over the years, Jorge and his employees developed specific funds of
knowledge (Vélez-Ibáñez and Greenberg 1992) that eased their workload and allowed them to keep costs down. These funds of knowledge
consisted of strategies to efficiently and effectively transport thousands
of dollars in cash and merchandise across the border and to manage the
risks involved in this operation. Although Jorge and his drivers were
legal residents of the United States and could go back and forth at will,
crossing the international boundary with money, mostly used goods,
passengers, and no formal permit to conduct these activities required a
constant interaction and negotiation with customs agents and other officials at different ports of entry along the Texas-Mexico border.

For instance, one particular fund of knowledge had to do with the
management of interactions with Mexican customs and highway police
and being able to choose alternative ports of entry when customs agents
wanted to extract excessive bribes to allow the van's cargo to come into
Mexico. As it is shown in detail below, such negotiations were not always
successful, occasionally provoking critical incidents that compromised the
viability of the entire business. Another important knowledge reserve was
related to the familiarity with the urban geography of the two metropolitan areas. Jorge and his employees developed substantial expertise on the
geographic location of migrant households in Houston and Monterrey,
which was used to drop off the *cartas* containing remittances, packages,
and passengers directly to clients' homes. There were other skills that
made up this repertoire of knowledge and that were particular to the
characteristics of the small company: learning how to fix the mechanical
malfunctions of the vans, knowing how to solve the occasional loss of
money and packages, and satisfactorily administering the operation.

## Social Capital and Network Membership in the Initiation of a Migration Industry Business

What allowed for Jorge's transformation from a wage worker into a
migration industry entrepreneur? A fundamental precondition was the
gradual emergence of an actual migratory circuit linking Houston and
Monterrey in the 1970s and 1980s, that is, a critical mass of the Monterrey immigrant population in the Bayou City and a growing density of

its networks and activities. Second, Jorge's ability to become one of such entrepreneurs stemmed not from his personal attributes but rather from his membership in the network of immigrant industrial workers from Monterrey, namely, from his social capital. It was his membership in this network that allowed him to identify the needs of fellow *regiomontanos* and to detect the opportunity to make money as these immigrants sought to remit funds, send correspondence and parcels, and travel back home. In other words, Jorge, as opposed to an outsider, was particularly well positioned to take advantage of the potential business opportunity embedded in the social practices of these newcomers.[11]

But when Jorge García decided to turn his social capital into a launching pad for a business operation, he also changed the terms of his nexus to fellow migrants, which shifted from feelings of trust, reciprocity, and solidarity to the expectations of efficiency and effectiveness that characterize a commercial transaction. There is no doubt, then, that the prolonged survival of Transportes García had to do with the efficiency and low cost of the multiple services that Jorge and his assistants provided to customers. Like the Salvadoran *viajeros* (travelers) studied by Mahler (1999), the *camionetas* continued existence as a successful small-business operation was largely anchored on such efficiency and not solely on personal relations based on trust (i.e., between Jorge and his clients–fellow immigrants). Jorge himself acknowledged that it was the regularity and uninterrupted character of his services that attracted and kept the patronage of other *regiomontanos*. For instance, he emphatically asserted that his passenger vans *never* skipped the Friday trip to Monterrey, since this was the day when most migrants cashed their weekly checks and remitted money to their families in Mexico. Thus, even though Jorge's ability to initiate his remittances business was intimately connected to his relationship with fellow immigrants from Monterrey, as the nature of his relationship to them changed (from *paisanos* to customers) and the circle of clients expanded over time, the entire enterprise became dependent on the ability to deliver a service and not on trust and personal acquaintance. From just another member of the network with access to free resources to be used in case of need, Jorge García became the successful owner of a profit-seeking enterprise.

In my interviews with Jorge, he often produced an account of his migration industry enterprise that described his clients' trust in him and the moral obligation he felt toward his clients and the members of the extended family employed in the business. He explained these notions with the example of the secondhand items that people shipped from Houston to Monterrey. During an interview at a Houston restaurant, Jorge and his brother-in-law argued about whether they would have to raise the fees charged for the *paquetería* service to make the shipment of parcels a profitable activity. Most of these fees were utilized at the border to bribe Mexican customs officials. This was necessary because people sent mostly used goods, such as secondhand clothing, that could not be legally introduced into Mexico. Jorge saw two impediments to a service fee increase. First, his clients tended to remit items with very little or no commercial value, making it difficult to estimate the appropriate levy. Second, he stated that to make a profit with the parcels, he needed to charge $50 to $60 for small packages for which he was currently asking $10 to $12. In his view, immigrants earning $250 a week could not pay such an amount. He concluded that the trust and moral obligation that he felt toward the people that used Transportes García prevented him from raising the prices for shipping parcels. I interpret the motives provided in this account not as the real reason why prices of parcel shipping could not be increased but as part of Jorge's moral self-justification for what in the end was an economic decision.[12] As shown below, eliminating or even scaling down the parcel part of the business compromised the remittance segment of the venture (the most profitable one, in fact), as many customers patronized Transportes García because of the multiple services it offered, including its low cost and virtually duty-free package shipping service.

In contrast to Jorge's moral account, his customers and employees—members of the same migratory network—verbalized a different view of him and his operation. One of his customers reasoned that people used this and similar services simply because they did not want to pay the import taxes (on parcels sent to Mexico) and higher fees charged by formal courier and remittance firms. Others even argued that Jorge García was taking advantage of his customers by not delivering the exact amounts of cash remitted from Houston and by losing large sums of money and parcels quite often. One interviewee contended that Jorge García had been using the remittance business as a front to smuggle large numbers of goods, such as computer monitors, without having to pay taxes.

One of the drivers who used to deliver remittances and parcels in Monterrey also provided a dissonant account of the business, exposing some of the internal cleavages of Transportes García. The circumstances in which I talked to him helped reveal these inner tensions. I had gotten permission from Jorge to ride with the driver, Andrés, throughout his delivery route, which included La Fama and the two municipalities where most customers lived. Gustavo, Jorge's brother-in-law, was going to cover the rest of the metropolitan area. Andrés had seen me talking to Jorge during my visits to the *camionetas* home base in Monterrey, and so he immediately suspected that I was spying on him on behalf of the owner. Although Andrés did not say this, I could sense his discomfort from his body language and from the many questions he asked about what I was doing. Only after we spent several hours together and after lengthy explanations on my part about the purpose of my activities did he appear to soften his original reluctance, confessing his suspicion that I was Jorge's spy, ready to tell on him. Helping Andrés unload boxes, television sets, and other heavy items from the van and into clients' homes also contributed to establishing trust between us.

Andrés told me that customers had complained to Jorge about missing money, including lost envelopes and incomplete remittances. In fact, while assisting him along the delivery route, I witnessed how clients confronted Andrés about partial transfers and missing cash. Andrés believed that Gustavo was taking money from the envelopes for his own use when Jorge was late paying his salary without informing him (Jorge) of his actions. Throughout the day, Andrés bitterly complained about his low pay, about having to withstand a great deal of downtime as he waited for the arrival of the *camionetas* from Houston, and about having to use his own vehicle to make the deliveries. Although Jorge provided him with money for gas, the wear and tear on his already old pickup truck were not covered. Needless to say, all of these dynamics raised tensions and provoked distrust, especially between Andrés and Jorge. Soon after this conversation, Andrés left Transportes García.

These dissonant interpretations of the same business activity reflected cleavages that had unfolded as Jorge García became a successful entrepreneur. Even though he had been able to identify and pursue a business opportunity, thanks to his social capital, the profit-seeking nature of his flourishing venture had set him apart from the largely horizontal network of industrial workers from Monterrey. The consequences of such a cleavage would not show up until the operation faced its most critical juncture.

### The Demise of Transportes García: The Role of Sending and Receiving States

How do sending and receiving states affect the social organization, success, and demise of migration industry ventures such as Transportes García? The description of the origins and mode of operation of Jorge

García's business might suggest that this *camioneta* service was the text-book example of the ethnic economy enterprise developed by immigrants with the assistance of their networks and social capital. But I argue that Transportes García was more than an ethnic enterprise. As a migration industry business, this courier and passenger transport firm was part of the social and economic infrastructure that facilitates the mobility of people and monetary and in-kind remittances across international borders. Furthermore, Jorge and his Transportes García took advantage of the distinct and uneven institutional realities of the two countries to stay in business for nearly twenty years—often straddling a formal and informal existence in the United States but always operating informally in Mexico. As described before, Jorge regularly bribed Mexican customs officials at various ports of entry along the Texas-Mexico border to bring cash and parcels into the country with minimal inspection. On one occasion, while at his home base in Monterrey, Jorge was approached by a low-level representative of the Ministry of the Treasury who tried to get him to register his business or face fines and other penalties. Unable to bribe him, Jorge's response was to "hire" a local policeman to intimi-date him and drive him out of the neighborhood.

Clearly, the different institutional realities of the two countries cre-ated opportunities for Jorge García and his employees, shaping the orga-nization and strategies of the operation. But at the same time, frequent interactions with state officials, especially at the border, created risks.[13] One of these encounters in the late 1990s brought the *camionetas* to the brink of bankruptcy. On that particular occasion, U.S. customs agents in Laredo, Texas, seized $27,000 in remittances that Transportes García was taking to Monterrey. The agents confiscated the money because it exceeded the $10,000 in cash that a person is allowed to take outside the United States without declaring it to customs. This problem had been solved in the past by having one or two assistants take part of the funds (while the rest was kept in the van) and walk across the border to get on the vehicle again on the Mexican side. Jorge was not traveling with the van at the time this incident happened, and when the customs officer asked the driver how much currency he was transporting in cash and he hesitated, stating that he did not know, the agents moved in, counted the whole amount, and confiscated the money. It is worth not-ing that although Texas authorities often fine bus and *camioneta* firms for engaging in currency transportation without the proper permits, local state officials do not confiscate either funds or vehicles—something their federal counterparts obviously do.[14]

Even before trying to get the remittances back from U.S. customs, Jorge had to figure out how to deliver the money to the families in Monterrey. The incident had occurred during the weekend, and he could not withdraw large sums of cash from a bank's ATM. In light of this situation, Jorge asked some of his clients to wait a few days until he could either manage to get the remittances back or pool some funds together. According to him, most of his customers did not accept this proposition and asked to have their remittances handed over to them immediately. Only a few agreed to his request. Such a reaction led Jorge to a rather discouraging conclusion: People were not returning in kind the support and favors that he had extended to many of them over the years. Jorge was nonetheless able to borrow $11,000 from a *compadre,* which he pooled together with some savings to deliver the remittances to his clients in Monterrey. Nonetheless, the confiscation of the money put him under such financial strain that he considered leaving the remittance transportation business altogether. In order to retrieve the $27,000 from customs, Jorge had to hire a lawyer, who charged him $3,000, and to pay a $4,000 fine. In the end, with other expenses tallied, the incident had cost him $8,000. The viability of the business was also in doubt because, as a reaction to these events, a sizable number of customers stopped utilizing the services of Transportes García. The drop in the number of deliveries was significant: from a normal average of one hundred to one hundred twenty remittances to only thirty to forty after the border episode took place. As a consequence, Jorge's earnings had dropped to about $200 to $300 per trip.

To make things worse, all of Jorge's vehicles started to break down at nearly the same time. These circumstances forced him not only to spend additional money to fix them but also to temporarily halt the shipping of packages. Since they could not get their parcels delivered, many customers decided not to use the *camionetas* to send remittances. Not surprisingly, when Jorge openly expressed to individual clients the possibility of ending the remittance transportation service—an interaction I witnessed at a cantina in La Fama—many urged him to continue with the operation.

To cope with the financial problems derived from these events, Jorge began to consider selling one of the houses that he had bought in Monterrey—the home where his father had lived until his death. This was the house that Transportes García used as a home base and also where his sister, Beatriz, and brother-in-law, Gustavo, were living with their children. When he mentioned the idea to them, they rejected it immediately, arguing that this was their home. Jorge had actually registered the property title under Beatriz's name, and there was little he could do, given that she appeared as the legal owner of the house. Needless to say, Jorge's proposition to sell this asset provoked heightened conflict within the extended family, evidencing underlying tensions and contradictions. Although all of these individuals participated in the operation of the *camioneta* business and were members of the network of migrants of the Monterrey-Houston circuit, there were significant differences in the sharing of power and resources among them. Lacking any kind of migratory experience, Jorge's sister and brother-in-law were subordinate to him in various ways; they depended on him for living quarters and for wages, as Gustavo worked for him delivering the shipments and had no other source of income. But tensions were not new to the family. Jorge had been thinking about removing Gustavo from the reception and delivery of remittances in Monterrey because his brother-in-law had been taking cash for his own use without notifying him. When remittances were missing, Jorge had to put back money from his own pocket. Still, firing Gustavo was not an easy thing to do, given that Jorge himself acknowledged his sister's and brother-in-law's dependence on the income provided by Transportes García.

The small transportation company survived this prolonged crisis that nearly drove it out of business, but not for long. Customers continued to use the service, and the number of remittances sent regained its normal level. Gustavo stayed in charge of delivering *cartas* and parcels in Monterrey, even as both he and his wife reasserted their right to the house and blocked any efforts on the part of Jorge to sell it. Moreover, the house remained the home base of the *camionetas* in Mexico. Nevertheless, similar problems continued to emerge, underscoring the risks of the constant interface with state officials on both sides of the border. Agents of the Mexican Ministry of Communications and Transportation seized one of Jorge's vans because he did not have the permit and insurance to transport passengers. Although these encounters with state officials were not new, the outcome confirmed the perilous effect of regulation on this informal migration industry enterprise. In a separate incident, U.S. authorities had jailed Jorge's most reliable driver and a friend as they were trying to introduce an American car into Mexico. Jorge had been paid by the owner of the vehicle to take it to Mexico to probably sell it there—an illegal but rather common practice. Although the title documents of the car were in order, the two men were detained. Jorge realized that the owner of the vehicle, in a clear abuse of his trust, had reported the car as stolen, with the purpose of claiming the value of the automobile from the insurance company. Given his indirect responsibility in the affair, Jorge felt compelled to pay the $15,000 bail bond to set the two men temporarily free.

Shortly after this string of incidents, Transportes García went out of business. Still, just as important was the way in which it ceased operating. According to customers and acquaintances of Jorge García, the final months of the courier service's operation were fraught with conflict between him and his employees, on the one hand, and between him and his clientele, on the other. A fellow *regiomontano* and longtime patron claimed, "Jorge and his crew were stealing from people" and that, "at the end, folks were constantly complaining to him." As Transportes García closed down, Jorge disconnected his phone and basically "disappeared" from sight. Although he was still living in town, his new low-key profile appeared to be the result of missing money he owed to his former customers. One interviewee stated that he had momentarily seen Jorge and that he had gone back to do factory work in Houston. I later found out that the house used as the home base of the *camionetas* in Monterrey had been sold and that Beatriz and Gustavo had moved to Houston.

## CONCLUSION

The shutdown of Transportes García did not leave the migrants from La Fama and surrounding neighborhoods without a *camioneta* service to tend to their remittance and transportation needs. Immediately after the closing of Jorge García's business, at least two others sprung up to replace this long-established operation. Both were set up by "insiders" of the Monterrey-Houston migratory network: One was established by Jorge's most trusted driver, while the other was launched by Antonio and Raquel, the couple introduced in the previous chapter. During a 2003 visit to the Summerland area of Houston, I identified yet another service, also founded by a *regiomontano* and also specializing in distributing *cartas* and parcels in La Fama and the westernmost districts of the Monterrey metropolitan area.

The fact that not one but several *camioneta* operations emerged as Transportes García went out of business attests to the persistence and growth of the migration industry. The reason why only *regiomontano* migrants and no "outsiders" took advantage of the chance to launch a similar venture had to do with the highly embedded nature of this money-making opportunity. Just like Jorge García himself, all of the new migration entrepreneurs arising in his wake were members of the same social network as their clients, were acquainted with the needs of fellow migrants, and had a sense of how to satisfy them in a cost-effective manner. At the same time, they were all aware of the juncture opened by the failure of Transportes García. Still, the ultimate reason why all of them flocked to seize the opportunity was clear: This was simply a highly profitable venture.

Even though I never got a firm answer from Jorge García regarding what kind of profit margin he was making on each trip, one of his successors did share this information with me. Antonio, the asbestos laborer who threw a lavish *quinceañera* party for his daughter, told me that he could make $1,000 profit on a single trip (or $4,000 a month, as a result of four weekend trips). It is evident that even for a "reluctant" *camionetero* like Antonio, who always downplayed his incursion in the business and never quit his regular job in asbestos removal, these were handsome earnings. Indeed, two years after he became one of Jorge's successors and despite the fact that he serviced a small number of clients on his weekly trip to Monterrey, Antonio, his wife, Raquel, and their four children were able to move from the rundown apartment where they had lived for more than a decade into a single-family home. As related in chapter 4, profits from the van courier operation also helped pay for his daughter's $10,000 *quinceaños* celebration. Still, neither Antonio's insider status nor the sheer profitability of the opportunity was enough to guarantee a successful and durable business operation. The financial and personal cost of two highway accidents—one in 2003 in Mexico and another in 2005 in Texas—ended up driving Antonio out of business, narrowing the number of *camioneta* providers specializing in La Fama to two.

But the *camionetas* that link the urban neighborhoods of Houston and Monterrey are part of a larger matrix of businesses catering to the mobility, communication, legal, and financial needs of immigrants and their families and households on both sides of the border. This matrix—the migration industry—is not getting smaller. On the contrary, it is growing and becoming more varied. In addition to the migration industry entrepreneurs and businesses rooted in the Monterrey-Houston circuit (or entrepreneurs using these cities to conduct far-reaching operations), over the past ten years, new actors, big and small, have entered this market. It is worth noting the establishment of alliances between firms traditionally identified with separate services (i.e., remittances versus transportation) and the participation of large corporations in the remittance business and the already-discussed remittance in-kind sector of the migration industry. For instance, wire transfer corporations, such as Western Union and MoneyGram, are partnering with transportation firms, like Senda, in Mexico, turning bus depots into outlets where customers can send and receive remittances. In establishing these partnerships and despite their already large share of the remittance market, companies like Western Union are catching up and competing with options immigrants have enjoyed for some time, enterprises like Transportes García and Autobuses Adame.

The emergence of new actors, novel strategic alliances, and innovative modalities trying to capture a share of the remittance market raises questions about the long-term survival of small, informal courier services like Transportes García and its successors. Together with the above-mentioned corporations, medium- and small-sized money transfer businesses (i.e., Sigue, Orlandi Valuta, King Express) and banks (i.e., Bank of America, Wells Fargo) are now part of the migration industry landscape, generating heightened competition between old and new service providers, all of them trying to get a piece of the more than $23 billion Mexican immigrants sent back home in 2006 (Banco de Mexico 2007).[15] Competition, together with political pressure to bring down transaction costs and legal challenges by immigrant organizations, has fostered a decline in fees for sending cash and in-kind remittances to Mexico and the drop of such fees across regions in the United States (Orozco 2002; Banco de México 2007). Given the availability of multiple low-cost options, can the *camionetas* compete and survive? Although obviously only time will tell, I would argue that these types of courier services are unlikely to disappear, at least in the short run. So long as they can offer some reliability to customers, the *camionetas* will continue to build on the very competitive advantages outlined in this chapter: specialization and social embeddedness in distinct migratory circuits, a combination of multiple services under one roof, and the negotiation of risks and costs by moving between formality and informality in the two political and legal contexts where they operate.

# CHAPTER 6

# Metropolitan Migrants

*A New Dimension of Mexico-U.S. Migration*

What lessons should be drawn from the migration of Monterrey's skilled manufacturing workers to the United States? How does their experience compare to the experiences of rural Mexicans, who for so long have represented the paradigmatic Mexico-U.S. migrant? The story of *regiomontano* sojourning to Houston yields four instructive findings about the causes and the socioeconomic and sociopolitical organization of migration stemming from an urban setting. These findings can be cautiously extrapolated to other Mexican urban and metropolitan areas of the broader binational flow.

## CAUSES OF URBAN MIGRATION

This book has shown that the residents of the country's third-largest metropolis are resorting to U.S.-bound migration as a result of the sea change transformation of Mexico's urban-industrial base. Although this transformation has been accompanied by successive crises in the 1980s and 1990s, such crises have only heralded the more lasting and profound passage from an economic model of ISI to an outward-looking policy of EOI. It is this process of urban-industrial economic restructuring that has displaced—at times rapidly and at times more gradually—members of Mexico's skilled manufacturing working class, forcing them to contemplate international migration. As I have argued above, economic dislocation does not automatically translate into an actual move abroad in search of work. In urban centers, such as Monterrey, where international sojourning is a new phenomenon and a culture of migration has not taken hold, the alternative to join the cross-border labor market is part of a broader and complex structure of opportunities available to local residents, which include employment in services, informal sector jobs, and export-oriented assembly.

The story of migration from La Fama and its surrounding districts illustrates how the causes of urban-origin international migration are intimately connected with the changing political economy of the metropolitan area where these neighborhoods are nested. In Monterrey, economic restructuring has given way to the progressive elimination of the regime of industrial-labor relations that prevailed during the period of ISI and that afforded male workers and their families relatively high wages, comprehensive benefits, and employment stability—elements that collectively made migration an unattractive alternative for the social reproduction of urban households. Thus, new generations of manufacturing workers have come to bear the brunt of the modernization of Mexico's industry, as firms call for and implement increased flexibility within plants and in the labor market to compete internationally. In this context, as economic restructuring has eroded the structure of work opportunities, stints of unemployment, declining local opportunities, shrinking benefits, and downward occupational mobility have become antecedents to U.S. migration. Just as peasants and small *ejidatarios* (communal land farmers) resorted to temporary international migration to deal with effects of ISI and rural disinvestment, urbanites and their households are now forced to consider cross-border sojourning to mitigate the impact of EOI—a process that has dislocated and made redundant scores of skilled and semiskilled manufacturing workers. Thus, instead of using migration as a risk-management strategy (Massey et al. 1993), urban households appear to be using migration to cope with the effects of restructuring.

The experience of *regiomontano* workers also provides a window into the social processes that explain why and how cities south of the border have become part of the Mexico-U.S. migratory flow. To be sure, Mexican urban and metropolitan centers have long been linked to the social process of international migration, most notably as settlement areas for returning braceros (during the 1950s and 1960s) who chose not to go back to their rural hometowns. In addition, a few cities, including Monterrey, functioned as temporary centers for the recruitment of such workers. Today, Mexican cities are becoming sending areas of U.S.-bound sojourners and, in some cases, hubs for migration industry services. This development has begun to confront scholars with issues regarding the specificity of international flows stemming from metropolitan settings, including questions about their causes, about the nature and dynamics of support networks and social capital in cities, about whether migration theories developed in rural communities actually apply to metropolitan areas, and about the migration-related consequences of economic restructuring, not only in the countryside but also in urban Mexico. Still, the metropolitan case study of Monterrey confirms one of the findings uncovered in rural environments: the centrality of recruitment in the initiation of migratory flows (Durand 1998; Massey et al. 1987). Like their late-nineteenth-century counterparts who discovered in western Mexico a demographically dense region they could use as recruitment grounds for the mines, fields, and railroads of the southwest, during the 1960s and 1970s, U.S. employers found in Monterrey a wealth of skilled manufacturing workers to enlist as machinists in aviation and oil-related industries.

But are La Fama and its neighboring districts (and to that extent Monterrey) an exceptional case study, making any extrapolation to other Mexican cities a questionable exercise? There is no doubt that Monterrey is in some respects unique among cities in Mexico because of its peculiar history of early industrialization and its hyperconcentration of manufacturing activities. La Fama was not only the local cradle of this experience of industrialization but also a company town of sorts, with many social interactions structured around the textile mill and union membership. Yet all cities have distinct sociohistorical configurations that set them apart from other urban areas. Thus, despite obvious variation, the country's urban centers and Mexico's urbanization process during the twentieth century unfolded under one common macroeconomic model, that of ISI. It is the dismantling of ISI and of its corresponding regime of industrial-labor relations, enshrined in federal and state labor codes and in informal practices, that have exposed the formerly protected urban working class to global competition and economic dislocation.

I have observed firsthand the presence of other displaced Mexican urban-industrial workers elsewhere in the United States. Conducting fieldwork in the suburbs of the Atlanta metropolitan area, I discovered clusters of former oil workers from Tampico, Tamaulipas. Located in the gulf region, the Tampico-Ciudad Madero-Altamira metropolitan area is one of Mexico's most important petroleum refining centers, developing in close connection with the ISI regime. Whereas in Monterrey private capital was the chief force behind industrialization, in Tampico this was a state-led process. Similarly, while in Monterrey industrialists and their *sindicatos blancos* assumed a key role in the provision of a social wage, in Tampico this role corresponded to the government-owned oil monopoly Petróleos Mexicanos and its powerful union. After clamping down on the union and its leadership, which opposed the privatization of state-owned enterprises during the 1980s, the federal government fired thousands of skilled as well as casual workers, revised the collective bargaining agreement, and dramatically downsized the social provision capacity of the union (Cravey 1998). This campaign paved the way for the government's reorganization of the industry, a process that entailed the closing of major refineries, including one in Mexico City, and laying off thousands of additional employees (Cravey 1998; Uhlig 1991).

Former oil workers from Tampico had clearly established a beachhead in the suburbs of Atlanta, where they had converged with Mexicans coming from different parts of the country. After a handful of conversations with these *tampiqueños*, it was clear that they were highly skilled workers, previously occupied in oil refining and in the maintenance of production facilities. They argued that the cause for their sojourning was the growing difficulty of securing jobs in the oil industry back home. However, unlike Monterrey workers in Houston, these skilled operatives did not appear to have transferred their technical know-how to their new residence. In fact, most of them were holding various low-paying jobs in the service and construction sectors. Still, this is not the only type of occupational incorporation these skilled workers endure in the United States. In their study of the oil industry in southern Louisiana, Katherine Donato and associates (2001, 2005, 2008) report the presence of industrial operatives from Tampico, hired through formal and informal recruitment strategies. Other studies have reported a growing out-migration from Mexico City and the presence of these sojourners in destinations such as New York (Smith 2005), but in general, there is still little research on flows stemming from Mexico's urban and metropolitan areas. If any lessons can be drawn from this book for future studies of migration, it is that researchers need to pay more attention to urban settings, the places where the majority of Mexicans live, which are also being swept by a momentous economic transformation.

## SOCIAL NETWORKS

This book has also offered a qualitative and ethnographic window into the kinds of social networks urban migrants deploy. The evidence collected in Monterrey shows that, in addition to kinship networks, these Mexican urbanites use the weak ties that connect them to their neighbors and coworkers to support their cross-border sojourning. In this sense, the findings from La Fama are similar to findings stemming from the ethnographic study of low-income urban populations in Latin America and the United States, a diverse literature which shows that, under certain conditions, cities can be fertile ground for the emergence of webs of solidarity and support (Lomnitz 1975; Suttles 1968; Fernández-Kelly 1994; Gutmann 2002). The working-class households of La Fama are part of the close-knit, kinship-based networks that are central to U.S.-migration. This is to be expected. But had these clusters of strong networks functioned like small islands, migration would have remained in the realm of a handful of families. Instead, the weak ties that link friends, neighbors, and coworkers have contributed to make U.S.-bound migration a widespread behavior by connecting kinship groups to each other. This finding comes as a surprise, running against the canon of American urban sociology and its emphasis on anonymity, social heterogeneity, and isolation in the city. But as explained in chapters 3 and 4, just the opposite took place in La Fama and its surrounding districts. Here, ISI gave rise to stable urban neighborhoods that over time produced and sustained relatively durable social relations among local residents, who were sharing the space of the barrio, working in the same factories, attending the same schools, and establishing and joining institutions and associations, such as unions and soccer clubs. All of this accounts for the sense of obligation neighbors expressed about assisting each other in their migratory endeavors.

And yet, this sense of obligation had clear limitations, some of which can be exposed by contrasting the weak ties of urban migrants with the strong networks of rural-origin sojourners. To sustain and minimize the costs of their migratory sojourning, rural Mexicans have long utilized networks based on kinship and *paisanaje*. As I argued previously, in the towns and villages of Mexico, these ties reinforce each other through endogamic marriage practices. In the end, *paisanos* are often also *parientes* (kin), and many *parientes* are also *paisanos*. This mutually supporting relationship is strengthened even more by economic cooperation in agricultural activities—sharing communal lands, water, and other resources, including labor. These multiplex ties, with their economic, social, and ecological underpinnings, tend to produce clearly bound social capital and strong, enforceable trust. In La Fama, in the absence of these conditions, network members could withdraw support to fellow migrants from Monterrey without fear of substantial group reprisal.

Still, that these individuals were able to, at least in part, rely on their weak networks to launch and sustain their international sojourning shows that urban-origin migration to the United States was not either atomized or socially disorganized. Furthermore, in contrast with findings reported in other studies, most notably *Return to Aztlan* (1987), these city migrants did not have to resort to the rural *paisano* networks which connect them, at times only remotely, to their parents' hometowns in northeast and north-central Mexico. Clearly, the social infrastructure for their cross-border trips did not depend on such rural-origin ties, imported into the city via domestic migration, but was developed on the basis of the combination of family connections and networks rooted in the urban barrio.[1]

In this context, women play a seldom-analyzed role, not only as migrants themselves but also as providers of migratory social capital for men, especially husbands. Thus, males whose families have little or no international migratory experience can access U.S. labor markets through their in-laws. Migrating using a father-in-law or a brother-in-law as the chief contact for lodging and finding work has important consequences, particularly for socially controlling the behavior of men who have left their families behind. In urban settings, where migratory social capital is less commonly available than in small rural settlements, women might be the conduit for men to access social networks.

The workings of these different kinds of networks have left a visible footprint in the social and spatial organization of *regiomontano* migration, helping establish Houston as the main destination of this flow. It is evident that other factors have been at play as well: recruitment, Houston's own economic specialization, the geographic proximity of Monterrey and the Bayou City, and the highly developed communications infrastructure connecting the two metropolitan areas. Still, there is no question that networks have done their job channeling men and women of the western section of metropolitan Monterrey to clearly identifiable districts of Houston, where people from La Fama and surrounding neighborhoods have formed a daughter community of sorts, dispersed in the apartment complexes and houses along the I-10 cor-

ridor. These same networks have funneled these individuals to a variety
of workplaces and have contributed to the formation of occupational
niches in skilled industrial trades as well as unskilled service and construction jobs.

## THE SIGNIFICANCE OF BORDERS

Monterrey and Houston form a distinct international migratory circuit. The word *circuit* does not refer here to the circulation of migrants
between seasonal jobs in the United States and rest periods in Mexico.
*Regiomontano* sojourners have never really engaged in such a pattern of
migration, which is typical yet steadily eroding in recent decades among
rural Mexicans. As urban migrants displaced by restructuring at home
and moving to an urban destination abroad, these individuals have usually obtained year-round jobs. Monterrey and Houston constitute a
circuit because of the constant migration-driven movement of people,
information, money, and goods in both directions across the border—to
paraphrase Durand (1988). And yet, what differentiates this international migratory circuit from the multiple domestic circuits that connect
Monterrey with other localities in Mexico is precisely that, in this case,
the two poles are separated by a border. Thus, the geographic space
occupied by this circuit is not seamless. In fact, it is fundamentally made
discontinuous by the presence of the common border of two nation-
states (Foucher 1991).

To emphasize this point, however, is not to say that nation-states
function like perfect containers of social relations, nor to deny that the
various stakeholders of the social process in question—migrants, governments, employers, intermediaries, and anti- and pro-immigrant activists—regularly engage in border-spanning behavior. It is to say, though,
that borders matter, especially for international migration, a definite
trans-state (and transborder) phenomenon. However, with its emphasis
on the border-spanning capacity of social networks, much of the migration scholarship has paid little attention to the transformation of such
networks and the changes in social and political status of their members
as they traverse the boundaries of nation-states, entering or leaving distinct polities.

In my analysis of the Monterrey-Houston circuit, I have shown that
states, their borders, and their corresponding immigration policies have
transformed a relatively homogenous and horizontal working-class population into a population stratified according to legal status. An immi-

grant's position—as a citizen, legal permanent resident, holder of a work permit or a border-crossing card, or undocumented sojourner—was by no means inconsequential. On the contrary, how these *regiomontanos* crossed the border and what legal documentation they possessed once in Houston had deep implications for their occupational opportunities, binational orientation, and long-term social mobility. As shown in chapters 4 and 5, naturalized citizens and legal permanent residents could travel regularly between the two cities and take advantage of entrepreneurial opportunities providing services to fellow immigrants, especially to those whose mobility was limited due to their clandestine presence in the United States. Despite their technical skills, the lack of papers restricted undocumented immigrants to low-wage jobs and occupational niches where salaries remained stagnant. In several respects, their lives resembled those of the native working poor. These experiences confirm that legal status plays a key role in the process of stratification and class formation among immigrants (Griffith 2005).

These findings have implications for the study of immigrant transnationalism. In my analysis of the Monterrey-Houston circuit, I conclude that the ability of immigrants to engage in transnational or crossborder activities is contingent upon factors such as border enforcement and immigrants' legal status. Not surprisingly, those possessing U.S. citizenship and legal permanent residence were able to participate in many transborder activities, including travel, entrepreneurial opportunities, family functions, and cultural, religious, and sports initiatives linking Monterrey and Houston. Sojourners who had entered the country using a tourist visa or who had crossed the border clandestinely faced multiple constraints, especially regarding cross-border mobility, which limited potential transnational orientation on their part. Perhaps one can argue that by breaching the borders and challenging the enforcement apparatus of the state, migrants had engaged in the most transnational of practices (Rodríguez 1996; Waldinger and Fitzgerald 2004). Yet this very transgression, combined with heightened vigilance at borders and ports of entry and an increasingly restrictive and punitive immigration policy, produced immobility and clamped down on meaningful transnational participation in the dual contexts in which immigrants were embedded.

Here, it is worth revisiting the case of Rafael, the skilled machinist portrayed in chapters 3 and 4 who had shuttled between a job in Houston and his family in La Fama for almost ten years using a border-crossing card. Although Rafael visited his spouse and children every other weekend, always at the risk of being detected by authorities upon reentry into the United States, his wife bluntly told me that this pattern of mobility had turned him into an absent father who had forsaken his sons' entire childhood. According to some definitions of immigrant transnationalism, Rafael would represent the textbook example of simultaneous embeddedness in two national societies. But as his wife would likely claim, his migratory pattern as a single target earner, shuttling back and forth across the border, had over the years limited his presence in the lives of those left at home. Thus, in addition to raising questions about the contingency of transnationalism, the case of Rafael and his family raises questions about what constitutes meaningful dual participation (or presence) and who is making such an assessment.

Needless to say, neither the example of Rafael nor even the case of the larger Monterrey-Houston circuit can be utilized to dismantle the transnationalist approach (nor is that my goal). Still, both shed light on an important shortcoming of this emerging theoretical perspective. Even though recent contributions have shown how transnational fields are partly the result of sending state activism in response to internal and international realities (Smith 2003), the broader literature has ignored the significance of the often more powerful receiving polities and their geopolitical interests in facilitating, segmenting, limiting, or thwarting immigrant transnationalism.[2] In contrast, I have argued that host states' immigration and border control policies and the array of legal statuses conferred to immigrants are central in explaining why, when, and how some newcomers become active participants in transnational fields while others do not. The reasons that account for this fundamental variation cannot be found solely within the world of those with a strong transnational orientation—no matter how intense, durable, and complex their transnational experiences are.

Ultimately, this study shows that international migration is fundamentally a trans-state social process, where the spanning of borders and the embeddedness of immigrants and other social actors in two or more national societies is the *normal* state of affairs. This claim has fundamental methodological and practical implications. Perhaps the most important of them is that scholars cannot fully understand immigration if they do not systematically study the economic, political, and sociological realities of sending localities and countries. By the same token, students of international migration will not achieve a comprehensive view of this social process if they do not analyze the dynamics of immigration at the destination. Although a number of classic studies, such as *Return to Aztlan* (1987), and more recent contributions, such as Robert Smith's

*Mexican New York* (2006), have adopted these principles, too many analyses pay lip service or simply ignore them, holding on to the illusion that all that is relevant happens in either origin or destination but not in (and through the connection of) both places.

## THE MIGRATION INDUSTRY

Over the past two decades, many researchers have used social networks to explore the trans-state nature of international migration. In this study, I have demonstrated that the migration industry constitutes a parallel social and economic infrastructure facilitating cross-border mobility, with multiple and complex connections to immigrants and their social networks but also sufficiently distinct from said networks. Often marginalized and viewed as an appendage to the core phenomenon and its central actors, the migration industry and migration entrepreneurs make several important contributions to the social process of international migration, opening markets for foreign labor, establishing regular connections between origin and destination, and structuring opportunities for immigrants. In an era of increasing restrictions on both legal and clandestine human mobility across international borders, the migration industry provides an effective and efficient means to bridge (but not erase) the boundaries of nation-states—something individual migrants and their networks might be incapable of doing on their own. Given the advent of heightened enforcement along the U.S.-Mexico international boundary and its constraining effect on the cross-border mobility of undocumented immigrants, the back-and-forth movement of *camioneteros,* bus operators, *coyotes,* recruiters, and remittance couriers has become ever more relevant for the individuals and households inhabiting the Monterrey-Houston migratory circuit.

Although many migration entrepreneurs emerge from the ranks of immigrants and their networks and are consequently bound to them through ethnic and other types of ties, I contend that these entrepreneurs mainly offer mobility-related services to pursue financial gain. This motivation structures relationships between migration entrepreneurs and their customers and sets up the context for social differentiation and a growing asymmetry between them. Viewed through this lens, migration entrepreneurs, such as the *camionetero* portrayed in chapter 5, might be cataloged as a distinct type of ethnic entrepreneur specializing in the migration-driven mobility of people, remittances, and goods across international borders and moving between formality and informality, legality and illegality, depending on the activity, financial resources, and other circumstances.

In the business of transgressing borders, Jorge García and his *camionetas* faced constant risk. Tellingly, this risk resulted primarily from regular exposure to and interaction with U.S. and Mexican state officials guarding the border and regulating the flow of persons, money, and products. García and his employees sought to minimize or avoid encounters with U.S. officials and to favorably manipulate interactions with Mexican customs, treasury, and highway agents by bribing them. Operating largely in the realm of informality, Jorge García knew that any potentially unfavorable encounter with the authorities could bring his business to the brink of disaster. Still, that Transportes García existed for nearly twenty years and that several similar operations sprouted once it shut down attest to the profitability and durability of the migration industry.

## COMPARING URBAN- AND RURAL-ORIGIN MIGRATION TO THE UNITED STATES

Scholars of Mexico-U.S. migration have argued that there are fundamental differences between rural- and urban-origin migratory flows and that, consequently, existing theories might not apply to metropolitan contexts without significant revisions (Massey, Goldring, and Durand 1994; Flores, Hernández-León, and Massey 2004; Fussell and Massey 2004). A straightforward comparison of rural- and urban-origin migrations is no simple task given the profound transformations that rural flows have undergone in the past few years. Disentangling the causes and social dynamics of urban and rural streams is also difficult because of old and new connections between city and countryside and between internal and international migration.[3]

In recent decades, technological and organizational changes in agricultural industries and new border enforcement strategies in the United States, coupled with the decline of the peasant household economy in rural Mexico, have eroded old patterns of seasonal migration, tying workers to jobs and receiving areas year round (Griffith and Kissam 1995; Cornelius and Myhre 1998). During the 1980s and 1990s, the paralysis of the construction industry and the overall saturation of urban labor markets in Mexican cities have deflected established domestic temporary streams, turning them into new international flows—further illustrating how rural migrations can have urban causes (Binford 2004). On a general level, one can argue that the two seemingly separate flows have been caused by the same policies of economic liberalization that have swept through Mexico from the mid-1980s to the present. At the destination, the distinction between urban and rural migrants might get blurred as the two flows converge in service industries and, perhaps less commonly, in agribusiness across the United States (Griffith and Kissam 1995).

Despite these caveats, I retain the comparative lens because it helps shed light on the specificity of urban-origin migration. Regardless of their multiple interconnections, rural and urban flows stem from different political economies and sets of social institutions: Whereas rural migratory flows have been historically embedded in the peasant household economy—prompting sojourners to use migration as a way to acquire insurance and capital and to engage in temporary and circular mobility—urban streams are nested in wage labor markets. In urban and metropolitan settings, migration responds to different opportunity structures and motivations. Mexican urbanites appear to migrate internationally as a result of dislocations produced by industrial modernization and the declining quality of urban-industrial labor markets. In their case, migration substitutes for local employment instead of supplementing it (as was long the case with rural sojourners, although less so nowadays). Despite the fact that a few *regiomontanos* combined work stints abroad with employment at home and others moved between Houston and Monterrey, responding to the boom and bust cycles of the oil industry, the majority sought stable, year-round jobs, which produced long-term stays and permanent migration to the United States.

Yet another significant difference between urban and rural flows has to do with the kinds of networks migrants deploy as social capital to support their U.S. sojourns. As discussed at length previously, rural migrants rely on a combination of strong, mutually reinforcing kinship and *paisano* networks supplemented by an array of casual ties at the destination (Krissman 2005; Griffith and Kissam 1995). In contrast, urbanites mix family (strong) ties with friend and neighbor (weak) ties. A wealth of studies on rural communities in western and north-central Mexico have shown that strong kinship and *paisano* networks have been the most effective in spreading migratory behavior, reducing the costs and risks associated with international sojourning, creating a culture of migration among sending populations, and producing the self-feeding effect that lies at the heart of the cumulative causation of migration. The handful of studies on Mexican cities as sources of U.S.-bound migration have uncovered more precarious ties (Massey et al. 1987; Hernández-León

1999; Lozano Ascencio 2000; Arias and Woo Morales 2004), prompting researchers to ask whether urban-based networks, especially nonfamilial ones, could sustain the cumulative causation dynamics observed
in small towns and villages. The answer to this question has been negative, not only because of the relative fragility of urban ties (vis-à-vis rural
ones) but also because city-origin migration is unlikely to provoke the
same types of transformations in the political economy of the sending
area the way rural migration does. In sharp contrast with their peasant
and small farmer counterparts, urbanites simply do not return and use
their remittances to buy the single most important productive resource
in the countryside—land—and therefore are less likely to produce the
same sense of relative deprivation found among stay-at-home individuals and households (Fussell and Massey 2004).

Does this mean that Mexico's urban-origin migration is unlikely to
increase? I argue the opposite. The reason for the likely increase is that
the growth of migration stemming from urban areas does not depend
solely on the types of network dynamics found in cities. Extending the
arguments I have made in the case of Monterrey to the national context,
I contend that the continuation and deepening of economic restructuring in Mexico will advance the dislocation of urban-industrial workers,
creating conditions for their migration to the United States. During the
administration of President Vicente Fox, private corporations, government officials, and top union leaders agreed on a plan to reform Mexico's
labor law. The intended reform sought to modernize the labor code by
introducing clauses that mirrored the process of economic restructuring.
These clauses gave employers more flexibility in the hiring and firing
of workers through temporary contracts and training periods, allowed
management to extend the workday according to the variable needs of
companies, promoted operatives on the basis of skill rather than seniority, limited the power of unions to call strikes, and prepared employees
to be multiskilled workers, among other provisions (Martínez 2002).

Although the reform was stalled in Congress throughout the Fox
administration, it will likely come back to the legislative agenda in the
near future. Still, as labor leaders, lawyers, and analysts have observed,
corporations are already putting into practice many of the conditions
included in this initiative, violating existing law and taking advantage of
its lax enforcement. This de facto implementation involves the growth of
subcontracting and outsourcing (therefore avoiding collective bargaining agreements), which increases the numbers of nonunionized employees because fewer workers are hired through formal contracts (which by

law include social security and other benefits); they are appointed instead through temporary and casual agreements (Alcalde Justiniani 2004; Martínez 2005; Muñoz Ríos 2006; Palacios 2003). Taken together, these transformations will reduce job security and stability, dislocating a growing number of previously rooted urban-industrial workers in Mexico and setting the stage for their migration to the United States.

In this context, the migration industry and its array of entrepreneurs can only acquire an even more salient role. As I noted above in chapter 5, migration industry actors are already present in Mexican cities, structuring the separation between urban and rural streams. Although labor contractors had a foothold in La Fama, they apparently chose not to recruit there, preferring instead to draw workers from *ejidos* (communal farms) in northern Mexico. Following on the footsteps of these migration entrepreneurs, the state government, through its Oficina de Atención al Migrante, explicitly decided not to recruit H2-B prospects in the Monterrey metropolitan area, a move that (I hypothesize) could have upset the city's industrialists. Instead, the *oficina's* staff advertised these opportunities in the state's rural hinterland.[4]

More important, this study has shown that cities have become important hubs of migration industry services and that urban neighborhoods, with their networks of immigrants, have given rise to home-grown migration entrepreneurs, including smugglers and remittance couriers. Given that new urban migrants are likely to be disproportionately clandestine, the demand for the services of *coyotes, remeseros, transportistas,* and other migration entrepreneurs is bound to increase. These intermediaries will continue to open labor markets and to provide regular connections between sending and receiving areas of migratory circuits. The extent to which these entrepreneurs will effectively structure the labor market opportunities of urban newcomers compared to their rural counterparts working in agricultural labor markets, however, is less evident (see Griffith and Kissam 1995; Griffith 2005). Since city-origin migrants rely more on skills and weak ties to find jobs, it is possible that they be less dependent on recruiters and *contratistas* (who often work closely with *coyotes*) and on the opportunities and conditions they afford to their clients.

Interestingly, urban migrants are generally better positioned to take advantage of recent changes in the remittance industry, particularly the entry of large American financial institutions, which have partnered with Mexican banks to offer cheaper and more efficient ways to transfer money between the two countries. Whereas in rural areas, the sheer absence of banks turns *remeseros* and *camioneteros* into the de facto financial institutions of towns and villages, urban areas enjoy a growing menu of options to wire and cash money.

## CODA

By 2005, the walled-in residential complex that replaced the demolished textile mill in La Fama was almost finished. The complex included houses priced well beyond the reach of most of the working-class families in the area and clearly aimed at middle-class homeowners. A seven-foot-tall perimeter wall separated the new housing development from the older, modest working-class dwellings and from local landmarks, including the Plaza del Obrero (Workers' Square), the remains of the original textile factory and aqueduct built in the nineteenth century, and an open-air market catering to local residents. This final chapter in the history of the textile mill in La Fama suggests other insights into and questions about the future of migration in this urban district. On the one hand, the restructuring and closing of Textiles Monterrey had clearly propelled many operatives to look for work in the United States. On the other hand, the closing of the factory, the downfall of the union, and the ensuing gentrification of at least a section of the neighborhood suggest that La Fama is becoming a more heterogeneous place.

Even though, as argued above deepening economic restructuring is likely to create conditions for additional migration, the demise of key local institutions, like the plant and the union, and growing socioeconomic heterogeneity might undermine the networks on which migration was built. These networks were established on the basis of a highly homogeneous and stable working-class world, which today is undergoing profound transformations. For now, however, the migratory social capital developed in La Fama over the last two decades is likely to channel former mill workers to Houston and other U.S. labor markets. Dislocated once, some of these operatives are likely to be excluded from industrial job opportunities because of age and membership in a so-called red union, circumstances that will force them to turn their sights abroad.

# Methodological Appendix

This study is the result of nearly ten years of (discontinuous) field research: surveying, interviewing, and observing the lives of hundreds of migrants and nonmigrants in Monterrey and Houston. In this appendix, I address the methodological issues I confronted while researching urban Mexican migration to the United States. Having realized more than a decade ago that researchers had paid scant attention to urban and metropolitan areas as sources of international flows, I decided to center my inquiry on such flows, trying to understand both their causes and their social organization. Despite this effort to underscore what is distinct about this type of migration, urban-origin flows need to be understood as part of the broader Mexico-U.S. migratory system, characterized, as Durand (2000) has argued, by its one-hundred-fifty-year history, its geographic peculiarity, and its massive yet predominantly rural sources.

This study also follows on the footsteps of the long and fruitful tradition of Mexico-U.S. migration research dating back to the 1920s, which is largely dominated by the genre of qualitative community studies. Although community studies have been criticized on the basis of several salient and recurrent limitations (Durand and Massey 1992), this tradition boasts fundamental analytical and methodological contributions, utilized to mount innovative research endeavors. This scholarly tradition includes the works of Manuel Gamio and Paul Taylor (Durand 1991), the myriad single case studies of source communities conducted during the 1970s and 1980s (see Cornelius 1976; Dinerman 1978; Reichert

1982), as well as Massey's and Durand's rolling community survey design (Massey 1987; Durand and Massey 1992).

Aware of the criticisms leveled against community studies, I took active steps to address potential pitfalls. Instead of relying on a single method and source of data, I sought to combine a variety of research methodologies and techniques to select sites and respondents, to collect evidence, and to triangulate sources of data (see Hammersley and Atkinson 1995). As in most cases where field research is a central component of a study, the specific mix of techniques resulted in part from choices limited by the time and resources available. Although the methods I used are mostly qualitative, I also resorted to quantitative techniques, especially in the case of La Fama, where I implemented a survey to a randomly selected sample of households (see below).

An important characteristic of the research presented here is that it was conceived from its inception as a binational, multisite study, remaining so throughout its different stages. As I argued previously, international migration is by definition a trans-state social process, namely, a phenomenon defined by the border-spanning behavior of its chief actors (i.e., state institutions, migration entrepreneurs, and individual migrants and their households). This implies that "the phenomenon (located in space/time) about which data are collected and/or analyzed, and that corresponds to the type of phenomena to which the main claims of the study relate" (Hammersley 1992: 184) should always include binational (or multinational) data collection in origin and destination countries of migratory flows. Surprisingly, this methodological strategy has not necessarily become the norm. During the 1970s and 1980s, community studies of Mexico-U.S. migration often tended to concentrate on sending localities, neglecting the experience of sojourners as *immigrants* in the host society. Thus, many of these analyses failed to appreciate the transformation of this flow as a result of the urbanization of Mexican immigration to the United States in the 1970s and the passage and implementation of new immigration legislation in the late 1980s. The full impact of these developments could not be captured by researching sending localities alone.

*Return to Aztlan* (Massey et al. 1987) broke with existing methodological practice by showing that the study of "the social process of international migration in western Mexico" (to quote the subtitle of the book) required understanding the experiences of migrants not only in the United States in general but also in distinct places of settlement, such as Los Angeles and Chicago. Since then, a growing number of studies have adopted a binational (or multinational), multisite research design—a trend strengthened by the advent of the transnational perspective in migration studies. But old habits die hard. Nowadays, scholars often rush to label immigrants as transnational on the basis of observations collected at the destination without systematically analyzing the effect of noncyclical migrations on the home country and its sending localities.

Another common criticism of community studies is that researchers frequently use findings from one or two sending localities to generalize about the entire Mexico-U.S. migratory flow. Thus, Durand and Massey caution that "the field is replete with general statements about the nature of Mexico-U.S. migration based on the experience of a single community" (1992: 13). Needless to say, such a critique raises questions about the uses of case study research, about how representative cases actually are, and about the validity of extrapolating from particular instances to the general phenomena—questions that cannot be solved with a two or three case study research design.

Clearly, this study does not seek to use the case of La Fama or even the broader case of Monterrey to make general statements about all U.S.-bound migratory flows stemming from Mexican cities. Although throughout this study I contend that there might be causes, network dynamics, and forms of social capital particular to the migratory flows originating in cities, I also recognize that different urban experiences produce migrations with distinct features. The characteristics of these migrations depend, at least in part, on the diversity of urban and regional experiences that exist in Mexico. The specificity of urban-origin migrations will depend on the histories of different cities, the position they occupy in the national urban hierarchy, and the distinct regional economies in which they participate as central places. The characteristics of urban-origin migrations will also be influenced by a city's location in a given region of U.S.-bound migration. Durand (2000) has identified four regions of migration (border, historic, central-south, and southeastern), arguing about the significance of such regions for the analysis of the history and patterns of migration from distinct sending localities. Indeed, Monterrey's proximity to the border does have an impact on migratory strategies, as it lowers the cost of international sojourning. In addition, Monterrey has had a long historical connection to the United States and to Texas in particular. But the city is also intimately connected to states located in the historic region of migration such as Zacatecas and San Luis Potosí (and even Guanajuato and

Durango) through internal migrations. Thus, even though a region may be characterized by the prevalence of certain migratory dynamics, the case of Monterrey suggests that in urban areas, multiple patterns of migration may overlap. In short, the findings presented here apply primarily to Monterrey and to the labor flows between this metropolitan area and Houston.

At the same time, it is undeniable that I expect these findings to have some value as "provisional generalizations" that "may advance our general sociological knowledge" (Merton 1987: 14) about the nature of urban-origin migration from Mexico to the United States. In other words, I expect the findings and conclusions of this study to hold some truth for other metropolitan areas in Mexico that are also starting points of international migratory flows. As I discuss below in the context of the different methodological choices made, cases have an instrumental value when they are turned by the researcher into strategic research materials, useful for generalization, when "the empirical material . . . exhibits the phenomena to be explained or interpreted to such an advantage and in such accessible form that it enables the fruitful investigation of previously stubborn problems and the discovery of new problems for further inquiry" (Merton 1987: 10–11). The case of La Fama and its surrounding neighborhoods and of the larger Monterrey metropolitan area and its cross-border linkages with Houston provide such an opportunity— one in which I see that it is possible to bring together "intrinsic interest in the particular sociocultural case with instrumental interest in it as leading to provisional general conclusions" (Merton 1987: 15).

Although the case in question cannot be the basis to formulate a general theory about either the causes or the social organization of international migration stemming from urban settings, it has been possible to use it to push the boundaries of existing theories of migration (Fitzgerald 2006b). Researchers have for some time now questioned whether theories largely formulated in rural contexts, where the central actor is the peasant household and its social networks, apply to urban and metropolitan areas (Massey, Goldring, and Durand 1994). My study validates aspects of established theories but also raises questions about previous findings. Instead of concurring with prior studies, which argue that urban anonymity, isolation, and heterogeneity impede the development of social capital, I have shown that under certain conditions, metropolitan environments give rise to their own migratory social capital. Instead of agreeing with formulations which explain migration as the result of the lack of insurance and capital in developing economies, I have demonstrated that urban flows in Mexico are the outcome of the profound transformation of the country's urban-industrial economy. In this context, international migration is not a risk-management strategy as much as it is a way for urban households to cope with the destabilizing effects of economic restructuring.

I have also used this case study to critically engage less-established paradigms, such as the transnational approach, affirming instead the significance of nation-states and their borders in shaping the contours of migrants' social experiences and cross-border activities. Finally, by including a whole chapter on the migration industry, a dimension of the social process of international migration that has received little systematic attention, I have also sought to "broaden the field of the visible and the intelligible" (Froud et al. 1998: 303) in migration studies.

## THE SELECTION OF SITES AND STRATEGIC RESEARCH CASES

The identification and selection of strategic research cases for this study was the result of the process of ethnographic discovery set out to detect the social ecology of international migration in the city. I was specifically interested in identifying urban neighborhoods with a density of households with international migratory experience. This was a first step to then collecting observations on the causes and social organization of international mobility. Determining a starting point posed a major challenge. In contrast with the small towns and villages frequently used as sites in community studies of Mexico-U.S. migration, a metropolitan area with a population of four million did not provide a self-evident starting point. Selecting and sampling an entire municipality, as Zúñiga (1993) did in Guadalupe, a dormitory municipality of the Monterrey metropolitan area, would not have provided the type of data that was necessary to answer the study's research questions.

In contrast to studies that have sought to establish a nexus between economic crisis and urban out-migration to the United States by analyzing data collected at the Mexico-U.S. border (Cornelius 1992), I decided to resort to the long tradition of community studies to research the case of a working-class neighborhood whose inhabitants have long been employed in the types of large-scale industries that have given Monterrey the reputation as Mexico's center of heavy manufacturing. In contrast to the transit points of migrants, urban communities of origin are the sites where the short- and long-term effects of crisis and restructuring are being felt by individuals and their families and households.

I identified La Fama and its surrounding districts as a potential research site by going first to Houston, where community activists got me in touch with *regiomontano* immigrants who had settled either temporarily or permanently in that city. I undertook this strategy following Cornelius's methodological suggestion "to begin by interviewing a group of migrants living in the U.S. Their responses to questions about place of origin in Mexico can be examined to identify clusters of migrants coming from particular communities or regions. Those places can then be selected as sites for fieldwork in Mexico, among relatives and friends of the initial group of interviewees" (1982: 390). These initial contacts took place in the winter of 1995–96, paving the way for several weeks of fieldwork in Houston during the summer of 1996. I concretely targeted Monterrey-origin households, studying their labor market incorporation and their pattern of contacts with their home city. I also used this fieldwork to map out the specific neighborhoods where these migrants used to live back in Monterrey

As fieldwork progressed, it became evident that many migrants from La Fama and nearby districts of the Monterrey metropolitan area were concentrated in Houston's Summerland section. As reported in chapter 4, it was evident from the interviews and the observed clustering of immigrants in this neighborhood that social networks played a role in organizing this migration. As soon as I completed fieldwork in Houston, I left for Monterrey, where I started conducting observations in La Fama and surrounding neighborhoods. Still, full-blown data collection in La Fama did not begin until the spring of 1997. Besides gathering data on the forty *regiomontano* households, the research activities carried out in Houston produced another important result, namely, the acquaintance with Jorge García and my familiarity with Transportes García. At the same time I implemented the household survey in La Fama, I managed to develop a relationship with Jorge García, conducting numerous observations of the business and multiple interviews with him, his employees, and his relatives about the operation of the *camionetas* (see below). Between 1997 and 1999, I visited the *regiomontano* "daughter" community in Summerland several times, verifying prior observations and findings. I met with the same families on almost every occasion I visited Houston, keeping track of their experiences of incorporation into the United States.

The field experience in La Fama was more extensive than intensive, combining the implementation of the survey with interviews and ethnographic fieldwork. During the first two years I researched this historic industrial district, I was able to establish a relationship of trust with active and inactive migrants, gaining access to numerous households and to the networks that link La Fama with Summerland. Because of the extensive nature of fieldwork, I also observed a number of events as they unfolded. For example, as I was beginning my entry into the setting, I found out that the local *coyote* (smuggler) had been arrested by the Border Patrol and was in prison in Laredo, Texas. I had interviewed him in Houston without knowing that he was a smuggler, and I was able to interview him again in Monterrey several times once he was released from prison. These events are analyzed in chapter 5.

Between 2000 and 2005, I returned to La Fama and Summerland for short fieldwork stints several times a year. Throughout this period, I also conducted research in El Naranjo and the Atlanta metropolitan area, experiences that I used for brief comparisons with *regiomontano* immigrants in chapters 3 and 4. Over these years, I closely followed the demise of Transportes García and the rise of similar operations, which took over the *camioneta* business that serviced the migrants of La Fama once Jorge García exited this activity. The period 2003–2005 included crucial events, such as the closing of Textiles Monterrey, the workers' takeover of the plant's facilities, and, on a more symbolic level, the commemoration of the one hundred fiftieth anniversary of the foundation of the original textile mill. In the summer of 2003, I returned to Houston to interview new *regiomontano* immigrants and interview others I had originally met in 1996 again, tracking their experiences seven years after our initial encounter.

STRATEGIC RESEARCH CASES

*Chapter 3: Restructuring and International Migration in a Mexican Urban Neighborhood*

The households studied in the working-class neighborhood of La Fama were selected through random sampling. The total number of households selected was 203 out of 1,105, which constituted the sampling frame. There were 166 fully completed and 2 partially completed questionnaires, for a final sample of 168 households. In 31 households, the targeted respondent refused to answer, hence yielding a rejection rate of a little over 15 percent. In 4 households, respondents were unreachable but could not be substituted. Although the survey instrument elicited data about the household head and his or her spouse and about all persons with either internal or international migratory experience, the targeted respondent was the adult who was most knowledgeable about the activities of the other household members. The category "most knowledgeable adult" is certainly subjective and not always effective, yet it offers particular advantages. Responding to the long and detailed survey actually required an interviewee that would be well informed about a variety of issues related to the head and spouse, their children, and other members of the domestic unit. Thus, selecting a respondent randomly would not have produced the right kind of informant given that, for instance, younger adults are generally less informed about the experiences of parents and older household members. On the other hand, asking the household head to respond to the questionnaire could have produced a mostly male pool of respondents and an undesirable gender bias. In most cases in the sample, men are identified as heads (90.5 percent). Applying the survey to the most knowledgeable adult produced instead a more balanced pool of actual interviewees and a majority of women as respondents—61 percent were female and 39 percent were male.

The survey used for data collection in La Fama gathered information at both the household and extended family levels. Households included all of the individuals living in a particular residence who shared a common budget and common cooking facilities. Extended families included the members of the household (typically related by kin) and the children of the head who had moved away and established their own separate households. As Selby, Murphy, and Lorenzen (1990) have noted, these children often remain connected to the parental household through various rights and obligations. Moreover, households were classified following González de la Rocha's (1986) characterization of three different stages of the domestic life cycle as described in Anderson and de la Rosa (1991). These stages are "(1) the expansion phase, in which the family is growing and the mother is under forty; (2) the consolidation phase, in which at least some of the children are old enough to join the labor market and contribute to family income; and (3) the dispersion phase, in which the children leave home" (Anderson and de la Rosa 1991: 55).

The survey instrument gathered basic demographic information about all household residents, including the children of the main cohabiting couple who had moved away. The questionnaire also collected basic residential histories of all individuals fifteen years and older with internal or international migratory experience. If either the head or the spouse had conducted or were currently engaged in cross-border migration, the questionnaire elicited detailed information about labor market experience in the United States. The instrument then dealt with the social networks of head and spouse by asking about the international migratory background of kin, neighbors, and coworkers. A short section inquired about family remittances. The rest of the instrument concentrated on the present and past occupational experiences of the head and spouse, reconstructing their entire work careers and self-employment activities. Two final sections addressed questions dealing with episodes of economic hardship and household well-being and with plans for U.S. migration. The instrument was constructed following the model of the ethnosurvey (Massey 1987). The ethnosurvey has been widely used in the study of Mexico-U.S. migration by Massey and Durand and their associates (Massey et al. 1987). The ethnosurvey instrument seeks to combine surveying and in-depth ethnographic interviewing to benefit from both methodologies' respective features: on the one hand, close-ended questions that allow for a rapid systematization of the data and, on the other, open-ended queries aimed at better understanding the interviewee's strategies and conceptions of migration (Massey 1987).

The decision to collect most of the data around the work and migratory experiences of the household head and the spouse merits discussion. Although the notion of "household head" is widely used as a sociological category in the study of the political economy of households, it is also a cultural and ideological construct. It assumes a particular family structure in which a single, usually male breadwinner earns a family wage, therefore enjoying power and moral authority over the rest of the domestic unit. The flip side of this notion is that women are not actively incorporated into the labor market and that instead they are exclusively engaged in the biological reproduction of the family and the day-to-day reproduction of the household. In Mexico, these assumptions have begun to break down as a result of the growing rates of female labor participation over the past twenty years. Secular trends, economic crises, and the programs of structural adjustment account for these increasing rates of labor market participation. This process is not exclusive to Mexico. It has also occurred in other Latin American countries and in the rest of the developing world. Despite these social and economic changes, the ideological and cultural underpinnings of the notion of headship remain, and women who become breadwinners are frequently not acknowledged as household heads (Acosta 1994). Instead of asking the respondent to identify the "head of household" right away, the La Fama survey called for identifying the person who made the largest income contribution to the family budget. This was the survey's operational definition of the concept. Still, slightly more than 90 percent of the identified household heads were males, and less than 10 percent were women. This percentage contrasts with the fact that nearly one-third of the mostly female spouses of the main cohabiting couple were working at the time of the interview.

Yet another methodological complication that the concept of household head presented had to do with the often overlooked issue of changes in headship as the domestic life cycle progresses. As discussed in chapter 3, a substantial proportion of La Fama households were already in the dispersion stage of their life cycle. In households where the parents had reached old age, grown-up children who remained at home had begun to assume the role of heads. In other cases, where an older parent had become a widow or widower, one of the children shared responsibility as family head. The role of household head, then, is not fixed in time and may change with shifts in the family life cycle and other circumstances.

A disadvantage of studying a neighborhood with a large number of households in the dispersion stage is that at that point of the domestic life cycle, heads have a current (and future) low or very low likelihood of migration. Key studies of Mexico-U.S. migration have shown that the likelihood of an undocumented move across the border is strongly associated with an individual's position as family head and with the household's life cycle stage (Massey et al. 1987). Households that are in the initial expansion stage of their life cycle have a higher probability of having a member (usually the head) undertake international migration. In La Fama, many households and their heads had this risk behind them. Thus, one of the disadvantages of conducting migration-related research with "older" households is precisely that heads and other members were not presently under pressure to migrate to satisfy family needs. Still, economic restructuring intersected with demographic profiles in highly relevant ways: by reinforcing the migratory pressure young heads (with expanding households) faced and by turning older, displaced industrial workers into U.S.-bound migrants.

As reported in chapter 3, one-third of all households in La Fama have at least one member with international migratory experience. Although due to reasons explained below, these figures overstate the prevalence of cross-border migration in this neighborhood, they still support one basic finding: For these urban households, U.S.-bound migration is not an uncommon experience. In some families, as many as five members have migrated to the United States. However, overestimation of the prevalence of migration may result from the way migratory events have been tallied. For example, not all who had attempted to cross the border to work in the United States had been successful. Some had been detained by the Border Patrol within hours or days of their border crossing and had been sent back to Mexico immediately. A few had started their migratory journey and had actually returned to their places of origin before moving to La Fama or to the Monterrey metropolitan area. Others were the children of La Fama household heads who had begun migrating as adults and were responsible for their own separate households established in different neighborhoods. All of these occurrences have been registered as migratory events. Nonetheless, counting these instances offers the advantage of compensating for the underestimation of migration, which typically occurs because some individuals and households have migrated permanently to the United States without leaving anybody behind in the neighborhood, and because some others have actually died before data gathering had taken place.

## Chapter 4: The Monterrey-Houston Connection: The Social Organization of Migration and the Economic Incorporation of Immigrants

As related above, initial fieldwork in Houston took place in the winter of 1995–96. During the summer of 1996, I returned to the Bayou City to gather data on forty households in which at least one member of the adult cohabiting couple was from the Monterrey metropolitan area. In most cases in the sample, both partners identified Monterrey as home in Mexico. Households for this part of the study were selected using snowball-sampling procedures. This allowed the study to identify and follow particular migrant networks. Initial points of contact with potential respondents were established through immigrant service agencies and local Catholic churches. Once a first contact was established and the corresponding interview was completed, respondents were asked to provide the names of other families from Monterrey. To gain variation in this analytical sample, interviewees were asked not to refer their relatives. Subsequent contacts were usually to neighbors and coworkers. In a number of cases, they were friends and associates who had met in Monterrey. The sample was stratified by area of residence in Houston between eastern and western sections of the city. The purpose of such stratification was to capture households established in new as well as traditional Mexican settlements in Houston. Previous works on Latin American migrations to this city during the 1980s and 1990s have shown that recent waves of newcomers have settled in the eastern sections of Houston (Hagan and Rodríguez 1992; Rodríguez 1993). The criterion for stratification used in this study reflected different times of arrival and allowed for further distinguishing between recent and older immigrant cohorts. The largest Mexican neighborhoods in the eastern and western parts of the city are Summerland and Magnolia, respectively. Most of the households contained in the Houston snowball sample reside in these neighborhoods.

The interview instrument was designed to gather data on and from the point of view of household heads principally. In most cases, adult males identified themselves or were identified by other members as household heads. In total, thirty-one men and nine women were interviewed. Interviews were conducted using an instrument containing structured as well as unstructured questions. Interviews lasted approximately ninety minutes, depending on how extensive migratory, work, and household economic hardship histories were in each case. The instrument contained six sections. Section 1 of the interview elicited information on the demographic characteristics of the household, including age, number of children, years of education, place of birth, and current occupation. This segment also included questions related to the household division of labor. Section 2 asked questions about the work and migratory histories of the respondent, such as current occupation, number of jobs during the previous twelve months, description of current or most recent job, type of employer, salary, and annual household income. Work and migratory histories were reconstructed, starting with the first full-time job of the respondent.

Section 3 of the interview instrument made specific inquiries about migration to the United States, such as number and time of trips, reasons to migrate, legal status during first and last trips, intended U.S. destination, prospects for settlement and return, and recent visits to Monterrey. Section 4 was comprised of questions about contacts and forms of assistance between Houston and Monterrey, for instance, assistance received and given to migrate and find employment in the United States, help and services provided to and by relatives, neighbors, and friends in Monterrey, and participation in Houston-based Mexican clubs and social organizations. Section 5 asked about issues of adolescent development in the household and child-rearing strategies. Finally, section 6 posed questions about household experiences of economic hardship, sources of assistance, use of social services, housing tenure both in Mexico and the United States, and weekly household expenses.

## Chapter 5: The Migration Industry in
## the Monterrey-Houston Connection

Regarding the research design of the larger study, Transportes García represents a case within the case (Monterrey-Houston). On the one hand, I have presented the findings on this small firm as an example of how Monterrey is a hub for migration industry services catering to the needs of urban-origin migrants. In this sense, this *camioneta* business is part of the broader social infrastructure that sustains migration from working-class neighborhoods like La Fama to destinations in the United States. But on the other hand, I once again make a more instrumental use of the case study as "strategic research material" (Merton 1987; see also Stake 1995) to comment on the migration industry and its entrepreneurs.

The identification and selection of the small remittance and transportation business Transportes García resulted from the fieldwork I conducted in Houston during the summer of 1996. Researching the social ties that link migrants in Monterrey and Houston, I was able to identify businesses, such as Transportes García, which provide important services to immigrants and their stay-at-home relatives. Some of these businesses do not advertise their services in either newspapers or the electronic media. This was the case for Jorge García's operation, which basically relied on word of mouth and on the continuing demand for its services on the part of its binational customer base to stay in business. But many other small firms regularly publicized their travels between Monterrey and Houston. The classified ad section of most Monterrey daily newspapers featured advertisements offering the services of micro and small businesses that transport people, parcels, correspondence, and money between the two cities.

In Houston, a stroll along the main street of the Mexican neighborhood of Magnolia quickly reveals the great variety of companies specializing in the cross-border market for passenger transportation and remittance shipping. The classified ads that these businesses post in the local Spanish press corroborate these observations. In some of these weekly newspapers, which cater to the Latin American immigrant community in Houston, readers can find dozens of such ads. Without having firm numbers to support this claim, my impression is that the sheer number of these types of migration industry business grew substantially over the entire study period, reflecting the sizable growth of the Mexican immigrant population in the United States during the past decade. As

I conducted a last round of observations at an Autobuses Adame bus depot in Monterrey in January 2006, I noticed that the neighborhood where this company has been located for nearly ten years has become populated with similar businesses (which do not include those operating from Monterrey's main bus station).

Data gathering for this case study was carried out using qualitative methods: ethnographic observation, participant observation, and in-depth structured and unstructured interviews. I conducted observations in the Monterrey and Houston transportation company "offices" and interviewed the owner, employees, and relatives that worked in the delivery of remittances and parcels in Monterrey. As I mentioned in chapter 5, I accompanied the drivers of Transportes García as they delivered remittances and parcels in the two municipalities where most clients lived. As I helped these employees carry television sets, tires, bundles of used clothes, and other items from the van into the customers' homes, I was able to observe, in a relatively unobtrusive manner, who was receiving the remittances and goods, the conditions of the dwellings, the composition of the households, and, very importantly, the interaction between the driver and the clients. My relationship with the owner of Transportes García evolved throughout the course of multiple interviews in both Monterrey and Houston between 1996 and 1999. During these four years, I followed the ups and downs of his small business until its closing in 2000. I also interviewed the customers of Transportes García and closely followed one of the operations that replaced Jorge García's venture once it shut down. It is worth mentioning that in addition to my participant observation experience as delivery hand for the *camionetas,* I was also a participant observer as passenger and client of the courier service and other transportation firms traveling the Monterrey-Houston migratory circuit.

# Notes

1. By 1965, two-thirds of the city's population had been born in places other than Monterrey (Balán, Browning, and Jelin 1973).

2. In fact, by the early 1990s, Monterrey had the highest number of *maquila* plants of any city not on the border.

3. The traditional region comprises the states of Aguascalientes, Colima, Durango, Guanajuato, Jalisco, Michoacán, Nayarit, San Luis Potosí, and Zacatecas. Together, these states constitute the historic migratory heart of the country. The rest of the states make up the nontraditional migratory region (Lozano Ascencio 2001; see also Durand and Massey 2003).

4. See also Jones (1995), who argues that there is a geographic shift in Mexico's migratory heart.

5. The Mexican consulate in Houston issues the largest percentage of consular identification cards *(matrículas consulares)* to migrants from Nuevo León in the United States—28 percent in 2006. Since more than 85 percent of Nuevo León's 4.2 million people are concentrated in the metropolitan area of Monterrey, this datum attests, albeit indirectly, that Houston is the most important destination for *regiomontano* migrants (see Instituto de los Mexicanos en el Exterior 2007; INEGI 2007).

6. I owe this observation to Mariano Sana of Louisiana State University.

7. Arguably, these reforms have been undertaken by the Mexican state to confront the generalized crisis of the country's agriculture, in general, and the low productivity of small agricultural units, in particular. Agriculture's share of the GNP continued to decline, from 11.51 percent in 1970 to 8.75 percent in 1980. The proportion of economically active population engaged in agricultural activities also decreased, from 29.2 percent in 1980 to 22.7 percent in 1990 (Garza and Rivera 1993).

8. Martin (1997) uses the term "agricultural revolution."

9. In combination with other factors, these forces have contributed to slowly but surely transform the dynamics of rural-origin migration to the United States, including its seasonal and temporal nature as well as its foundations in the peasant household economy (see for example Binford 2004). I return to this issue in the conclusion.

10. The one notable exception is the debate about whether employment in the export-oriented *maquiladoras* of Mexico's northern border cities fosters international migration by bringing workers closer to the United States. The *maquiladoras,* or export assembly plants, were part of the Border Industrialization Program initiated by the Mexican government to provide employment to former braceros and internal migrants who had moved to border cities. Until recent years, the scholarly consensus was that the *maquiladora* industry did not employ either returning bracero workers or prospective international migrants (mostly men) and that assembly plants actually recruited female workers from local and regional labor markets (Bustamante 1983; Fernández-Kelly 1983; Kopinak 1996). A critique of this consensus can be found in Zabin and Hughes 1995.

11. Reciprocity has been defined as "the norm . . . [which] holds that people should help those who have helped them and, therefore, those whom you have helped have an obligation to help you" (Gouldner 1973: 246). Similarly, Mair (1965) conceptualizes reciprocity as a type of cooperation in which "every service deserves a return, and he who helps his neighbor can expect the neighbor to help him" (1965: 66).

12. The theory of cumulative causation also contends that migration fosters other important transformations in sending and receiving areas that contribute to perpetuate population movement. For example, immigrants carve out niches in labor markets at the destination, attain legal status, and form daughter communities, facilitating the continuation of migration. At home, the availability and use of remittances changes local socioeconomic stratification structures and the use of productive resources in ways that stimulate people's desire for the material and symbolic goods attained through migration (Durand and Massey 1992; Massey 1990; Massey, Goldring, and Durand 1994).

13. In *The Age of Migration,* Castles and Miller refer to the existence of a migration industry "with a strong interest in the continuation of migration," conceptualizing such industry as "a 'maso-structure' which acts in the space between micro and macro-structures, by linking individual activities to the state and the economy" (Castles and Miller 1998: 26). In a subsequent edition of their text, these authors describe the migration industry as composed of "the many people who earn their livelihood by organizing migratory movements as travel agents, labour recruiters, brokers, interpreters and housing agents. Such people range from lawyers who give advice on immigration law, through the human smugglers who transport migrants illegally across borders" (Castles and Miller 2003: 114).

CHAPTER 2

1. The definition of "urban area" has obviously changed over time. In 1940, a human settlement of more than ten thousand people was defined as an urban area. In 1990, twenty thousand people constituted an urban area.

2. The exchange rate remained at 12.50 pesos to the dollar between 1954 and 1976 (Guillén Romo 1985).

3. Natural demographic growth cannot be overlooked as a source of urban expansion during this period. In fact, the 1940–82 period is one of rapid demographic growth in Mexico and reached rates of 3.5 percent during the mid-1960s. During the decades between 1940 and 1960, as living standards improved and public health measures spread, mortality declined dramatically and life expectancy reached fifty-nine years, rising by a total of eighteen years. At the same time, fertility levels remained rather high. Thus, the national population doubled between 1950 and 1970, reaching 50 million people (Ordorica Mellado 1994).

4. One of the consequences of this process of population redistribution was that, to this day, vast numbers of urban dwellers in the country's metropolitan areas trace their origins back to the small villages and towns of the rural hinterland. Indeed, many of the urban U.S.-bound sojourners studied in this book have prior experience as internal migrants in Mexico or are the children of such migrants.

5. A critique of using the notion of peripheral Fordism to study late industrialization can be found in Amsden 1990.

6. As I describe at length in the chapter, in Monterrey, substantial benefits packages were part of local industrialists' strategies of corporate paternalism, which were devised to secure workers' acquiescence. These strategies were conceived and implemented even before the rise of the Mexican welfare state, frequently as a response by local entrepreneurs to the federal government's support of union movements that were not subordinate to the companies.

7. Mexico has developed social welfare policies targeting the urban and rural poor. However, such policies have not been delivered through the labor market or the workplace. An analysis of social welfare policy directed toward low-income populations in Mexico can be found in Ward 1993.

8. See Escobar Latapí and Roberts 1991 for similar estimates.

9. Suddenly, Mexico became the sixth most important oil producer in the world (Guillén Romo 1985).

10. However, it is important to acknowledge that urbanization, service sector growth, and educational opportunities were already producing a secular trend during the 1970s toward the incorporation of more women into the labor market (García Guzmán 1993).

11. As stated above, informal work and the informal sector were present and played a significant role in urban economic development during ISI. Moreover, as De Oliveira and Roberts (1993) argue, informal work was important in smaller urban centers and cities where industrialization was structured around the production of basic consumer goods.

12. By the mid-1980s, conditions in rural areas had also significantly worsened (Friedmann, Lustig, and Legovini 1995; Gates 1996).

13. Still, by the end of the decade, 49.4 million people, or 60.8 percent of the national population, lived in urban areas (Garza and Rivera 1993).

14. There is some discussion as to whether the slowdown in the pace of urban growth and population concentration in the major metropolitan areas

was the result of the 1980s crisis or of a pattern of decentralization that had begun to emerge in previous decades. To be sure, the rate of urbanization had started to decline around 1960. During the 1960–70 period, the rate of urbanization was 1.8 percent, decreasing further to 1.3 percent during the 1970–80 decade. Similarly, Mexico City's population growth rate experienced a moderate decline over the decade. Researchers attribute the deceleration of urban growth to the policies of decentralization and regional development that the federal government undertook throughout the 1970s (Garza and Rivera 1993; Ruiz Chiapetto 1994).

15. Mexico's three regions are north, central, and south. See Lozano Ascencio, Roberts, and Bean (1997) for a detailed reference of the states included in these regions.

16. However, not all international migration occurring in the 1980s in Mexico was the result of the economic crisis. The Immigration Reform and Control Act (IRCA) of 1986 also had a powerful effect on Mexico-U.S. migration. The amnesty and Special Agricultural Worker (SAW) programs of IRCA legalized some 3 million immigrants, 2.3 million of whom were Mexican. The legalization of such large numbers of Mexicans in the United States has had long-lasting effects on the continuation of migratory flows between the two countries. Some of these effects are discussed in Baker 1997, Hernández-León and Zúñiga 2000, and Durand, Massey, and Parrado 1999. During the 1980s, the maturation of social networks between sending localities in Mexico and daughter communities in the United States was also playing a significant role in the perpetuation of migration (Massey et al. 1987).

17. The industrial sector in Mexico was (and still is) highly heterogeneous, comprising large modern firms that use advanced technology as well as small companies that operate as subcontractors to the leading corporations that utilize outdated equipment. Arguing for the analytical significance of the heterogeneity of manufacturing, Gutiérrez Garza (1992) identifies four industrial subsectors in Mexico: (1) large corporations that utilize modern technology and employ some 30 percent of the manufacturing labor force; (2) large- and medium-sized firms that produce exclusively for the internal market using outdated technologies; (3) small companies that produce under labor-intensive systems, operating as subcontractors for larger firms, also manufacturing some final goods, and (4) the *maquiladora* industry, which in recent years has begun to include not only firms that do basic assembly but also companies that use high-tech and highly automated equipment. This subsector, however, shows very little integration with the national industry, except for the case of Monterrey.

18. Gutiérrez Garza (1992) has further argued that in Mexico's industrial context, firms have implemented what she terms "static flexibility"—a type of reform that emphasizes cutting down the cost of labor (i.e., direct and social wages) and intensifying its use. Static flexibility is largely synonymous with deregulation, that is, the attempt to do away with the labor codes of the Fordist era, which are viewed by industrial capitalists as an obstacle to creating an internationally competitive manufacturing sector. The implementation of static flexibility strategies does not exclude the implementation of dynamic flexibility, namely, the kind of strategy that privileges changes in the labor process via new

technologies and new forms of industrial organization. The two kinds of flexibility have coexisted during Mexico's transition to EOI, although static flexibility has arguably been the dominant type (Gutiérrez Garza 1992: 380).

19. The strategies that Mexican corporations have used to access new technologies are analyzed in Pozas 1997.

20. For an analysis of restructuring in the auto part industry, which holds multiple similarities to and linkages with the automobile industry, see Zapata, Hoshino, and Hanono (1994).

21. As part of the restructuring process, the strategy of liberalizing and opening the economy has comprised different policies and reforms, including the reprivatization of banks and the privatization of state-owned companies, the deregulation of foreign direct investment and foreign participation in Mexico's financial system, and strict monetary policy (Dussel Peters 1998, 2000; Heath 1998). Not all these measures can be analyzed here. I focus on those that have a stronger connection and relevance to job markets and international migration.

22. *Maquiladora* activities are included in this figure. If *maquiladora* activities are excluded from the calculation of the balance of trade, the deficit for 1994 reaches 27.3 billion dollars (Dussel Peters 1998).

23. According to Gereffi, "Maquiladoras are assembly plants that import parts and supplies duty-free into Mexico and export their production, largely to the United States" (1996: 87). Much literature has addressed in detail the characteristics and development of the *maquiladora* industry along the U.S.-Mexico border, including Bustamante 1983; Carrillo Huerta 1991; de la O. and Quintero 1995; Fernández-Kelly 1983; Kopinak 1996; Sklair 1993; and Tiano 1990. See also the works collected in *Industria Maquiladora y Mercados Laborales* (1992).

24. This figure was obtained by dividing the number of people employed in *maquiladoras* (operatives, technicians, and administrative personnel) in December 1998 (1,038,783) by the number of people employed in manufacturing in 1998 (4,213,566) (INEGI 2005).

25. At the end of 1999, there were 429,301 men and 531,620 women working as operatives in *maquila* plants (INEGI 2005).

26. Nevertheless, researchers such as Gereffi (1996) have questioned whether export processing may constitute a sound strategy for long-term development. He argues that this is not the case and that *maquiladoras* need to be promoted as a transitional strategy that should evolve into a type of industrialization with better paid and more secure jobs (Gereffi 1996: 98).

27. In contrast, nearly six hundred miles separate Monterrey from Mexico City.

28. At the end of the nineteenth century, these states (Chihuahua, Durango, Zacatecas, Coahuila, and Nuevo León) were the leading producers of lead, silver, gold, copper, and ferrous ores in Mexico (Cerutti 1992a).

29. For instance, the brewery Cervecería Cuauhtémoc was seized by revolutionary forces and its production confiscated from 1914 to 1916 (Saragoza 1988).

30. Monterrey's corporations also needed to negotiate their external debt, and some of them had to turn over part of their stock to creditors. It is worth noting that the federal government played a fundamental role in bailing these

corporations out of financial trouble through different programs and loans (Pozas 1993a).

31. These percentages need to be interpreted with caution since they represent the overall economically active population and not only working-class individuals.

32. By 1989, 58.4 percent of the economically active population in Monterrey was employed in commerce and services (Ramones Saldaña 1995).

33. The concentration of industrial activity in a few subsectors has remained a feature of the Monterrey metropolitan area. In 1988, the metallic goods, machinery, and equipment subsector contained 34.3 percent of industrial firms and 36.1 percent of manufacturing employment in the city. In 1980, however, the basic metals industry was the dominant manufacturing subsector. The decline of this subsector was closely tied to the closing of Fundidora, which generated 12 percent of the local industrial product (Aguilar Barajas 1993; Garza 1995a).

34. Pozas (1993a) argues that, given their economic prowess and historical experience with international markets, the Monterrey corporations were the best prepared to take advantage of state policies promoting exports and opening of the national economy.

35. According to ALFA's president, the transaction allowed the Mexican corporation to slash its debt and to become concentrated in strategic sectors such as petrochemicals, food, and auto parts ("Dejan ir Hylsa; crecen con Alfa," *Reforma,* May 26, 2005).

36. See http://www.ternium.com/sp/prensa/default.asp (accessed May 2, 2007); "Sale personal de Hylsamex," *Reforma,* November 14, 2005.

37. See "Toma Ternium control de IMSA," *Reforma,* April 30, 2007; "Tienen extranjeros siderurgia nacional," *Reforma,* July 25, 2005; "Huracán de acero," http://www.cnnexpansion.com/expansion/reportajes/2006/12/27/huracan-de-acero (accessed May 2, 2007); "La industria acerera mexicana?" http://www.cnnexpansion.com/negocios/la-industria-acerera-bfmexicana (accessed May 2, 2007).

CHAPTER 3

1. Needless to say, in a 4-million-people metropolitan area, this is one of many such starting points for U.S. migration, not all Houston or even Texas bound. Fieldwork I have conducted in other Monterrey neighborhoods and at U.S. destinations showed that working-class *regiomontanos* have established circuits between this city and localities in Georgia, North Carolina, and Illinois.

2. The Fábrica de Hilados y Tejidos El Porvenir was shut down in February 2004.

3. In contrast, 36 percent of the households are in the expansion stage, which means that young children live in the household, and 18 percent are in the consolidation phase, indicating that some of the offspring are employed while still living at home and contribute to the household budget.

4. Respondents identified 152 men (90.5 percent) and 16 women (9.5 percent) as household heads (n = 168). For purposes of the survey, the head was

defined as the adult who contributed the most money to the household. A discussion of some of the problems posed by the concept of household head can be found in the methodological appendix.

5. Lower proportions of spouses were born in the rural areas of Nuevo León, San Luis Potosí, and Zacatecas and a higher proportion in rural Coahuila and Tamaulipas, suggesting some degree of exogamy, which might be linked to the experience of internal migration.

6. The textile mill in Villa de Santiago, called El Porvenir, was established in 1871, some fifteen years after the creation of La Fama (Rojas Sandoval 1997).

7. On-the-job training has in many cases provided the skills that these posts require.

8. Some of these children have already moved away from the parental home to establish their own independent household. For comparative purposes, the last two columns of table 2 provide statistics for La Fama's current residents fifteen years of age and older and all family members also fifteen and over, regardless of where they live.

9. This number includes individuals who have moved away and are no longer residents of the neighborhood.

10. These are individuals who were born in Monterrey (52 percent of all U.S. migrants) or who were born elsewhere but spent their formative years (ages five to fifteen) in the city.

11. An obvious caveat to this finding is that since they are the oldest migrant cohort in the sample, at least some La Fama residents with U.S. experience during the Bracero program years are likely to have died already.

12. Unfortunately, there is no published historical analysis about the workings of the bracero recruitment center in Monterrey to triangulate with the qualitative and quantitative findings from La Fama.

13. This section uses data drawn from fieldwork conducted in both La Fama and Houston.

14. Established by private investors in 1900, Fundidora had become a parastate enterprise in the late 1970s. In 1986, the federal government declared the company bankrupt due to severe financial losses over the previous four years and a mounting debt. Yet beneath the question of the financial viability of the firm there were problems of productivity, labor relations, and technological modernization (Rojas Sandoval 1997).

15. It is worth noting that in the two previous sketches, women have been the sources of support networks for the migration of men.

CHAPTER 4

1. Census data need to be interpreted with caution given the common underreporting of undocumented workers.

2. By the late 1970s, six of these major corporations—Exxon, Gulf, Shell, Conoco, Chevron, and Mobil—controlled the production of 37 percent of crude oil in Texas (Shelton et al. 1989).

3. This phenomenon may be repeating itself during the present decade.

4. Still, Houston's political landscape is undergoing important changes. In

2005, the Service Employees International Union managed to organize more than five thousand janitors in the largely Latino-immigrant cleaning services industry. In October 2006, the union launched a strike, demanding higher wages and mobilizing thousands of workers and their supporters. A month later, the strikers and their employers reached an agreement that included a raise of almost 50 percent over two years, health insurance, two extra hours of work per shift, and paid holidays. This settlement gave the labor movement one of its most important victories in Houston, and in the South, ever (Greenhouse 2006a, 2006b).

5. See the study of Arias and Woo Morales (2004) for a similar finding in the metropolitan area of Guadalajara using data from the Mexican Migration Project.

6. Needless to say, changes in U.S. immigration policy have made obtaining a visa a more difficult and expensive endeavor. And yet, as I mentioned before, many skilled industrial workers already possess border-crossing cards and tourist visas.

7. This is worth noting, because, as the methodological appendix indicates, in Houston I cast my fieldwork net in wider terms than in La Fama, using any subject as long as he or she was from Monterrey.

8. For a study analyzing the impact of the ups and downs of the global oil industry on employers' hiring practices of native workers and Mexican immigrants in the southern Louisiana labor market, see Donato and Bankston 2008.

9. The border-crossing card (BCC) is a visa issued to residents of Mexican border cities and states with the purpose of allowing them entry into United States to conduct certain commercial activities and short visits. A BCC holder may stay in the country for up to seventy-two hours and is required to remain in the border area. I do not intend to argue that all or most BCC and tourist visa holders necessarily use these documents to enter the United States and find employment. However, many Mexican border residents take advantage of the visa to work and undertake a broad array of commercial transactions (some of which are allowed under the terms of the visa) *en el otro lado* (on the other side). This fact has been part of the fabric of border towns (and interior cities, such as Monterrey, located in border states) for decades, although few studies have documented its multiple implications. It is not uncommon, for instance, for women residents of Mexican border cities to use their BCCs to work as domestics on the U.S. side. Just like the *regiomontanos* depicted in this chapter, these women have also developed many strategies to avoid detection by immigration authorities. During the initial stages of my fieldwork in Houston, I interviewed a former industrial worker from Monterrey who, for years during the 1970s, used his BCC to go to El Campo, Texas, to play Mexican music in cantinas and at weddings and baptisms. A skilled manufacturing operative in a large glass-making corporation in Monterrey, this man used his musical stints to supplement his wage, traveling to Texas only during his vacation. At times, however, border officials would deny him entry, alleging that he needed a professional performer's visa. His solution was to leave his guitar at home and borrow one once he had managed to cross into the United States.

10. Guadalupe's actions also announced a trend that has unfolded with full force during the past ten years: the U.S. corporations' courting of the undocumented population as part of their consumer base (Grow 2005).

11. It is also telling that in the early 1990s, some La Fama migrants were not even using the services of *coyotes* to get across the border.

12. These emergencies always exposed how the border effectively kept families apart. In one specific case in La Fama, no family member from Monterrey was able to attend the funeral of a close relative in Houston because of the lack of U.S. visa documents.

13. However, states and municipalities have for some time tried to pass and enforce laws and ordinances discouraging or preventing undocumented immigrants from integrating into the fabric of local communities, effectively deflecting newcomers to more welcoming parts of the country (see Light 2006). The most famous of such efforts in recent history is Proposition 187, approved by California voters in 1994. The dispersion of Mexican immigrants to new destinations has been met by literally hundreds of ordinances and laws, which range from barring laborers from soliciting work on street corners to penalizing landlords for renting to the undocumented and training local police to identify "illegals." The fact that many of these ordinances are often shut down in the courts has not prevented state and local governments from passing them and therefore becoming actors once again in the immigration policy debate.

CHAPTER 5

1. Two notable exceptions are Griffith and Kissam's (1995) multisite study of farm workers, which deals at length with the role of contractors and transportation providers in the social organization of immigrant-dominated agricultural labor markets in the United States, and Kyle's (2000) study of migrant merchants "profiting, legally or illegally, from the commodification of the international migration process, [forming] a larger system or informal network" in Ecuador (67).

2. Still, many of the small, informal operations specializing in distinct migratory circuits connecting Houston with locations in Mexico and relying on word of mouth instead of advertising, like Transportes García, also use vans as the preferred means of transportation. By the same token, some bus firms, such as the aforementioned Autobuses Adame, also offer connections from Houston to cities in the U.S. interior using a fleet of buses.

3. A more recent phenomenon has to do with Houston's rise as a recruitment center for agricultural labor (and now construction, services, and light manufacturing) all across the southeast, a role long held by the towns of the Texas-Mexico borderlands. In this informal system of recruitment, contractors work closely with *raiteros* (ride providers) and *troqueros* (truck drivers) who, doubling as *transportistas* (transportation providers) and recruiters, are able to charge one fee for transportation from Houston to the worksite and another fee for selecting the worker. Thus, in a chainlike system, to secure access to labor, employers resort to contractors, who in turn rely on *raiteros* operating in Houston.

4. Newspaper reports have counted as many as fifty small van operations in Houston (Hegstrom 2002). In August 2003, twenty-one such companies advertised their services in the Spanish weekly *La Subasta*. Nineteen of them appeared to offer travel exclusively to the U.S. interior.

5. The success of bus companies such as Adame, El Conejo, and El Expresso has been such that Greyhound has made several overtures to acquire them or establish partnerships with them (Beachy 1996).

6. The services that van operators render to undocumented immigrants are by no means a secret. These firms advertise in local papers, stating both their destinations in the U.S. interior and their pickup points in Houston, and are the subject of regular journalistic reports. Some of these van line operators have been prosecuted, accused of smuggling immigrants (Hegstrom 2002).

7. Although my field research has dealt very little with female participation in and perspectives about the operation of this business, it is clear that a woman, Jorge's wife, played a central role in the history and day-to-day administration of the *camionetas*. First, Jorge was able to adjust his migratory status through his wife, Rosy, who is Mexican American. For Jorge it was essential to become a legal permanent resident to be able to go back and forth across the border without major problems and therefore develop this business. Second, as a U.S. citizen, Rosy was the only one who could register the company, and the commercial insurance for the vehicles was under her name. Third, despite her active involvement with the business, Rosy continued working full time in a salaried job. This job provided the household with income and health insurance for all family members.

8. Observations made while delivering van shipments allowed for a firsthand look into the characteristics of the migrant households receiving money, letters, and packages. Most of these households seemed to be comprised of young women with small children or young adolescents, with other domestic units made up of older men and women. Yet other households consisted of women and both small children and elderly persons. Thus, there were few recipient families composed of middle-aged adults. In these observations, the apparent absence of adult males in the households receiving shipments was notable. The latter corresponds with Jorge's assertions that the majority of his clients were men living alone in the United States. Some of these men traveled with the *camionetas* every weekend to see their wives and children who stayed behind in Mexico. For details on the strategy used to conduct these observations, see the methodological appendix.

9. These items were often secondhand merchandise—goods purchased in the weekend flea markets located in the Latino immigrant settlements in Houston. In Monterrey, families would resell these items in local street markets to raise household income. This is the most likely case for those households receiving secondhand clothing.

10. The shipment of medicine is particularly significant because access to medication in the United States requires a doctor's prescription. The high cost of medication and medical services forced some migrants to satisfy these needs using Jorge's transportation company. One phone call to a family member in Monterrey on a Tuesday or Saturday afternoon asking for a particular medicine

guaranteed that the item would arrive at the Houston Transportes office the following morning.

11. As a counterpoint, it is worth noting that other studies have shown that under certain circumstances, money capital can bypass the social closure set by social capital, hence allowing outsiders access to highly embedded economic opportunities (Spener and Roberts 1998).

12. In invoking trust and moral arguments, Jorge might have been trying to rebuild, at the discursive level, the bonds that linked him to fellow *regiomontanos* before he became a successful migration entrepreneur.

13. Another potential risk that the vans faced were the robberies taking place along Mexican highways. It is somewhat surprising that, given the large cash sums Transportes García carried twice a week on its sojourn from Houston to Monterrey, it never experienced a robbery. However, other remittance transportation services were not so lucky, showing that this was a looming threat. In November 1999, a similar company was robbed as one of the vehicles was making deliveries in Monterrey. The attackers took $22,000 with them (Alvarez 1999).

14. See the Proposal for Decision no. B346–00–143 of the Finance Commission of Texas (http://www.fc.state.tx.us/ALJ/DECIDE/B346PFD.HTM; accessed January 27, 2006).

15. U.S. and Mexican financial institutions are now offering low-cost and even free remittance services to customers with checking accounts. The goal of these institutions is not to carve out a substantial piece of the remittance market. Instead, their objective is to sell a variety of services to documented and undocumented Mexican immigrants, populations that contain large segments of "unbanked" individuals. These financial services include credit cards, mortgages, savings accounts, and investment schemes. The potential of this new frontier has prompted bankers to talk about establishing a "binational financial culture" (González Amador 2007; see also Reckard 2007).

CHAPTER 6

1. However, some *regiomontanos*, native or adopted, do utilize their contacts with a hinterland rich in migratory social capital to sustain their U.S.-bound moves. In fact, in my research into other neighborhoods in Monterrey with more recent experience of internal migration, I encountered household heads who would call on their friends and family in their rural Nuevo León hometowns to launch a migratory trip to the United States (see Hernández-León 1999). As noted by Massey and associates (1987), by stretching the resources that facilitate sojourning from towns and villages to cities, this strategy also has the potential of spreading the migratory behavior to urban neighborhoods and households, where the experience had been largely absent.

2. As suggested by Karthick Ramakrishnan of UC Riverside at a 2007 conference on immigration politics at UCLA, an excellent illustration of this phenomenon are the efforts of the United States and other Western governments to restrict or shut down Islamic charitable organizations, which in the aftermath of 9/11 are often accused of funneling money to terrorist groups.

3. Recent studies have shown that in some regions of Mexico, internal migration functions as a stepping stone for international migration (Rivera Sánchez and Lozano Ascencio 2006). In others, internal migration substitutes for cross-border mobility (Zamudio Grave et al. 2004).

4. Interestingly, the jobs of the H2-B program were not all in agriculture, preempting the argument that rural residents had to be matched with field tasks. For example, some of the H2-B posts were located in the hospitality industry.

# Bibliography

Acosta, Félix. 1994. "Hogares con Jefes Mujeres. ¿Qué Sabemos? ¿Qué Sigue?" Paper presented at the Sociedad Mexicana de Demografía (SOMEDE-INEGI) Conference, Hogares, Familias: Desigualdad, Conflicto, Redes Solidarias y Parentales, Aguascalientes, June 27–29.

Aguilar, Adrian G. 1997. "The Urban Labor Market in Mexico: Global Change, Informality, and Social Polarization." *Urban Geography* 18(2): 106–134.

Aguilar Barajas, Ismael. 1993. "Industria Manufacturera en Nuevo León, 1985–1988: Un Análisis de su Concentración Sectorial y Territorial." In *TLC: Impactos en la Frontera Norte*, edited by A. Dávila Flores, 73–99. Mexico City: UNAM.

Aguilar Camín, Héctor, and Lorenzo Meyer. 1993. *In the Shadow of the Mexican Revolution: Contemporary Mexican History, 1910–1989*. Austin: University of Texas Press.

Alarcón, Rafael. 1992. "Norteñización: Self-Perpetuating Migration from a Mexican Town." In *U.S.-Mexico Relations: Labor Market Interdependence*, edited by J.A. Bustamante, C.W. Reynolds, and R.A. Hinojosa Ojeda, 302–318. Stanford, CA: Stanford Universvity Press.

Alba Vega, Carlos, and Bryan Roberts. 1991. "Crisis, Adjustment and Employment in the Manufacturing Industry of Jalisco." In *Migration Impacts of Trade and Foreign Investment*, edited by S. Díaz-Briquets and S. Weintraub, 255–278. Boulder, CO: Westview Press.

Alcalde Justiniani, Arturo. 2004. "¿Y la Reforma Laboral?" *La Jornada*, www.jornada.unam.mx/2004/04/10/012a1pol.php?origen = opinion.php&fly = 2, accessed August 16, 2007.

Alvarez, Mario Alberto. 1999. "Roban 22 Mil Dólares Enviados por Paisanos." *El Norte*, http://busquedas.gruporeforma.com/elnorte/Documentos/Documento Impresa.aspx?, accessed August 16, 2007.

Amsden, Alice H. 1990. "Third World Industrialization: 'Global Fordism' or a New Model?" *New Left Review* 182: 5–31.

Anderson, Joan, and Martin de la Rosa. 1991. "Economic Survival Strategies of Poor Families on the Mexican Border." *Journal of Borderland Studies* 6(1): 51–68.

Arias, Patricia, and Woo Morales, Ofelia. 2004. "La Migración Urbana hacia Estados Unidos. Tres Ejemplos de la Zona Metropolitana de Guadalajara." *Papeles de Población* 42 (October–December): 37–72.

Arreola, Daniel D. 1993. "Mexico Origins of South Texas Mexican Americans, 1930." *Journal of Historical Geography* 19(1): 48–63.

Arteaga, Arnulfo. 1985. "Innovación Tecnológica y Clase Obrera en la Industria Automotriz." In *Testimonios de la Crisis 1. Restructuración Productiva y Clase Obrera,* edited by Esthela Gutiérrez Garza, 146–169. Mexico City: Siglo XXI.

Baker, Susan González. 1997. "The 'Amnesty' Aftermath: Current Policy Issues Stemming from the Legalization Programs of the 1986 Immigration Reform and Control Act." *International Migration Review* 31(1): 5–27.

Balán, Jorge, Harley L. Browning, and Elizabeth Jelin. 1973. *Men in a Developing Society: Geographic and Social Mobility in Monterrey, Mexico.* Austin: University of Texas Press.

Banco de México. 2007. *Las Remesas Familiares en México.* Www.banxico.org. mx/audiencias/prensa/index.html, accessed April 19, 2007.

Barkin, David. 1991. *Un Desarrollo Distorsionado: La Integración de México a la Economía Mundial.* Mexico City: Siglo XXI-UAM Xochimilco.

Basch, Linda, Nina Glick Schiller, and Cristina Szanton-Blanc. 1994. *Nations Unbound: Transnational Projects, Postcolonial Predicaments, and Deterritorialized Nation States.* Amsterdam: Gordon and Breach.

Beachy, Debra. 1996. "Greyhound Takes Another Route." *Houston Chronicle,* July 11.

Binford, Leigh. 2004. "La Migración Internacional en el Contexto de la Crisis de la Industria Mexicana de la Construcción: El Caso de Santo Tomás Chautla, Puebla." In *La Economía Política de la Migración Internacional en Puebla y Veracruz: Siete Estudios de Caso,* edited by Leigh Binford, 215–256. Puebla, Mexico: Benemérita Universidad Autónoma de Puebla.

Bluestone, Barry, and Bennett Harrison. 1982. *The Deindustrialization of America.* New York: Basic Books.

Borden, Teresa. 2004. "On a Roll: Cross-border Bus Business Booms as Immigrants Help Others Go Home." *Atlanta Journal-Constitution,* July 12.

Bortz, Jeffrey. 1992. "The Effect of Mexico's Postwar Industrialization on the U.S.-Mexico Price and Wage Comparison." In *U.S.-Mexico Relations: Labor Market Interdependence,* edited by J.A. Bustamante, C.W. Reynolds, and R.A. Hinojosa Ojeda, 214–234. Stanford, CA: Stanford University Press.

Boruchoff, Judith A. 1999. "Equipaje Cultural: Objetos, Identidad y Transnacionalismo en Guerrero y Chicago." In *Fronteras Fragmentadas,* edited by Gail Mummert, 499–518. Zamora, Mexico: El Colegio de Michoacán-CIDEM.

Boudreaux, Richard. 2003. "Migrants' Dollars Cross Border, Brick by Brick." *Los Angeles Times,* June 1.

Browning, Harley, and Rodolfo Corona. 1995. "La Emigración Inesperada de los Chilangos." *DemoS* 8: 16–17, 55–56.

Bustamante, Jorge A. 1983. *"Maquiladoras:* A New Face of International Capitalism on Mexico's Northern Frontier." In *Women, Men, and the International Division of Labor,* edited by J. Nash and M.P. Fernández-Kelly, 224–256. Albany: State University of New York Press.

Calvo, Dana. 2005. "In the New Houston, Oil Is No Longer King." *Los Angeles Times,* September 4, C1.

Cano, Gustavo. 2002. "Understanding Immigrant Political Mobilization: The Mexican Communities in Chicago and Houston." Paper presented at the annual meeting of the American Political Science Association, August 29–September 1, Boston.

Capps, Randy. 1999. "Characteristics of Asian and Latino/a Immigrants in Houston." Paper presented at the conference Coming to America: Asian and Latino/a Experiences in the 1990s, April 15, University of Houston.

Carrillo, Jorge V., and Alfredo Hualde. 1992. "Mercados de Trabajo en la Industria Maquiladora de Exportación." In *Ajuste Estructural, Mercados Laborales y TLC,* 157–177. Mexico City: Colegio de México.

Carrillo Huerta, Mario M. 1991. "The Impact of *Maquiladoras* on Migration in Mexico." In *The Effects of Receiving Country Policies on Migration Flows,* edited by S. Díaz-Briquets and S. Weintraub, 67–102. Boulder, CO: Westview Press.

Castles, Stephen, and Mark J. Miller. 2003. *The Age of Migration.* 3rd ed. New York: Guilford.

———. 1998. *The Age of Migration.* 2nd ed. New York: Guilford.

Cerutti, Mario. 1995. "Brote Fabril, Empresariado y Expansión Demográfica, 1890–1910." In *Atlas de Monterrey,* edited by Gustavo Garza, 89–93. Monterrey: Gobierno del Estado de Nuevo León/UANL/INSEUR-NL/COLMEX.

———. 1992a. *Burgesía, Capitales e Industria en el Norte de México.* Mexico City: Alianza Editorial/UANL.

———. 1992b. "Monterrey and Its *Ambito Regional,* 1850–1910: Historical Context and Methodological Recommendations." In *Mexico's Regions: Comparative History and Development,* edited by Eric Van Young, 145–165. San Diego: Center for U.S.-Mexican Studies, University of California, San Diego.

Colegio de la Frontera Norte/Universidad Autónoma de Ciudad Juárez. 1992. *Industria Maquiladora y Mercados Laborales.* Ciudad Juárez: COLEF and UACJ.

CONAPO. 2002. "Índice de Intensidad Migratoria México-Estados Unidos, 2000." Mexico City: Consejo Nacional de Población, www.conapo.gob.mx, accessed August 9, 2007.

Contreras, Oscar F., and Miguel Angel Ramírez Sánchez. 1992. "Mercado de Trabajo y Relaciones Laborales en Cananea: La Disputa en Torno a la Flexibilidad." In *Ajuste Estructural, Mercados Laborales y TLC,* 337–350. Mexico City: Colegio de México.

Cook, Maria Lorena, Kevin J. Middlebrook, and Juan Molinar Horcasitas, eds. 1994. *The Politics of Economic Restructuring: State-Society Relations and Regime Change in Mexico.* San Diego: Center for U.S.-Mexican Studies, University of California, San Diego.

Coriat, Benjamin. 1992. *Pensar al Revés: Trabajo y Organización en la Empresa Japonesa.* Mexico City: Siglo XXI.

———. 1991. *El Taller y el Cronómetro: Ensayo sobre el Taylorismo, el Fordismo y la Producción en Masa.* Mexico City: Siglo XXI.

Cornelius, Wayne A. 1998. *"Ejido* Reform: Stimulus or Alternative to Migration?" In *The Transformation of Rural Mexico: Reforming the* Ejido *Sector,* edited by Wayne A. Cornelius and David Myhre, 229–246. San Diego: Center for U.S.-Mexican Studies, University of California, San Diego.

———. 1992. "From Sojourners to Settlers: The Changing Profile of Mexican Immigration to the United States." In *U.S.-Mexico Relations: Labor Market Interdependence,* edited by J.A. Bustamante, C.W. Reynolds, and R.A. Hinojosa Ojeda, 155–195. Stanford, CA: Stanford University Press.

———. 1991. "Los Migrantes de la Crisis: The Changing Profile of Mexican Migration to the United States." In *Social Responses to Mexico's Economic Crisis of the 1980s,* edited by Mercedes González de la Rocha and Agustín Escobar Latapí, 155–193. San Diego: Center for U.S.-Mexican Studies, University of California, San Diego.

———. 1982. "Interviewing Undocumented Immigrants: Methodological Reflections Based on Fieldwork in Mexico and the U.S." *International Migration Review* 16(2): 378–411.

———. 1976. "Outmigration from Rural Mexican Communities." In *The Dynamics of Migration: International Migration,* edited by W.A. Cornelius et al., 1–40. Washington, D.C.: Smithsonian Institution.

Cornelius, Wayne A., and Philip L. Martin. 1993. *The Uncertain Connection: Free Trade and Mexico-U.S. Migration.* San Diego: Center for U.S.-Mexican Studies, University of California, San Diego.

Cornelius, Wayne A., and David Myhre, eds. 1998. *The Transformation of Rural Mexico: Reforming the* Ejido *Sector.* San Diego: Center for U.S.-Mexican Studies, University of California, San Diego.

Corona Vázquez, Rodolofo. 1993. "La Migración de Mexicanos a los Estados Unidos: Cambios en la Década de 1980–1990." *Revista Mexicana de Sociología* 55(1): 213–233.

Cortés, Fernando, and Rosa María Rubalcava. 1993. "Desocupados Precoces: Otra Cara de la Maquila? *Estudios Sociológicos* 11(33): 695–723.

Cortés García, Jesús. 1991. *Semblanzas. Estampas y Apuntes de un Pueblo: La Fama, N.L.* Santa Catarina, Mexico: Ayuntamiento de Santa Catarina.

Crandall, Russell. 2005. "Mexico's Domestic Economy: Policy Options and Choices." In *Mexico's Democracy at Work: Political and Economic Dynamics,* edited by Russell Crandall, Guadalupe Paz, and Riordan Roett, 61–87. Boulder, CO: Lynne Rienner.

Cravey, Altha J. 1998. *Women and Work in Mexico's* Maquiladoras. Lanham, MD: Rowman and Littlefield.

————. 1997. "The Politics of Reproduction: Households in the Mexican Industrial Transition." *Economic Geography* 73(2): 166–186.

Cuellar, Margarito. 1996. "La Fábrica de Hilados y Tejidos La Fama de Nuevo León y el Desarrollo Poblacional en Santa Catarina." In *Santa Catarina: Un Acercamiento a su Historia,* edited by Jesús Cortés García et al., 115–124. Santa Catarina, Mexico: Presidencia Municipal de Santa Catarina.

De la Garza, Rodolfo O., and Briant Lindsay Lowell. 2002. *Sending Money Home: Hispanic Remittances and Community Development.* Lanham, MD: Rowman and Littlefield.

De la O., María Eugenia, and Cirila Quintero. 1995. "Trayectorias Laborales y Estabilidad en las Maquiladoras de Matamoros y Tijuana." *Frontera Norte* 7(13): 67–91.

Delaunay, Marina. 2002. "Las Remesas en Especie." *Expansión,* October 16–30, 117–126.

De León, Arnoldo. 1989. *Ethnicity in the Sunbelt: A History of Mexican Americans in Houston.* Houston: Mexican American Studies Program, University of Houston.

De Oliveira, Orlandina, and Bryan Roberts. 1993. "La Informalidad Urbana en Años de Expansión, Crisis y Restructuración Económica." *Estudios Sociológicos* 11(31): 33–58.

Dinerman, Ina R. 1978. "Patterns of Adaptation among Households of U.S.-Bound Migrants from Michoacan, Mexico." *International Migration Review* 12(4): 485–501.

Donato, Katharine M. 1993. "Current Trends and Patterns of Female Migration: Evidence from Mexico." *International Migration Review* 27(4): 748–771.

Donato, Katharine M., and Carl L. Bankston. 2008. "The Origins of Employer Demand for Immigrants in a New Destination: The Salience of Soft Skills in a Volatile Economy." In *New Faces in New Places: The Changing Geography of American Immigration,* edited by Douglas S. Massey, 124–148. New York: Russell Sage Foundation.

Donato, Katharine M., Carl L. Bankston, and Dawn T. Robinson. 2001. "Immigration and the Organization of the Onshore Oil Industry: Southern Louisiana in the Late 1990s." In *Latino Workers in the Contemporary South,* edited by Arthur D. Murphy, Colleen Blanchard, and Jennifer A. Hill, 105–113. Athens: University of Georgia Press.

Donato, Katharine M., Melissa Stainback, and Carl L. Bankston. 2005. "The Economic Incorporation of Mexican Immigrants in Southern Louisiana: A Tale of Two Cities." In *New Destinations: Mexican Immigration in the United States,* edited by Víctor Zúñiga and Rubén Hernañdez-León, 76–100. New York: Russell Sage Foundation.

Durand, Jorge. 2000. "Tres Premisas para Entender y Explicar la Migración México–Estados Unidos." *Relaciones* 21: 17–36.

————. 1998. *Política, Modelo y Patrón Migratorios.* San Luis Potosí: El Colegio de San Luis.

————. 1994. *Mas Allá de la Línea: Patrones Migratorios entre México y Estados Unidos.* Mexico City: CONACULTA.

————, ed. 1991. *Migración México-Estados Unidos: Años Veinte.* Mexico City: CNCA.

————. 1988. "Circuitos Migratorios." In *Movimientos de Población en el Occidente de México,* edited by Thomas Calvo and Gustavo López, 25–49. Zamora, Mexico: El Colegio de Michoacán.

Durand, Jorge, and Douglas S. Massey. 2003. *Clandestinos: Migración México–Estados Unidos en los Albores del Siglo XXI.* Mexico City: Universidad Autónoma de Zacatecas and Porrúa.

————. 1992. "Mexican Migration to the United States: A Critical Review." *Latin American Research Review* 27(2): 3–42.

Durand, Jorge, Douglas S. Massey, and Fernando Charvet. 2000. "The Changing Geography of Mexican Immigration to the United States, 1910–1996." *Social Science Quarterly* 81(1): 1–15.

Durand, Jorge, Douglas S. Massey, and Emilio Parrado. 1999. "The New Era of Mexican Migration to the United States." *Journal of American History* 86: 518–536.

Durand, Jorge, Douglas S. Massey, and René M. Zenteno. 2001. "Mexican Immigration to the United States: Continuities and Changes." *Latin American Research Review* 36(1): 107–127.

Dussel Peters, Enrique. 2000. *Polarizing Mexico: The Impact of Liberalization Strategy.* Boulder, CO: Lynne Rienner.

————. 1998. "Recent Structural Changes in Mexico's Economy: A Preliminary Analysis of Some Sources of Mexican Migration to the United States." In *Crossings: Mexican Immigration in Interdisciplinary Perspectives,* edited by Marcelo M. Suárez-Orozco, 55–74. Boston: Harvard University and David Rockefeller Center for Latin American Studies.

Eschbach, Karl, et al. 1999. "Death at the Border." *International Migration Review* 33(2): 430–454.

Escobar Latapí, Agustín. 1992. "El Nuevo Estado Mexicano y el Trabajo Informal." In *El Nuevo Estado Mexicano: I. Estado y Economía,* edited by Jorge Alonso, Alberto Aziz, and Jaime Tamayo, 253–280. Mexico City: UdeG-Nueva Imagen-CIESAS.

Escobar Latapí, Agustín, and M. de la O. Martínez Castellanos. 1991. "Small-Scale Industry and International Migration in Guadalajara, México." In *Migration, Remittances, and Small Business Development,* edited by S. Díaz-Briquets and S. Weintraub, 133–173. Boulder, CO: Westview Press.

Escobar Latapí, Agustín, and Bryan Roberts. 1991. "Urban Stratification, the Middle Classes, and Economic Change in Mexico." In *Social Responses to Mexico's Economic Crisis of the 1980's,* edited by Mercedes González de la Rocha and Agustín Escobar Latapí, 91–113. San Diego: Center for U.S.-Mexican Studies, University of California, San Diego.

Escobar Latapí, Agustín, et al. 1998. "Aspects That Influence Migration." In *Mexico–United States Binational Migration Study. Migration between Mexico and the United States.* Austin: Mexican Ministry of Foreign Affairs and U.S. Commission on Immigration Reform, Morgan Printing.

Espinosa, Víctor M. 1998. *El Dilema del Retorno: Migración, Género y Perte-*

*nencia en un Contexto Transnacional.* Zamora, Mexico: El Colegio de Michoacán.

Faist, Thomas. 2000. *The Volume and Dynamics of International Migration and Transnational Social Spaces.* Oxford, England: Oxford University Press.

Feagin, Joe R. 1988. *Free Enterprise City: Houston in Political-Economic Perspective.* New Brunswick, NJ: Rutgers University Press.

———. 1987. "The Secondary Circuit of Capital: Office Construction in Houston, Texas." *International Journal of Urban and Regional Research* 11(2): 172–192.

———. 1985. "The Global Context of Metropolitan Growth: Houston and the Oil Industry." *American Journal of Sociology* 90(6): 1204–1230.

Fernández-Kelly, M. Patricia. 1994. "Towanda's Triumph: Social and Cultural Capital in the Transition to Adulthood in the Urban Ghetto." *International Journal of Urban and Regional Research* 18(1): 88–111.

———. 1983. "Mexican Border Industrialization, Female Labor Force Participation and Migration." In *Women, Men, and the International Division of Labor,* edited by J. Nash and M.P. Fernández-Kelly, 205–223. Albany: State University of New York Press.

Finance Commission of Texas. 2006. "Proposal for Decision No. B346–00–143." Www.fc.state.tx.us/ALJ/DECIDE/B346PFD.HTM, accessed January 27, 2006

Fitzgerald, David. 2006a. "Inside the Sending State: The Politics of Mexican Emigration Control." *International Migration Review* 40(2): 259–293.

———. 2006b. "Towards a Theoretical Ethnography of Migration." *Qualitative Sociology* 29(1): 1–24.

Flores, Nadia. 2001. "Place of Origin and Social Networks of Migration from Mexico to the United States." Master's thesis, University of Pennsylvania, Philadelphia.

Flores, Nadia, Rubén Hernández-León, and Douglas S. Massey. 2004. "Social Capital and Emigration from Rural and Urban Communities." In *Crossing the Border: Research from the Mexican Migration Project,* edited by Jorge Durand and Douglas S. Massey, 184–200. New York: Russell Sage Foundation.

Flores, Oscar. 2000. *Monterrey Industrial, 1980–2000.* San Pedro Garza García, Mexico: Universidad de Monterrey.

Foner, Nancy. 2000. *From Ellis Island to JFK: New York's Two Great Waves of Immigration.* New York: Russell Sage Foundation.

Foucher, Michel. 1991. *Front et Frontières: Un Tour du Monde Géopolitique.* Paris: Fayard.

Fox, Jonathan, and Gaspar Rivera-Salgado, eds. 2004. *Indigenous Mexican Migrants in the United States.* San Diego: Center for U.S.-Mexican Studies, University of California, San Diego.

Frankenberg, R.J. 1966. *Communities in Britain.* Harmondsworth, England: Penguin.

Friedmann, Santiago, Nora Lustig, and Arianna Legovini. 1995. "Mexico: Social Spending and Food Subsidies during Adjustment in the 1980s." In

*Coping with Austerity: Poverty and Inequality in Latin America,* edited by
N. Lustig, 334–374. Washington, D.C.: Brookings Institution.

Froud, Julie, et al. 1998. "Breaking the Chains? A Sector Matrix for Motoring."
*Competition and Change* 3: 293–334.

Fussell, Elizabeth, and Douglas S. Massey. 2004. "The Limits to Cumulative
Causation: International Migration from Mexican Urban Areas." *Demogra-
phy* 41(1): 151–171.

Gabayet, Luisa, and Silvia Lailson. 1991. "The Role of Female Wage Earners in
Male Migration in Guadalajara." In *The Effects of Receiving Country Policies on Migration Flows,* edited by S. Díaz-Briquets and S. Weintraub, 175–
203. Boulder, CO: Westview Press.

Gaetz, Stephen. 1992. "Planning Community-Based Youth Services in Cork,
Ireland: The Relevance of the Concepts, 'Youth' and 'Community.'" *Urban
Anthropology* 21(1): 91–113.

Galarza, Ernesto. 1964. *Merchants of Labor: The Mexican Bracero Story.* Charlotte: McNally and Loftin.

García, Edwin, Michelle Levander, and Ricardo Sandoval. 1998. "Rates Burden
Mexicans." *San Jose Mercury News,* April 13.

García Guzmán, Brígida. 1993. "La Ocupacion en México en los Años Ochenta:
Hechos y Datos." *Revista Mexicana de Sociología* 55(1): 137–153.

Garza, Gustavo. 1995a. "Crisis Industrial, 1980–1988." In *Atlas de Monterrey,*
edited by Gustavo Garza, 139–145. Monterrey: Gobierno del Estado de
Nuevo León/UANL/INSEUR-NL/COLMEX.

———. 1995b. "Estructura Macroeconómica, 1960–1988." In *Atlas de Monterrey,* edited by Gustavo Garza, 102–109. Monterrey: Gobierno del Estado
de Nuevo León/UANL/INSEUR-NL/COLMEX.

———. 1995c. "Expansión y Diversificación Industrial, 1960–1980." In *Atlas
de Monterrey,* edited by Gustavo Garza, 132–138. Monterrey: Gobierno del
Estado de Nuevo León/UANL/INSEUR-NL/COLMEX.

———. 1992. *Desconcentración, Tecnología y Localización Industrial en
México.* Mexico City: El Colegio de México.

Garza, Gustavo, and Salvador Rivera. 1993. "Desarrollo Económico y Dis-
tribución de la Población Urbana en México, 1960–1990." *Revista Mexicana
de Sociología* 55(1): 177–212.

Garza, Gustavo, and Marlene Solís. 1995. *Municipio de Monterrey: Geografía
de las Desigualdades Económicas.* Monterrey: Instituto de Estudios Urbanos
de Nuevo León.

Gates, Marilyn. 1996. "The Debt Crisis and Economic Restructuring: Prospects
for Mexican Agriculture." In *Neo-liberalism Revisited: Economic Restructuring and Mexico's Political Future,* edited by Gerardo Otero, 187–208.
Boulder, CO: Westview Press.

Gereffi, Gary. 1996. "Mexico's 'Old' and 'New' *Maquiladora* Industries: Con-
trasting Approaches to North American Integration." In *Neo-liberalism
Revisited: Economic Restructuring and Mexico's Political Future,* edited by
Gerardo Otero, 85–105. Boulder, CO: Westview Press.

Gereffi, Gary, and Martha A. Martínez. 2005. "Mexico's Economic Transformation under NAFTA." In *Mexico's Democracy at Work: Political and Eco-*

*nomic Dynamics,* edited by Russell Crandall, Guadalupe Paz, and Riordan Roett, 119–150. Boulder, CO: Lynne Rienner.

Girón, Jaime Rogerio. 1985. "Proceso de Trabajo, Automatización y Clase Obrera en la Industria del Cemento en México." In *Testimonios de la Crisis 1: Restructuración Productiva y Clase Obrera,* edited by Esthela Gutiérrez Garza, 115–145. Mexico City: Siglo XXI.

Glick Schiller, Nina, Linda Basch, and Cristina Blanc-Szanton. 1992. "Transnationalism: A New Analytic Framework for Understanding Migration." In *Towards a Transnational Perspective on Migration,* edited by N. Glick Schiller, L. Basch, and C. Blanc-Szanton, 1–24. New York: New York Academy of Sciences.

Goldring, Luin. 2002. "The Mexican State and Transmigrant Organizations: Negotiating the Boundaries of Membership and Participation." *Latin American Research Review* 37(3): 55–99.

González Amador, Roberto. 2007. "Impulsa Banorte un Sistema Financiero Binacional con EU." Www.jornada.unam.mx/2007/03/26/index.php?section =economia&article=025n1eco, accessed May 7, 2007.

González de la Rocha, Mercedes. 1986. *Los Recursos de la Pobreza: Familias de Bajos Ingresos in Guadalajara.* Guadalajara, Mexico: El Colegio de Jalisco/ CIESAS/SEP.

González de la Rocha, Mercedes, and Agustín Escobar Latapí, eds. 1991. *Social Responses to Mexico's Economic Crisis of the 1980s.* San Diego: Center for U.S.-Mexican Studies, University of California, San Diego.

González Quiroga, Miguel A. 2001. "Los Inicios de la Migración Laboral Mexicana a Texas (1850–1880)." In *Encuentro en la Frontera: Mexicanos y Norteamericanos en un Espacio Común,* edited by Manuel Ceballos Ramírez, 345–372. Mexico City: Colegio de México, El Colegio de la Frontera Norte, and Universidad Autónoma de Tamaulipas.

———. 1993. "La Puerta de México: Los Comerciantes Texanos y el Noreste Mexicano, 1850–1880." *Estudios Sociológicos* 11(31): 209–236.

Gouldner, Alvin W. 1973. *For Sociology: Renewal and Critique in Sociology.* New York: Basic Books.

Granovetter, Mark S. 1973. "The Strength of Weak Ties." *American Journal of Sociology* 78(6): 1360–1380.

Greater Houston Partnership. 2000. "Mission Accomplished, Houston! Trade Delegation Visit to Monterrey, Mexico, a Success." Www.houston.org/media Relations/pressReleases/0323002.html, accessed April 19, 2004.

Greenhouse, Steven. 2006a. "Cleaning Companies in Accord with Striking Houston Janitors." *New York Times,* www.nytimes.com/2006/11/21/us/21 janitor.html, accessed November 21, 2006.

———. 2006b. "Janitors' Union, Recently Organized, Strikes in Houston." *New York Times,* http://query.nytimes.com/gst/fullpage.html?sec = health &res = 9507E4DF103FF930A35752C1A9609C8B63, accessed November 21, 2006.

Grieco, Elizabeth. 2003. *The Foreign Born from Mexico in the United States.* Migration Information Source, www.migrationinformation.org/USfocus/ print.cfm?ID = 163, accessed January 13, 2005.

Griffith, David. 2005. "Class Relations among Old and New Immigrants."
    *Journal of Latino/Latin American Studies* 1: 89–106.
Griffith, David, and Ed Kissam. 1995. *Working Poor: Farmworkers in the
    United States.* Philadelphia: Temple University Press.
Grindle, Merilee S. 1991. "The Response to Austerity: Political and Economic
    Strategies of Mexico's Rural Poor." In *Social Responses to Mexico's Eco-
    nomic Crisis of the 1980s,* edited by M. González de la Rocha and A. Esco-
    bar Latapí, 129–154. San Diego: Center for U.S.-Mexican Studies, University
    of California, San Diego.
Grow, Brian. 2005. "Embracing Illegals." *BusinessWeek,* July 18, 56–64.
Guarnizo, Luis Eduardo. 1998. "The Rise of Transnational Social Formations:
    Mexican and Dominican State Responses to Transnational Migration."
    *Political Power and Social Theory* 12: 45–94.
Guarnizo, Luis Eduardo, and Luz Marina Díaz. 1999. "Transnational Migra-
    tion: A View from Colombia." *Ethnic and Racial Studies* 22(2): 397–421.
Guarnizo, Luis Eduardo, Arturo Ignacio Sánchez, and Elizabeth M. Roach.
    1999. "Mistrust, Fragmented Solidarity, and Transnational Migration:
    Colombians in New York and Los Angeles." *Ethnic and Racial Studies* 22(2):
    367–396.
Guarnizo, Luis Eduardo, and Michael Peter Smith. 1998. "The Locations of
    Transnationalism." In *Transnationalism from Below,* edited by Michael
    Peter Smith and Luis Guarnizo, 3–33. New Brunswick, NJ: Transaction.
Guillén Romo, Héctor. 1985. *Orígenes de la Crisis en México: Inflación y Ende-
    udamiento Externo (1940–1982).* Mexico City: ERA.
Gutiérrez Garza, Esthela. 1995. "Tendencias Recientes de la Industrialización,
    1988–1992." In *Atlas de Monterrey,* edited by Gustavo Garza, 146–152.
    Monterrey: Gobierno del Estado de Nuevo León/UANL/INSEUR-NL/
    COLMEX.
———. 1992. "Comentarios." In *Ajuste Estructural, Mercados Laborales y
    TLC,* 379–392. Mexico City: El Colegio de México, Fundación Friedrich
    Ebert, and El Colegio de la Frontera Norte.
———.1990. "La Crisis Laboral y la Flexibilidad del Trabajo: México, 1983–
    1988." In *Testimonios de la Crisis 4: Los Saldos del Sexenio,* edited by
    Esthela Gutiérrez Garza, 178–220. Mexico City: Siglo XXI.
——— .1988. "De la Relación Salarial Monopolista a la Flexibilidad del Tra-
    bajo: México, 1960–1986." In *Testimonios de la Crisis 2: La Crisis del
    Estado de Bienestar,* edited by Esthela Gutiérrez Garza, 129–173. Mexico
    City: Siglo XXI.
———. 1985. "La Regulación Competitiva como Trasfondo del Movimiento
    Obrero." In *Testimonios de la Crisis 1: Restructuración Productiva y Clase
    Obrera,* edited by Esthela Gutiérrez Garza, 28–65. Mexico City: Siglo XXI.
Gutmann, Matthew. 2002. *The Romance of Democracy: Compliant Defiance in
    Contemporary Mexico.* Berkeley: University of California Press.
Hagan, Jacqueline Maria. 1998. "Social Networks, Gender, and Immigrant
    Incorporation: Resources and Constraints." *American Sociological Review*
    63(1): 55–67.

———. 1994. *Deciding to Be Legal: A Maya Community in Houston.* Philadelphia: Temple University Press.

Hagan, Jacqueline Maria, and Susan Gonzalez Baker. 1993. "Implementing the U.S. Legalization Program: The Influence of Immigrant Communities and Local Agencies on Immigration Policy Reform." *International Migration Review* 27(3): 513–36.

Hagan, Jacqueline Maria, and Néstor P. Rodríguez. 1992. "Recent Economic Restructuring and Evolving Intergroup Relations in Houston." In *Structuring Diversity: Ethnographic Perspectives on the New Immigration,* edited by Louise Lamphere, 145–171. Chicago: Chicago University Press.

Hammersley, Martyn. 1992. *What's Wrong with Ethnography?* London: Routledge.

Hammersley, Martyn, and Paul Atkinson. 1995. *Ethnography: Principles in Practice.* London: Routledge.

Harney, R.F. 1977. "The Commerce of Migration." *Canadian Ethnic Studies/ Etudes Ethniques du Canada* 9: 42–53.

Harris, Nigel. 1995. *The New Untouchables: Immigration and the New World Workers.* London: Penguin.

Harvey, David. 1990. *The Condition of Postmodernity.* Oxford, England: Blackwell.

Harvey, Neil. 1996. "Rural Reforms and the Zapatista Rebellion: Chiapas, 1988–1995." In *Neo-liberalism Revisited: Economic Restructuring and Mexico's Political Future,* edited by Gerardo Otero, 187–208. Boulder, CO: Westview Press.

Heath, Jonathan. 1998. "The Impact of Mexico's Trade Liberalization: Jobs, Productivity, and Structural Change." In *The Post-NAFTA Political Economy: Mexico and the Western Hemisphere,"* edited by Carol Wise, 171–200. University Park: Pennsylvania State University Press.

Hegstrom, Edward. 2002. "Van Tours Called Front for *Coyotes.* " *Houston Chronicle,* March 3, 2002, 1A–20A.

Hennesy-Fiske, Molly. 2004. "N.C. Recruiter Gets Jobs for Mexicans." *(Raleigh) News & Observer,* www.journalismfellowships.org/stories/mexico/ pf_mexico_recruiter.htm, accessed March 12, 2005.

Hernández, Kathleen Lytle. 2002. "Entangling Bodies and Borders: Racial Profiling and the History of the U.S. Border Patrol." PhD diss., University of California, Los Angeles.

Hernández-León, Rubén. 2005. "The Migration Industry in the Mexico-U.S. Migratory System." California Center for Population Research, University of California, Los Angeles, Online Working Paper Series, www.ccpr.ucla.edu/ asp/papers.asp, accessed January 18, 2006.

———. 1999. "A la Aventura!: Jóvenes, Pandillas y Migración en la Conexión Monterrey-Houston." In *Fronteras Fragmentadas,* edited by Gail Mummert, 115–143. Zamora, Mexico: El Colegio de Michoacán.

———. 1997. "El Circuito Migratorio Monterrey-Houston." *Ciudades* 35: 26–33.

Hernández-León, Rubén, and Víctor Zúñiga. 2000. "'Making Carpet by the

Mile': The Emergence of a Mexican Immigrant Community in an Industrial Region of the U.S. Historic South." *Social Science Quarterly* 81(1): 49–66.

Hibino, Barbara. 1992. "Cervecería Cuauhtémoc: A Case Study of Technological and Industrial Development in Mexico." *Mexican Studies/Estudios Mexicanos* 8(1): 23–43.

Hill, Richard Child, and Joe R. Feagin. 1987. "Detroit and Houston: Two Cities in Global Perspective." In *The Capitalist City,* edited by R.C. Hill and J.R. Feagin, 155–177. Oxford, UK: Blackwell.

Hirsch, Jennifer S. 2003. *A Courtship after Marriage: Sexuality and Love in Mexican Transnational Families.* Berkeley: University of California Press.

Hondagneu-Sotelo, Pierrette. 1992. "Overcoming Patriarchal Constraints: The Reconstruction of Gender Relations among Mexican Immigrant Women and Men." *Gender and Society* 6(3): 393–415.

INEGI. 2007. *Consulta de Localidades ITER 2005.* www.inegi.gob.mx/est/ contenidos/espanol/sistemas/conteo2005/iter2005/default.aspx, accessed August 10, 2007.

———. 2005. *Banco de Información Económica.* Http://dgcnesyp.inegi.gob. mx/cgi-win/bdieintsi.exe/, accessed July 8, 2005.

———.1995. *Sistema para la Consulta de Información Censal (SCINCE 1995).* Compact disc.

Instituto de los Mexicanos en el Exterior. 2007. *Sistema de Información Origen-Destino de Comunidades Mexicanas.* Www.ime.gob.mx/estados.htm, accessed August 7, 2007.

Jones, Gareth A., and Peter M. Ward. 1998. "Deregulating the *Ejido:* The Impact of Urban Development in Mexico." In *The Transformation of Rural Mexico: Reforming the* Ejido *Sector,* edited by Wayne A. Cornelius and David Myhre, 247–275. San Diego: Center for U.S.-Mexican Studies, University of California, San Diego.

Jones, Richard C. 1995. *Ambivalent Journey: U.S. Migration and Economic Mobility in North-Central Mexico.* Tucson: University of Arizona Press.

Kearney, Michael. 1998. "Transnationalism in California and Mexico at the End of Empire." In *Border Identities: Nation and State at International Frontiers,* edited by Thomas M. Wilson and Hastings Donnan, 117–141. Cambridge, England: Cambridge University Press.

Kivisto, Peter. 2001. "Theorizing Transnational Immigration: A Critical Review of Current Efforts." *Ethnic and Racial Studies* 24(4): 549–577.

Kopinak, Kathryn. 1996. *Desert Capitalism:* Maquiladoras *in North America's Western Industrial Corridor.* Tucson: University of Arizona Press.

Krissman, Fred. 2005. "Sin Coyote Ni Patrón: Why the 'Migrant Network' Fails to Explain International Migration." *International Migration Review* 39(1): 4–44.

———. 2000. "Immigrant Labor Recruitment: U.S. Agribusiness and Undocumented Migration from Mexico." In *Immigration Research for a New Century,* edited by N. Foner, R. Rumbaut, and S. Gold, 277–300. New York: Russell Sage Foundation

Kyle, David. 2000. *Transnational Peasants: Migration, Networks, and Ethnicity among Andean Ecuador.* Baltimore: Johns Hopkins University Press.

Langley, Lester D. 1994. *MexAmérica: Dos Países, un Futuro*. Mexico City: Fondo de Cultura Económica.

Levitt, Peggy. 2001. *The Transnational Villagers*. Berkeley: University of California Press.

———. 2000. "Migrants Participate Across Borders: Toward an Understanding of Forms and Consequences." In *Immigration Research for a New Century: Multidisciplinary Perspectives*, edited by Nancy Foner, Rubén G. Rumbaut, and Steven J. Gold, 459–479. New York: Russell Sage Foundation.

Li, Wei. 1998. "Anatomy of a New Ethnic Settlement: The Chinese *Ethnoburb* in Los Angeles." *Urban Studies* 35(3): 479–501.

Light, Ivan. 2006. *Deflecting Immigration: Networks, Markets, and Regulation in Los Angeles*. New York: Russell Sage Foundation.

———. 2005. "The Ethnic Economy." In *The Handbook of Economic Sociology*, 2nd ed., edited by Neil J. Smelser and Richard Swedberg, 650–677. Princeton: Princeton University Press.

Lipietz, Alain. 1987. *Mirages and Miracles: The Crisis in Global Fordism*. London: Verso.

Lomnitz, Larissa. 1976. "Migration and Network in Latin America." In *Current Perspectives in Latin American Urban Research*, edited by A. Portes and H.L. Browning, 133–150. Austin: University of Texas Press.

———. 1975. *Cómo Sobreviven los Marginados*. Mexico City. Siglo XXI editores.

López Castro, Gustavo. 1989. "Impactos de la Migración Internacional en un Pueblo Michoacano." In *Estudios Michoacanos III*, edited by S. Zendejas, 151–161. Zamora, Mexico: El Colegio de Michoacan.

Lozano Ascencio, Fernando. 2001. "Nuevos Orígenes de la Migración Mexicana a los Estados Unidos: Migrantes Urbanos Versus Migrantes Rurales." *Scripta Nova: Revista Electrónica de Geografía y Ciencias Sociales*, www.ub.es/geocrit/sn-94-14.htm, accessed January 10, 2002.

———. 2000. *Migration Strategies in Urban Contexts: Labor Migration from Mexico City to the United States*. Paper presented at the Twenty-second International Congress of the Latin American Studies Association, March 16–18, Miami.

Lozano Ascencio, Fernando, Bryan R. Roberts, and Frank D. Bean. 1997. "The Interconnectedness of Internal and International Migration: The Case of the United States and Mexico." *Social Welt* 12: 163–178.

Lustig, Nora. 1992. *Mexico: The Remaking of an Economy*. Washington, D.C.: Brookings Institution.

Mahler, Sarah J. 1999. "La Industria Salvadoreña de Remesas." In *Fronteras Fragmentadas*, edited by Gail Mummert, 519–544. Zamora, Mexico: El Colegio de Michoacán–CIDEM.

———. 1995. *The Dysfunctions of Transnationalism*. Working Paper 73. New York: Russell Sage Foundation.

Mair, Lucy. 1965. *An Introduction to Social Anthropology*. London: Oxford University Press.

Martin, Philip L. 1997. "Do Mexican Agricultural Policies Stimulate Migra-

tion?" In *At the Crossroads: Mexico and U.S. Immigration Policy*, edited by
F.D. Bean et al., 79–116. Lanham, MD: Rowman and Littlefield.

———. 1993. *Trade and Migration: NAFTA and Agriculture*. Washington,
D.C.: Institute for International Economics.

———. 1991. "Labor Migration: Theory and Reality." In *The Unsettled Relationship: Labor Migration and Economic Development*, edited by D.G.
Papademetriou and P.L. Martin, 27–42. Westport, CT: Greenwood Press.

Martin, Philip L., and J. Edward Taylor. 1992. "The North American Free
Trade Agreement and Rural Mexican Migration to the United States." In
*Proceedings of the Conference North American Free Trade Agreement:
Implications for California*, edited by the Agricultural Issues Center, 63–92.
Davis: Agricultural Issues Center, University of California, Davis.

Martínez, Fabiola. 2002. "Entregaron en la Cámara Iniciativa de Reforma
Laboral." *La Jornada*, www.jornada.unam.mx/2002/11/28/049n1soc.php
?origen = index.html, accessed August 16, 2007.

Martínez, María del Pilar. 2005. "Contratos a la Carta." *La Jornada*, www
.jornada.unam.mx/2005/05/30/004n1sec.html, accessed August 7, 2007.

Massey, Douglas S. 1990. "Social Structure, Household Strategies and the
Cumulative Causation of Migration." *Population Index* 56(1): 3–26.

———.1988. "Economic Development and International Migration in Comparative Perspective." *Population and Development Review* 14(2): 383–413.

———. 1987. "The Ethnosurvey in Theory and Practice." *International Migration Review* 21(4): 1498–1522.

Massey, Douglas S., Jorge Durand, and Nolan Malone. 2002. *Beyond Smoke
and Mirrors: Mexican Immigration in an Era of Economic Integration*. New
York: Russell Sage Foundation.

Massey, Douglas S., and Kristin E. Espinosa. 1997. "What's Driving Mexico-
U.S. Migration? A Theoretical, Empirical, and Policy Analysis." *American
Journal of Sociology* 102(4): 939–999.

Massey, Douglas S., L. Goldring, and J. Durand. 1994. "Continuities in Transnational Migration: An Analysis of Nineteen Mexican Communities." *American Journal of Sociology* 99(6): 1492–1533.

Massey, Douglas S., et al. 1993. "Theories of International Migration: A Review
and Appraisal." *Population Development Review* 19(3): 431–466.

Massey, Douglas S., et al. 1987. *Return to Aztlan: The Social Process of International Migration from Western Mexico*. Berkeley: University of California
Press.

Maxfield, Sylvia, and Adam Shapiro. 1998. "Assessing the NAFTA Negotia-
tions." In *The Post-NAFTA Political Economy: Mexico and the Western
Hemisphere*, edited by Carol Wise, 82–118. University Park: Pennsylvania
State University Press.

Mendirichaga, Rodrigo. 1995. "Monterrey Define Su Perfil, 1821–1888." In
*Atlas de Monterrey*, edited by Gustavo Garza, 76–83. Monterrey: Gobierno
del Estado de Nuevo León/UANL/INSEUR-NL/COLMEX.

Menjívar, Cecilia. 2006. "Liminal Legality: Salvadoran and Guatemalan Immigrants' Lives in the United States." *American Journal of Sociology* 111(4):
999–1037.

———. 2000. *Fragmented Ties: Salvadoran Immigrant Networks in America.* Berkeley: University of California Press.

———. 1997. "Immigrant Kinship Networks: Vietnamese, Salvadoreans and Mexicans in Comparative Perspective." *Journal of Comparative Family Studies* 28(1): 1–24.

Merton, Robert K. 1987. "Three Fragments from a Sociologist's Notebooks: Establishing the Phenomenon, Specified Ignorance, and Strategic Research Materials." *Annual Review of Sociology* 13: 1–28.

Meyerson, Harold. 2004. "A Tale of Two Cities." *American Prospect,* June, A8–A10.

Miraftab, Faranak. 1997. "Revisiting Informal-Sector Home Ownership: The Relevance of Household Composition for Housing Options of the Poor." *International Journal of Urban and Regional Research* 21(2): 303–322.

Mora-Torres, Juan. 2001. *The Making of the Mexican Border: The State, Capitalism, and Society in Nuevo León, 1848–1910.* Austin: University of Texas Press.

Moreno, Jenalia. 2003. "Founder of Mexico-Bound Bus Line Took Own Journey between Two Worlds." *Houston Chronicle,* www.chron.com/CDA/archives/archive.mpl?id = 2003_3627326, accessed August 16, 2007.

Morris, Arthur S., and Stella Lowder. 1992. "Flexible Specialization: The Application of Theory in a Poor-Country Context: Leon, Mexico." *International Journal of Urban and Regional Research* 16: 190–201.

Muñoz Ríos, Patricia. 2006. "Fox 'Impuso' en los Hechos la Reforma a la Ley Laboral." *La Jornada,* www.jornada.unam.mx/2006/05/10/056n1soc.php, accessed August 16, 2007.

Napolitano, Valentina. 1997. "Becoming a *Mujercita:* Rituals, Fiestas and Religious Discourses." *Journal of the Royal Anthropological Society* 3: 279–296.

Ordorica Mellado, Manuel. 1994. "Evolución Demográfica y Estudios de Población en México." In *La Población en el Desarrollo Contemporáneo de México,* edited by Francisco Alba and Gustavo Cabrera, 29–51. Mexico City: El Colegio de México.

Orozco, Manuel. 2002. "Remittances and Markets: New Players and Practices." In *Sending Money Home: Hispanic Remittances and Community Development,* edited by Rodolfo O. de la Garza and Briant Lindsay Lowell, 125–154. Lanham, MD: Rowman and Littlefield.

Otero, Gerardo, ed. 1996. *Neo-liberalism Revisited: Economic Restructuring and Mexico's Political Future.* Boulder, CO: Westview Press.

Palacios, Lylia Isabel. 2003. "Flexibilidad Laboral y Gran Industria en Monterrey." In *Del Mercado Protegido al Mercado Global: Monterrey, 1925–2000,* edited by Mario Cerutti, 135–177. Mexico: Trillas.

Pastor, Manuel, Jr. 1998. "Pesos, Policies and Predictions: Why the Crisis, Why the Surprise, and Why the Recovery?" In *The Post-NAFTA Political Economy: Mexico and the Western Hemisphere,"* edited by Carol Wise, 119–147. University Park: Pennsylvania State University Press.

Pastor, Manuel, Jr., and Carol Wise. 2005. "The Fox Administration and the Politics of Economic Transition." In *Mexico's Democracy at Work: Political and Economic Dynamics,* edited by Russell Crandall, Guadalupe Paz, and Riordan Roett, 89–118. Boulder, CO: Lynne Rienner.

———. 1998. "Mexican-Style Neoliberalism: State Policy and Distributional Stress." In *The Post-NAFTA Political Economy: Mexico and the Western Hemisphere,*" edited by Carol Wise, 41–81. University Park: Pennsylvania State University Press.

Piore, Michael J. 1979. *Birds of Passage: Migrant Labor and Industrial Societies.* Cambridge, MA: Cambridge University Press.

PNUD. 2007. *Informe sobre Desarollo Humano México, 2006–2007: Migración y Desarollo.* Mexico City: Programa de las Naciones Unidas para el Desarrollo.

Polaski, Sandra. 2006. "The Employment Consequences of NAFTA." Www. carnegieendowment.org/publications/index.cfm?fa = view&id = 18703&prog = zgp&proj = zted, accessed May 3, 2007.

———. 2004. "Mexican Employment, Productivity and Income: A Decade after NAFTA." Www.carnegieendowment.org/publications/index.cfm?fa = view &id = 1473&prog = zgp&proj = zted, accessed May 3, 2007.

Portes, Alejandro. 1999. "Conclusion: Towards a New World—Origins and Effects of Transnational Activities." *Ethnic and Racial Studies* 22(2): 463–477.

———. 1989. "Latin American Urbanization during the Years of the Crisis." *Latin American Research Review* 24(3): 7–44.

Portes, Alejandro, Luis E. Guarnizo, and Patricia Landolt. 1999. "The Study of Transnationalism: Pitfalls and Promise of an Emergent Research Field." *Ethnic and Racial Studies* 22(2): 217–237.

Portes, Alejandro, William J. Haller, and Luis E. Guarnizo. 2002. "Transnational Entrepreneurs: An Alternative Form of Immigrant Economic Adaptation." *American Sociological Review* 67(2): 278–298.

Portes, Alejandro, and Julia Sensenbrenner. 1993. "Embeddedness and Immigration: Notes on the Social Determinants of Economic Action." *American Journal of Sociology* 98(6): 1320–1350.

Posada García, Miriam. 2005. "Mexicanos Van Tras Rutas de Transporte de Pasajeros en EU." *La Jornada,* www.jornada.unam.mx/2005/10/03/030n1eco .php, accessed December 6, 2007.

Pozas, María de los Ángeles. 2002. *Estrategia Internacional de la Gran Empresa Mexicana en la Década de los Noventa.* Mexico City: El Colegio de México.

———.1997. *Competitividad Emergente y Capital Internacional: El Caso de Monterrey.* Paper presented at the Twentieth International Congress of the Latin American Studies Association, April 17–19, Guadalajara.

———.1993a. *Industrial Restructuring in Mexico.* San Diego: Center for U.S.-Mexican Studies, University of California, San Diego.

———. 1993b. "Mecanismos de Inserción de la Gran Industria Nacional en la Economía Internacional: El Caso de Monterrey." In *TLC: Impactos en la Frontera Norte,* edited by Alejandro Dávila Flores, 171–204. Mexico City: UNAM.

———.1992. "Modernización de las Relaciones Laborales en las Empresas Regiomontanas." In *Ajuste Estructural, Mercados Laborales y TLC,* 365–

378. Mexico City: El Colegio de México, Fundación Friedrich Ebert, and El Colegio de la Frontera Norte.

Pozos Ponce, Fernando. 1996. *Metrópolis en Reestructuración: Guadalajara y Monterrey, 1980–1989.* Guadalajara: Universidad de Guadalajara.

Pries, Ludger. 2001. "The Approach of Transnational Social Spaces: Responding to New Configurations of the Social and the Spatial." In *New Transnational Social Spaces: International Migration and Transnational Companies in the Early Twenty-first Century,* edited by Ludger Pries, 3–33. London: Routledge.

Ramones Saldaña, Jesús. 1995. "El Mercado de Trabajo." In *Atlas de Monterrey,* edited by Gustavo Garza, 196–205. Monterrey: Gobierno del Estado de Nuevo León/UANL/INSEUR-NL/COLMEX.

Reckard, E. Scott. 2007. "Bank of America to Offer Credit Cards to Illegal Immigrants." Www.latimes.com/business/la-ex-credit13feb14,0,6793875.story ?coll = la-home-headlines, accessed February 13, 2007.

Reichert, Joshua. 1982. "A Town Divided: Economic Stratification and Social Relations in a Mexican Migrant Community." *Social Problems* 29(4): 411–423.

Reuters. 2007. "Otorga Cemex Hipotecas a Migrantes." Www.reforma.com/ negocios/articulo/740315, accessed February 19, 2007.

Rivera, Salvador. 1995. "Santa Catarina: Contorno Industrial." In *Atlas de Monterrey,* edited by Gustavo Garza, 348–354. Monterrey: Gobierno del Estado de Nuevo León/UANL/INSEUR-NL/COLMEX.

Rivera Ríos, Miguel Angel. 1992. *El Nuevo Capitalismo Mexicano: El Proceso de Reestructuración de los Años Ochenta.* Mexico City: ERA.

Rivera Sánchez, Liliana, and Fernando Lozano Ascencio. 2006. "Los Contextos de Salida Urbanos y Rurales y la Organización Social de la Migración." *Migración y Desarrollo* 6: 45–78.

Roberts, Bryan. 1995. "Socially Expected Durations and the Economic Adjustment of Immigrants." In *The Economic Sociology of Immigration,* edited by A. Portes, 42–86. New York: Russell Sage Foundation.

———. 1994. "Informal Economy and Family Strategies." *International Journal of Urban and Regional Research* 18(1): 6–23.

Roberts, Bryan, and Agustín Escobar Latapí. 1997. "Mexican Social and Economic Policy and Emigration." In *At the Crossroads: Mexico and U.S. Immigration Policy,* edited by Frank D. Bean et al., 47–78. Lanham, MD: Rowman and Littlefield.

Roberts, Bryan, R. Frank, and F. Lozano Ascencio. 1999. "Transnational Migrant Communities and Mexican Migration to the U.S." *Ethnic and Racial Studies* 22(2): 238–266.

Roberts, Bryan, and Erin Hamilton. 2005. *The New Geography of Emigration: Emerging Zones of Attraction and Expulsion, Continuity and Change.* Center for Migration and Development, Princeton University, Working Paper 05–021, http://cmd.princeton.edu/papers/wp0502l.pdf, accessed May 10, 2007.

Rodríguez, Néstor. 1996. "The Battle for the Border: Notes on Autonomous

Migration, Transnational Communities, and the State." *Social Justice* 23(3): 21–37.

———. 1993. "Economic Restructuring and Latino Growth in Houston." In *In the Barrios: Latinos and the Underclass Debate,* edited by Joan Moore and Raquel Pinderhughes, 101–127. New York: Russell Sage Foundation.

———. 1987. "Undocumented Central Americans in Houston: Diverse Populations." *International Migration Review* 21(1): 4–26.

Rodríguez, Néstor, et al. 1994. "Political Mobilization in Houston's Magnolia." In *Barrio Ballots: Latino Politics in the 1990 Elections,* edited by Rodolfo O. de la Garza, Martha Menchaca, and Louis DeSipio, 83–114. Boulder, CO: Westview Press.

Rojas, Javier, and Luis Lauro Garza. 1985. *La Insurgencia en el Sindicalismo Blanco.* Monterrey: OIDMO.

Rojas Sandoval, Javier. 1997. *Fábricas Pioneras de la Industria de Nuevo León.* Monterrey: Universidad Autónoma de Nuevo León.

Rothstein, Jeffrey S. 2004. "Creating Lean Industrial Relations: General Motors in Silao, Mexico." *Competition and Change* 8(3): 203–221.

Ros, Jaime, and Nora Lustig. 2001. "Mexico: Trade and Financial Liberalization with Volatile Capital Inflows: Macroeconomic Consequences and Social Impacts during the 1990s." In *External Liberalization, Economic Performance, and Social Policy,* edited by Lance Taylor, 217–250. Oxford, England: Oxford University Press.

Rouse, Roger. 1989. "Mexican Migration to the United States: Family Relations in the Development of a Transnational Community." PhD diss., Stanford University, Stanford, CA.

Ruiz Chiapetto, Crescencio. 1994. "Hacia un País Urbano." In *La Población en el Desarrollo Contemporáneo de México,* edited by Francisco Alba and Gustavo Cabrera, 159–181. Mexico City: El Colegio de México.

Saragoza, Alex M. 1988. *The Monterrey Elite and the Mexican State, 1880–1940.* Austin: University of Texas Press.

Sassen, Saskia. 1991. *The Global City: New York, London, Tokyo.* Princeton: Princeton University Press.

———. 1990. "Economic Restructuring and the American City." *Annual Review of Sociology* 16: 465–490.

Scott, John. 1988. "Trend Report: Social Network Analysis." *Sociology* 22(1): 109–127.

Selby, Henry A., Arthur D. Murphy, and Stephen A. Lorenzen. 1990. *The Mexican Urban Household.* Austin: University of Texas Press.

Shelton, Beth Anne, et al. 1989. *Houston: Growth and Decline in a Sunbelt Boomtown.* Philadelphia: Temple University Press.

Singer, Audrey, and Douglas S. Massey. 1998. "The Social Process of Undocumented Border Crossing among Mexican Migrants." *International Migration Review* 32(3): 561–592.

Sklair, Leslie. 1993. *Assembling for Development: The Maquila Industry in Mexico and the United States.* San Diego: Center for U.S.-Mexican Studies, University of California, San Diego.

Smith, Michael P., and Matt Bakker. 2005. "The Transnational Politics of the Tomato King: Meaning and Impact." *Global Networks* 5(2): 129–146.

Smith, Michael P., and Joe R. Feagin, eds. 1987. *The Capitalist City*. Oxford, England: Blackwell.

Smith Robert C. 2006. *Mexican New York: Transnational Lives of New Immigrants*. Berkeley: University of California Press.

———. 2005. "Racialization and Mexicans in New York City." In *New Destinations: Mexican Immigration in the United States*, edited by Víctor Zúñiga and Rubén Hernández-León, 220–243. New York: Russell Sage Foundation.

———. 2003. "Diasporic Membership in Historical Perspective: Comparative Insights from the Mexican, Italian and Polish Cases." *International Migration Review* 37(3): 724–759.

———. 2001. "Comparing Local-Level Swedish and Mexican Transnational Life: An Essay in Historical Retrieval." In *New Transnational Social Spaces: International Migration and Transnational Companies in the Early Twenty-first Century*, edited by Ludger Pries, 37–58. London: Routledge.

———.1998. "Reflections on Migration, the State and the Construction, Durability and Newness of Transnational Life." *Soziale Welt* 12: 197–217.

Snodgrass, Michael. 2003. *Deference and Defiance in Monterrey: Workers, Paternalism, and Revolution in Mexico, 1890–1950*. Cambridge: Cambridge University Press.

Sobrino, Jaime. 1995. "Consolidación Industrial Autónoma, 1940–1960." In *Atlas de Monterrey*, edited by Gustavo Garza, 124–131. Monterrey: Gobierno del Estado de Nuevo León/UANL/INSEUR-NL/COLMEX.

Soja, Edward W. 1989. *Postmodern Geographies*. London: Verso.

Spener, David. 2004. "Mexican Migrant-Smuggling." *Journal of International Migration and Integration* 5(3): 295–320.

Spener, David, and Bryan Roberts (1998). "Small Business, Social Capital, and Economic Integration on the Texas-Mexico Border." In *The U.S.-Mexico Border: Transcending Divisions, Contesting Identities*, edited by David Spener and Kathleen Staudt, 83–103. Boulder, CO: Lynne Rienner.

Stake, Robert. 1995. *The Art of Case Study Research*. Thousand Oaks, CA: Sage Publications.

Story, Dale. 1990. *Industria, Estado y Política en México: Los Empresarios y el Poder*. Mexico City: CNCA-Grijalbo.

Suttles, Gerald D. 1968. *The Social Order of the Slum: Ethnicity and Territory in the Inner City*. Chicago: University of Chicago Press.

Tamez, José Ramón. 1996. "Fábrica de Hilados y Tejidos de Algodón La Fama de Nuevo León." In *Santa Catarina: Un Acercamiento a Su Historia*, edited by Jesús Cortés García et al., 127–142. Santa Catarina, Mexico: Presidencia Municipal de Santa Catarina.

Tiano, Susan. 1990. "*Maquiladora* Women: A New Category of Workers?" In *Women Workers and Global Restructuring*, edited by Kathryn Ward, 193–223. Ithaca, NY: ILR Press.

Trejo Reyes, Saul. 1992. "Mexican-American Employment Relations: The Mexican Context." In *U.S.-Mexico Relations: Labor Market Interdependence*, edited by J.A. Bustamante, C.W. Reynolds, and R.A. Hinojosa Ojeda, 257–268. Stanford, CA: Stanford University Press.

Uhlig, Mark A. 1991. "Refinery Closing Outrages Mexican Workers." *New York Times,* March 27, A11.

U.S. Census Bureau. 2005. *American FactFinder.* Www.census.gov/, accessed November 13, 2005.

———. 1999. *U.S. Gazetteer: 1990 Census Lookup.* Www.census.gov/cgi-bin/gazetteer, accessed May 22, 1999.

U.S. Department of Justice. 1997. *Illegal Immigration Reform and Immigrant Responsibility Act of 1996.* Http://uscis.gov/graphics/publicaffairs/factsheets/948.htm, accessed September 21, 2005.

Valenzuela, Abel, Jr., Lisa Schweitzer, and Adriele Robles. 2005. "*Camionetas:* Informal Travel among Immigrants." *Transportation Research Part A* 39: 895–911.

Valenzuela Feijóo, José. 1986. *El Capitalismo Mexicano en los Ochenta.* Mexico City: ERA.

Vélez-Ibáñez, Carlos. 1988. "Networks of Exchange among Mexican in the U.S. and Mexico: Local Level Responses to National and International Transformations." *Urban Anthropology* 17(1): 27–51.

Vélez-Ibáñez, Carlos, and James B. Greenberg. 1992. "Formation and Transformation of Funds of Knowledge among U.S.-Mexican Households." *Anthropology and Education Quarterly* 23(4): 313–335.

Vellinga, Menno. 1994. *Industry and Society in Northern Mexico: Monterrey and the American Connection.* Paper presented at the Seventeenth International Congress of the Latin American Studies Association, March 10–12, Atlanta.

———. 1989. *Industrialización, Burguesía y Clase Obrera en México.* Mexico City: Siglo XXI.

Verduzco Igartúa, Gustavo. 1990. "La Migración Urbana a Estados Unidos: Un Caso del Occidente de México." *Estudios Sociológicos* 8(22): 117–139.

Vizcaya Canales, Isidro. 1995. "Fluctuaciones de la Industria Regiomontana, 1910–1940. In *Atlas de Monterrey,* edited by Gustavo Garza, 119–123. Monterrey: Gobierno del Estado de Nuevo León/UANL/INSEUR-NL/COLMEX.

Waldinger, Roger. 1989. "Immigration and Urban Change." *Annual Review of Sociology* 15: 211–32.

Waldinger, Roger, and David Fitzgerald. 2004. "Transnationalism in Question." *American Journal of Sociology* 109(5): 1177–1195.

Ward, Peter M. 1993. "Social Welfare Policy and Political Opening in Mexico." *Journal of Latin American Studies* 25: 613–628.

———. 1991. *México: Una megaciudad: Producción y Reproducción de un Medio Ambiente Urbano.* Mexico City: CNCA-Alianza Editorial.

Wilson, Tamar Diana. 1994. "What Determines Where Transnational Labor Migrants Go? Modifications in Migration Theories." *Human Organization* 53(3): 269–278.

Wimmer, Andreas, and Nina Glick-Schiller. 2003. "Methodological Nationalism, the Social Sciences and the Study of Migration: An Essay in Historical Epistemology." *International Migration Review* 37(3): 576–610.

Wirth, Louis. 1938. "Urbanism as a Way of Life." *American Journal of Sociology* 44: 3–24.

Wise, Carol. 1998. "NAFTA, Mexico and the Western Hemisphere." In *The Post-NAFTA Political Economy: Mexico and the Western Hemisphere*," edited by Carol Wise, 1–37. University Park: Pennsylvania State University Press.

Wyman, Donald L. 1983. "The Mexican Economy: Problems and Prospects." In *Mexico's Economic Crisis: Challenges and Opportunities*, edited by Donald L. Wyman, 1–28. San Diego: Center for U.S.-Mexican Studies, University of California, San Diego.

Yúnez-Naude, Antonio. 1991. "Towards a Free Trade Agreement between Mexico and the U.S.A.: The Effects of Mexican Primary, Non-mineral Sectors." Centro de Estudios Económicos, El Colegio de México, Mexico City. Unpublished document.

Zabin, Carol, and Sally Hughes. 1995. "Economic Integration and Labor Flows: Stage Migration in Farm Labor Markets in Mexico and the United States." *International Migration Review* 29(2): 395–422.

Zamudio Grave, Patricia E., et al. 2004. "Geografía y Patrones de la Migración Internacional: Un Análisis Regional del Estado de Veracruz." In *Nuevas Tendencias y Desafíos de la Migración Internacional México-Estados Unidos*, edited by Raúl Delgado Wise and Margarita Favela, 145–172. Mexico City: Porrúa.

Zapata, Francisco, Taeko Hoshino, and Linda Hanono. 1994. *La Restructuración Industrial en México: El Caso de la Industria de Autopartes*. Mexico City: El Colegio de México.

———. 1992. "La Crisis del Control Sindical sobre la Dinámica del Mercado de Trabajo en México." In *Ajuste Estructural, Mercados Laborales y TLC*, 59–71. Mexico City: El Colegio de México, Fundación Friedrich Ebert, and El Colegio de la Frontera Norte.

Zolberg, Aristide R. 1999. "Matters of State: Theorizing Immigration Policy." In *The Handbook of International Migration: The American Experience*, edited by Charles Hirschman, Philip Kasinitz, and Josh DeWind, 71–93. New York: Russell Sage Foundation.

Zúñiga, Víctor. 1995. "El Crecimiento Migratorio, 1960–1990." In *Atlas de Monterrey*, edited by Gustavo Garza, 190–195. Monterrey: Gobierno del Estado de Nuevo León/UANL/INSEUR-NL/COLMEX.

———. 1993. "Evolución de la Migración Internacional en un Municipio de la Zona Metropolitana de Monterrey (El Caso de Ciudad Guadalupe)." In *TLC: Impactos en la Frontera Norte*, edited by A. Dávila Flores, 205–228. Mexico City: Investigación Económica UNAM.

———. 1992. "Tradiciones Migratorias Internacionales y Socialización Familiar: Expectativas Migratorias de los Alumnos de Secundaria de Cuatro Municipios del Norte de Nuevo León." *Frontera Norte* 4(7): 45–74.

# Index

Text:  10/13 Sabon
Display:  Sabon
Compositor:  BookMatters, Berkeley
Indexer:  Kevin Millham
Printer and binder:  Sheridan Books, Inc.